Waipahu ... Recollections from a Sugar Plantation Community in Hawaii

Michael T. Yamamoto
Nina Yuriko (Ota) Sylva
Karen N. Yamamoto

Copyright ©2005 by Michael T. Yamamoto
Printed in the USA.

No part of this publication may be reproduced or transmitted in any form or by any means electric or mechanical, including photocopy, recording, or any information storage and retrieval system now known or to be invented, without permission in writing from the publisher, except by a reviewer who wishes to quote brief passages in connection with a review written for inclusion in a magazine, newspaper or broadcast. Contact Innoventions, P. O. Box 9194, Albuquerque, NM 87119.

Waipahu . . . Recollections from a Sugar Plantation Community in Hawaii

10 9 8 7 6 5 4 3 2 1

ISBN 0-9679279-5-1

Library of Congress Catalog Card Number 2005905119

Printed in the United States of America

Dedication

This book is dedicated to the town of Waipahu, Hawaii, and its fine residents ... past, present, future, and if away, with their hearts still in Waipahu.

Acknowledgement

Many people contributed material for this book and we have mentioned all that helped us.

A cold call to Lani Nedbalek (she wrote *Waipahu*) led us to Mike Mauricio and Kay Yamada. Mike's interest in cultural anthropology led him to learn more about Waipahu and he very generously shared his knowledge with us and reviewed early versions of this book.

Kay Yamada gave us (yes, gave us) her entire collection of material on Waipahu. This very extensive library led us to many other areas and jump-started our research in those areas.

As we progressed with research and writing, Lani helped us more and more with her knowledge of Waipahu, sharing contact names, previous writings, and insights into the history of Waipahu.

Lani, Mike, and Kay have written extensively for local newspapers and publications featuring stories about Waipahu. All shared their immense background of information.

Of particular interest is that contingent of people that have been meeting frequently in Torrance, California. The common thread among these people is that they went to Waipahu High School because the school was the only high school serving Waianae, Ewa, Waipahu, Pearl City, and even Aiea. Through the years these people have been meeting and enjoying their memories of Waipahu. They kindly shared much of their thoughts and memories for this book.

Grace Santistevan of Albuquerque, New Mexico, translated numerous documents, scrolls, newspaper articles, and works written in Japanese so we could tell a more complete story.

Jack Tasaka's father, Yokichi Tasaka, was one of the central figures in the sugar workers' strike of 1909. Jack helped us immensely with his knowledge of the history of the Japanese in Hawaii. Here again, his personal library and writings were of great assistance. And, because Brian Suzuki was willing to help us, we were able to contact and interview Jack Tasaka! [Brian is the owner of Hawaii Air Cargo and he used his many contacts to get these books shipped to Hawaii.]

Hawaii's Plantation Village allowed us the use of its collected works on Waipahu's history and the history of the Oahu Sugar Co.

John Tasato loaned us his collected works on Waipahu. These works would have seen the trash bin long ago were it not for John's foresight that one day he could share it with us! We found John to be a veritable encyclopedia on Okinawan history both in Hawaii and in the world.

Harriet Uchigaki, retired secretary of Waipahu Elementary School, allowed us the use of her memorabilia; this helped immensely to re-create much of the history of Waipahu and Waipahu Elementary School. Liz Kaneshiro, librarian, and Mildred Kimura, teacher, both at Waipahu Elementary, also shared materials with us. Keith Sienkiewicz of the Waipahu Bicycle & Sporting Goods store shared information with us. Ali Kessner brought her dad, Buster Takayesu, down to the Pagoda Hotel so we could interview him and Ali's sister, Georgine Morita, graciously shared a photo of old Waipahu that showed the rice paddies of long ago. Carrie Kawamoto brought her uncle, Tommy Yasue, to a local Waipahu store so we could interview him. Saxon Nishioka had a previous commitment and so could not be at the interview that he nonetheless arranged for us with his dad, Charley Nishioka. Dr. Milton Oshiro and his sister, Grace Nakamura, arranged our interview with their mother, Lillian Oshiro. Tom Tanji gave us much information on Hiro Higuchi and his connections to the churches in Waipahu. Charmille Abe and Glenn Pang of the Waipahu District Park gave us much information on their facilities. Lorna Miyasaki of the Waipahu Library opened its files for us. Stephanie Whalen and Ann Marsteller of the Hawaii Agriculture Research Center (fomerly the Hawaii Sugar Planters Association) were helpful in our search for information about sugar.

In our search for Dallas McLaren's plaque on the opening of Waipahu High School, both Ray Kagemoto, librarian of the present Waipahu High School, and Sandra Dela Cuadra of Waipahu Intermediate School assisted us. Patricia Pedersen, principal of the present Waipahu High School, opened its files so we could search for some individual's names in the history of the school. Some of the people giving us the information to create maps were Nina Yuriko (Ota) Sylva, Hideo Ishihara, Christine (Matsumoto) Mayeda, Harold and Sharon (Hirotsu) Fujioka, Harry Hirotsu, Evelyn (Hirotsu) Niino, Charlotte (Hirotsu) Matsuda, Diana (Hirotsu) Herrst, Irwin Kawano, Bernice Hamai, Carole (Goya) Holokahi, Jeannette (Goya) Johnson, Ellen (Goya) Miyake, Takemi Goya, Barney and Deanne Horie, James Serikaku, and Shige Yoshitake.

Hugh Morita is another gem in our journey. We went to Hugh's home to interview his dad, Yuzuru Morita. Both Hugh and Yuzuru are former employees of the Oahu Sugar Co. Hugh's adeptness with the computer led us to many computer aided design (CAD) graphics. After our interview with Yuzuru, Hugh took his dad on drives around Waipahu to recall significant landmarks from old Waipahu and thereby preserve them in CAD graphics. The maps that Hugh produced should be examined carefully as each map tells much about many aspects of the history of Waipahu. Hugh melded much from the individual interviews we conducted into map "pictures that tell more than a thousand words."

Paul LaPierre of Albuquerque, New Mexico, took time from his very busy schedule to help us find our way through the computer maze that is today a part of writing a book on the computer. His patience and knowledge "saved the day" for us.

Tiffany Voorhees and Sue Leonard of McNaughton & Gunn, our printers, were immensely helpful in guiding us through the printing process.

Robert Castro was instrumental in our search for information on the Oahu Sugar Co. and Waipahu's history. He is active in Hawaii's Plantation Village as a board member, dedicated researcher, archivist, and volunteer docent.

William Balfour Jr., the last manager of the Oahu Sugar Co. before it closed its doors, graciously reviewed the early versions of the chapter on the Oahu Sugar Co. and made some critical suggestions.

Marlene (Okada) Hirata and her husband Richard, both staunch supporters of Hawaii's Plantation Village, were pivotal in our research and connecting us to many, many people.

Shigeyuki Yoshitake helped us immensely with his vast knowledge of Waipahu ... almost all of it from memory, a result of his very deep interest in the history of Waipahu and thirst for knowledge. He made valuable observations and corrections as we wrote many drafts to finally arrive at this printed book. While Shige modestly would not like to be called the editor of this book, we ultimately recognize his talents as the editor.

Shige was also one of two "eagle eyes" looking over the final drafts of the manuscript. The other, who wishes to remain anonymous, scrutinized the manuscript finding typographical, grammatical, spelling, omission(!), and content(!) errors as well as parts that needed clarifications as we went to press. What a job these two did!

The many that we have not mentioned, the many that passed a few sentences, "Do you know ___? He would be a good one to interview. Here's his phone number. I already told him you're gonna call." To those sharing their family memories and files of information,

Thank You!

Table of Contents

Dedication	iii
Acknowledgement	iii
Table of Contents	vii
List of Illustrations	ix
List of Tables	x
Foreword *by Sharlyn Y. Miyahara*	xi
Special Introduction *by Kay M. Yamada*	xiii
Preface	xv

Chapter

1	**Locating and defining Waipahu** ... *water, bursting forth from the ground ...*	1
2	**Oahu Sugar** ... *a horse ride and a broken leg ...*	19
3	**Along Waipahu St. and down Depot Rd.** ... *the road curved this way and then that way ...*	49
4	**Some culture we retain to this day** ... *we brought this and we brought that ...*	83
5	**Along Farrington Highway** ... *a connector highway, a by-pass highway ...*	97
6	**World War II** ... *we saw the pilots, we waved at the pilots ...*	105
7	**Tatsuichi Ota** ... *one of many immigrants ...*	117
8	**Life in Waipahu** ... *life in this little town ...*	141
9	**Notes on the history of Waipahu** ... *more about people, places, and events in Waipahu ...*	159

Epilogue At the end of our story ... *along the way ...*	183
About the Authors	189
Index	190
Back cover notes & water information	192

References - at end of each chapter
Front cover background photo credit - Masuye Akiyama

List of Illustrations

Chapter	Figure	Description of Illustration	Page
1	1-1	Locating Waipahu	2
	1-2	Waipahu Census Tract Map, ca. 2004	3
	1-3	Geologic Strata of Pearl Harbor & Waipahu Area	4
	1-4	Geologic History of the Pearl Harbor Loch Area	4
	1-5	Points of Interest, ca.1930	9
	1-6	First Artesian Well in Hawaii marker plaque	14
2	2-1	A Trip Through the Town	19
	2-2	Sources of Ground Water for Oahu	21
	2-3	Oahu Sugar Co. Lands and Camp Locations ca. 1960	24
	2-4	Sewerage System, Waipahu ca. 1960	28
	2-5	Koalipea Camp Layout	30
	2-6	One view of Koalipea	30
	2-7	Locomotive Puuloa	39
3	3-1	New pathway for Waipahu St.	49
	3-2	The old Bank of Hawaii Bldg.	58
	3-3	Aerial photo of Shoburo ca. 1952	60
	3-4	Pedal Pushers	61
	3-5	A Trip through town with significant locations	70
	3-6	Jizo-san statue	74
	3-7	Okinawan Center	74
5	5-1	The new Bank of Hawaii	99
7	7-1	Ota name on a ceramic tile	117
	7-2	Yasu Ota	118
	7-3	Invoice from T. Ota Store	119
	7-4	T. Ota Store ca. 1903	119
	7-5	Waipahu ca. 1920	120
	7-6	Calligraphy Award	120
	7-7	Brushes for calligraphy	121
	7-8	T. Ota's Philosophy of How to Live One's Life	121
	7-9	Sumi stone and Han	122
	7-10	Liquid Sunshine Soda Shop	124
	7-11	Liquid Sunshine Soda Shop Invoice	125
	7-12	Lanterns in Hiroshima	129
	7-13	Nishi Health System Apparatus	135
	7-14	Tatsuichi and Yasu Ota	135

	7-15	Medal	136
	7-16	T. Ota residence on Pahu St.	137
	7-17	T. Ota with scroll at age 98	138
9	9-1	Okada Educational Center	167
	9-2	Memorial Stone	168
	9-3	Logo and Theme of Waipahu Centennial Celebration	177
Back Cover	----	Spring Waipahu (Photos and Location Map)	

List of Tables

1-1	Population by Decades of Waipahu, Honolulu, and Hawaii	7
1-2	Immigrant Groups - Arrival dates of significant groups	11
8-1	Nicknames in Waipahu	155
9-1	People of Note in Waipahu's Athletic History	179

Foreword

The history of a plantation town in Hawaii comes alive through the recollections and memories of many special people who lived, worked, played, or went to school in this town called Waipahu on the island of Oahu in the State of Hawaii.

At first, the authors planned to write a book about Tatsuichi Ota, a Japanese immigrant who resided in Waipahu and became a very successful businessman. Then, as people shared stories, photos, and memories about Mr. Ota, the authors soon realized that there were so many wonderful stories to tell about Waipahu and its people.

You will experience many "chicken skin" or "goose bump" moments as you journey through the history of Waipahu and the recollections of many people who have memories of life in this plantation town. There may be a few surprises when you read about the important people who have a Waipahu connection.

You will be taken back to times when life was much simpler, when people didn't have to lock their front doors, and when multiple ethnic groups could communicate with each other even though they spoke different languages. The lives of people were intertwined within the community, and, yet, each ethnic group could preserve its own heritage.

People who live and grow up in Hawaii have similar "small kid time" stories; there is a special bond that develops which keeps them connected even though they move away from Hawaii. This special connection is why so many people were willing to share stories that eventually blossomed into this book.

The recollections in this book surely bring out the exceptional characteristics of Waipahu and its people, and you will discover, as the authors did, that these people are very humble, extremely generous, and filled with the Aloha spirit. This book will warm your heart.

The authors have successfully presented a history of Waipahu in an interesting, enjoyable, and easy-to-read format. They take you on such a wonderful journey that you may find it difficult to put this book down. You will have a great time!

- *Sharlyn Y. Miyahara*

Special Introduction

The kingdom of Hawaii was on a chain of islands located in the middle of the Pacific Ocean, and populated by a peaceful group of natives who embraced a simple life style. When the Americans arrived and carefully reviewed the situation, they perceived a great potential for growing sugar cane and manufacturing sugar. The contour of the land and the balmy climate appeared to perfectly fit such an agricultural undertaking.

In 1835, Koloa Sugar Plantation in Koloa, on the Island of Kauai, was the first sugar plantation and mill to be built in Hawaii.

Once this first sugar plantation began operating successfully, the idea of planting sugar cane and manufacturing sugar spread like wildfire throughout the island kingdom. Sugar plantations and mills sprang up on every major island. Within just a few decades, sugar became the principal industry and economic base of Hawaii.

A labor shortage of natives soon began to plague the plantations. As a result, planters recruited Norwegians, Swedes, Germans, Portuguese, and Spaniards from Europe then even recruited some from the Caribbeans and other countries, but still could not resolve their labor problems. Later, with the support of King Kalakaua of Hawaii, they began to reach out to Asian countries. It was not until 1852 that the first group of workers arrived from China. Subsequently, they brought in workers from Japan, Okinawa, Korea, and the Philippines.

When the immigrants arrived, they were assigned to living quarters in camps according to race; as a result they had Chinese camps, Japanese camps, Korean camps, Filipino camps, etc. Separating people according to race for whatever reason may raise some serious questions today; however, in the plantation days, most of the immigrants were glad to be with their fellow countrymen. Although living with their own countrymen was a positive factor, the living and sanitary conditions as well as privacy factors caused some concern.

The living conditions left much to be desired but working in the cane fields had its share of challenges. The workers toiled long hours in the hot Hawaiian sun cutting stalks of sugar cane and were paid very meager wages. They soon realized that after they purchased their food and other essentials, they had almost nothing to save.

This was during the 1800s when the business management mentality was not as sophisticated as it is today. It was the American Civil War period and management reflected the period of slavery in U. S. history. Immigrants could neither speak nor understand English and supervisors could speak and understand only English. Misunderstandings were frequent and frustrations as well as resentment of workers intensified. Workers had given up everything in their homeland to come to Hawaii and earn enough money so that they could return to their homeland and a better quality of life. They saw that this could not happen. Thus, after fulfilling contractual obligations, some immigrants returned to their homeland and others sought work elsewhere in Hawaii. Some remained on the plantations.

The number of workers remaining on the plantations was substantial and they resorted to strikes to address the matter of unfair treatment of workers. Labor unrest was initially limited to only a few workers. This gradually erupted into major strikes and the employers continued to resist the workers' demands. Eventually it became clear that both labor and management would have to meet on a common ground.

More funds were allocated to provide more comfortable living quarters and better sanitary conditions. Medical care was improved. Management also began to realize that married workers were more stable, productive, and emotionally-focused. To this end, management began to provide workers with living quarters large enough to accomodate families and with yard space so they could plant vegetables and fruits.

As these changes were taking place on the plantations, other changes occurred that affected all of Hawaii. In 1848, King Kamehameha III enacted the Great Mahele that made fee-simple land ownership possible. In 1876, the Treaty of Reciprocity was enacted by Congress. This allowed sugar from Hawaii to be shipped to the United States duty-free. In 1898, Hawaii was annexed to the United States. Hawaii was being Americanized and the children of immigrants knew in their hearts that they were Americans.

When Pearl Harbor was bombed by the Japanese on December 7, 1941, the people of Waipahu watched the bombing in horror; Waipahu is located only a short distance from Pearl Harbor. Many of the children of the immigrants volunteered to fight for their country. Those who survived the war, returned to their homes and communities, and gratefully accepted what the Congress of the United States enacted in the GI Bill of Rights: a college education. With this opportunity, many went to get a higher education and, while coming from plantation camps and humble immigrant parents, they returned to serve their towns, cities, and communities with dignity and honor.

The mixed background of the people of Waipahu allowed them to work well together. They experienced the positive and the negative aspects of plantation life and they helped to form the history of Waipahu. The principal author of this book reached out and interviewed many people who shared their experiences and their memories of Waipahu.

A Chinese gentleman, whose parents were immigrants from China asked and answered, "What good are names, dates, and places? They mean nothing to me." The stories from the past - experiences and perceptions - make the history of Waipahu come alive. They are stories told by real people to whom Waipahu is a special place. George Santayana said, "Those who cannot remember the past are condemned to repeat it." We all learn from life's experiences and all societies tend to grow and develop into something better by examining the past. This is why *"Waipahu ... Recollections from a Sugar Plantation Community in Hawaii"* needed to be recorded.

- Kay M. Yamada

Preface

Tatsuo Ota, the only son of Tatsuichi Ota had passed away in June, 2002, and his ashes had just been put to rest in the Columbarium at Punchbowl National Memorial Cemetery of the Pacific in Honolulu, Hawaii. As a grandson of Tatsuichi, I decided early in the fact-gathering stage that this book would consist of anecdotes and sometimes only a sentence or two woven into a narrative to describe Tatsuichi Ota. Where possible, dates, times, and places would be included but only if it seemed to me that the source was reliable. Certain facts would be verified to confirm their validity but, by and large, this book would be about recollections.

Upon Tatsuo's death, the family chose the Bank of Hawaii to be its personal representative in the settlement of the estate. Sharlyn Miyahara, V.P. of Private Client Services, was the representative of the bank. It turns out that Sharlyn has ties to Waipahu and when we incidentally told her that a book on Tatsuichi Ota was being planned, she told us about her aunt in Torrance, California, and the contingent of people living there with connections to Waipahu.

And so it went. From Hideo Ishihara to Goro and Shigemi Arakawa; from Goro Arakawa to Pete Tagalog and Mac Flores; from Lani Nedbalek to Mike Mauricio and Kay Yamada; from Glenn Oyama to Barbara Kawakami... the connections are incredible!
- *Michael T. Yamamoto*

I invited those who went to my brother's services to lunch at a nearby coffee shop. Everyone there was a relative of my father, Tatsuichi Ota, and his younger brother, Kaoru. The conversation leaned toward Tatsuichi Ota and I decided that if the stories and memories being recalled about him were not recorded now, they would be lost forever, and future generations would not have anything regarding their family history. Already, many of those closest to Tatsuichi Ota had passed away years ago. Only the few who remained today could be asked to contribute stories to his memory. I enlisted the aid of my nephew, Michael, and his wife, Karen, and together our best efforts resulted in this book. My recollections are to the best of my memory.
- *Nina Yuriko (Ota) Sylva*

I started helping Mike with the library research but as he made contacts with various people, it became clear that there was a larger story that could be told. More and more people began coming forward willing to share their recollections about life in Waipahu. We very appreciatively accepted as much as we could, recording and collecting stories, anecdotes, photos, and articles for the book. I did much of what is commonly called "library research" and found some surprises. We put it all together and recalled that Sharlyn Miyahara's husband, Dennis, had told us early on that we would be going on an incredible journey.
- *Karen N. Yamamoto*

The original narrative was for the period 1900 to about 1980. These boundaries cover the period when Tatsuichi Ota came to Hawaii and through 1978, when he died. As with all stories that use time as a reference, straying before the earlier time limits and beyond the latter limits happens often ... as it did with this book. The reader will see seemingly duplicated descriptions of the trip around Waipahu town but we have tried to group like stories together ... sometimes in different chapters if only to make the story more readable.

Much went on during this period and while we have tried to include as many of the stories that came our way, it would be impossible to include all of them. *Every* person that we interviewed had stories that would fill an individual book by himself or herself.

We hope that what we have recorded here will be part of a story of the 'old times' in Waipahu and evoke memories of times long gone.

"When you get old, you have to live with the memories."
- *Charles Ishikawa.*

And finally, some points we need to make:

1) The temptation to use 'mauka,' 'makai,' 'Diamond Head,' and 'Ewa' as directions fell to the selection of 'North,' 'South,' 'East,' and 'West,' if purely to give more universal readability and understanding.

2) The deletion of specific pronunciation marks for Hawaiian words should not be taken as an affront to Hawaii or its people. Again, we elected not to use them for more universal readability.

3) As an example of name usage, Nina Yuriko (Ota) Sylva is read as follows: **Nina** is the given English first name, **Yuriko** is the middle name in English/first name in Japanese, **(Ota)** is the maiden name, and **Sylva** is the married/family/surname.

4) Brackets, [ ] , indicate our insertion.

-1- Locating and defining Waipahu

. . . water, bursting forth from the ground . . .

The town of Waipahu is located west of downtown Honolulu on the Island of Oahu, in the State of Hawaii. Defining the limits or boundaries of Waipahu is not simple. Where certain communities might have specific lines of demarcation between one town or another, the entire island of Oahu is also the entire City and County of Honolulu.

Most Islanders think of Honolulu as being that downtown area around Honolulu Harbor and containing the financial hub of banks and businesses as well as the centers of the State of Hawaii and the City & County of Honolulu governments. The City levies no municipal tax but as the City & County of Honolulu, it levies a property tax. The State has only a general excise tax, sometimes called a sales tax. Any other taxes, including income taxes, are assessed to all citizens uniformly and without discrimination as to location. This makes boundaries unnecessary. There are no incorporated towns or cities in Hawaii. As such, towns exist as regions.

The police department is the HPD — the Honolulu Police Department, and while it has many sub-stations around the island, it is responsible for the entire island of Oahu. Various businesses or agencies might denote Waipahu as simply being an area described suitably to their needs. For example, the U.S. Postal Service designates Waipahu as the zip code 96797. The telephone company denotes Waipahu as having phone numbers beginning with 657, 671, 675, 676, 677, 678, 679, 680, 686, 688, or 691.

Michael Mauricio, writing in *Waipahu: Its People and Heritage*, locates Waipahu as being between present-day Pearl City on the east and Kunia Rd. on the west. This area is part of the early Hawaiian land *mahele* [division of land] of 1848* denoting *ahupuaa* [lands "from the mountains to the sea" assigned to Hawaiians by their Royalty] regions of Waipio, Waikele, and Hoaeae. These *ahupuaa* are located in the *moku* [land division] of the Ewa District (Fig. 1-1).

---

* oftentimes called the Great Mahele

These ahupuaa were given so that each land owner had equitable shares of products from the land to the sea.

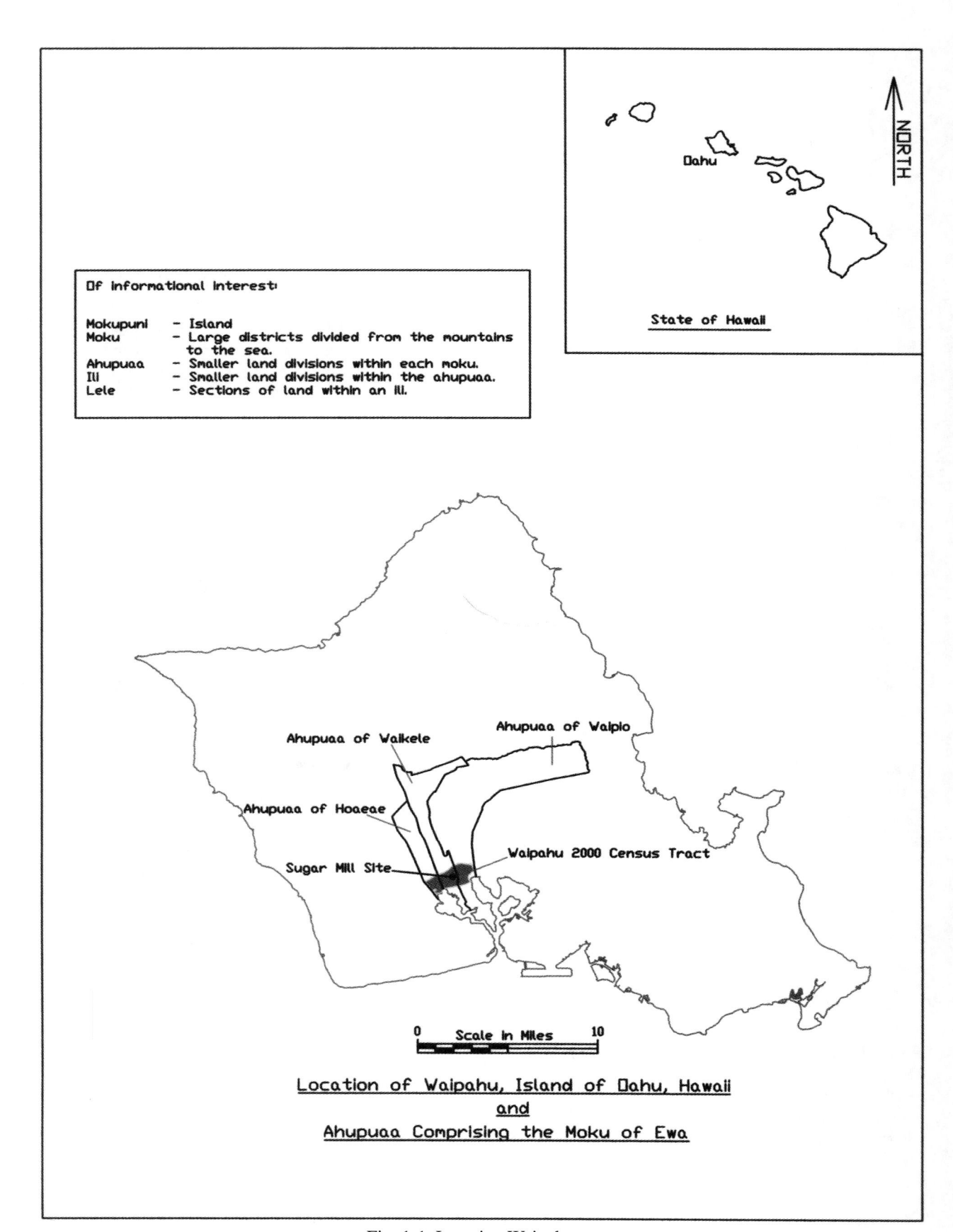

Fig. 1-1. Locating Waipahu

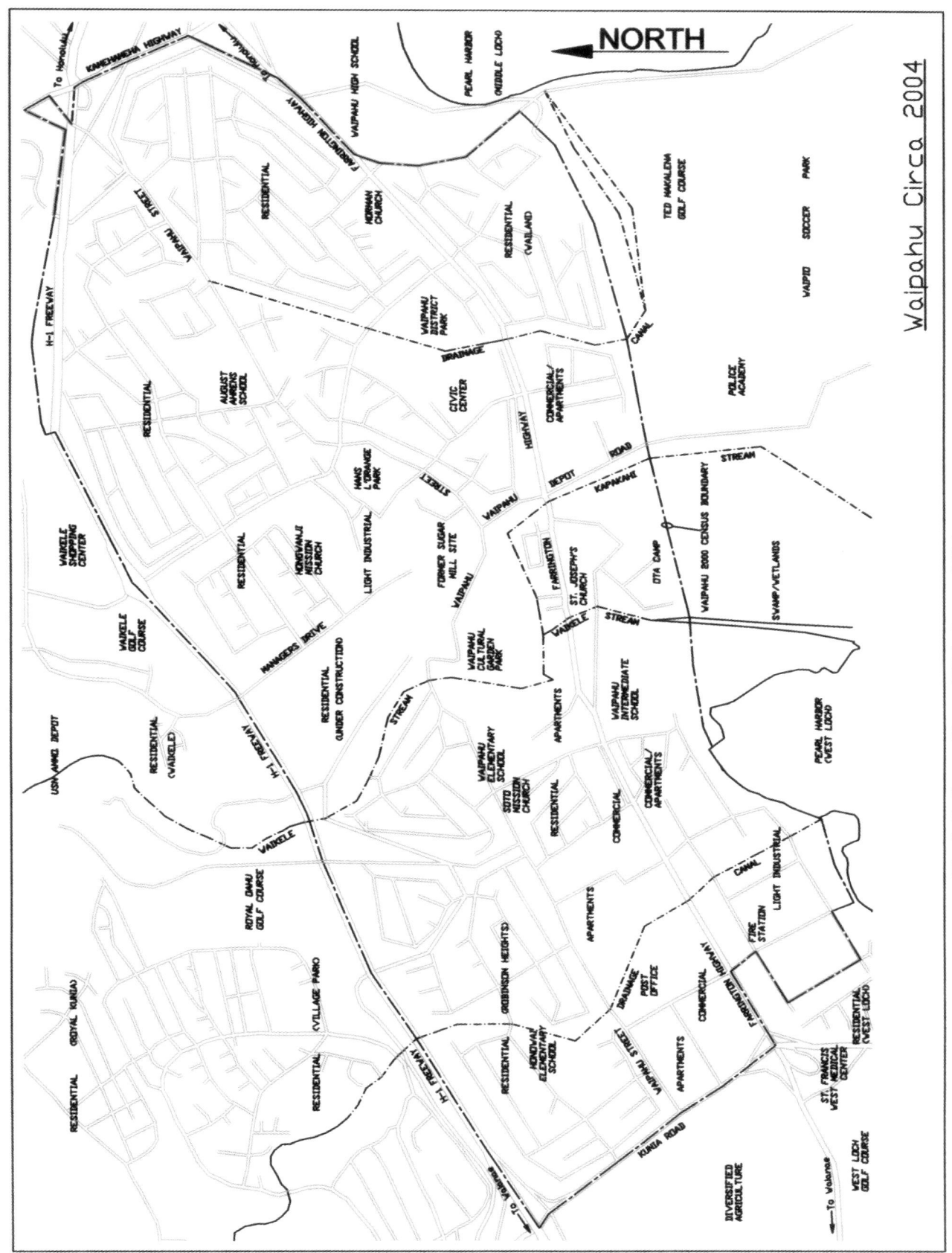

Fig. 1-2. Census Tract of Waipahu, ca. 2004.

More recently, the State of Hawaii enacted legislation defining the Waipahu town limits as shown in an island-wide map and detailed in a map (Fig. 1-2) showing streets as boundaries for census purposes in concurrence with the U.S. Census.

For property tax purposes, the State of Hawaii designates Waipahu as having Tax Map Keys (TMKs) with numbers prefixed and completed as 9-4-XXX-XXX or 9-3-XXX-XXX.

The climate in Waipahu is much like what it is over most of Hawaii. Low temperatures range from 62°F to 70°F and highs range from about 78°F to 87°F. The average year-round temperature is about 74°F. Precipitation is only from rain and a year-round average is about 2 inches per month.

About a 30-minute drive by freeway from Honolulu Harbor, and between the tips of the West and Middle Lochs of Pearl Harbor, Waipahu is today a residential community with many small businesses and a population with many ethnic backgrounds. Even with land at a premium in Hawaii, Waipahu has only a few high-rise buildings and these rarely go over six stories high.

One of the reasons for the lack of high-rise buildings or other structures of heavy mass may be that much of Waipahu has a coral underbed or a spongy ground. Stearns, writing in *Geology of the State of Hawaii*, shows in Fig. 1-3 the geologic strata of what is now the Pearl Harbor [and Waipahu areas south of Waipahu St.]; the sidebar shows sea levels around Pearl Harbor.

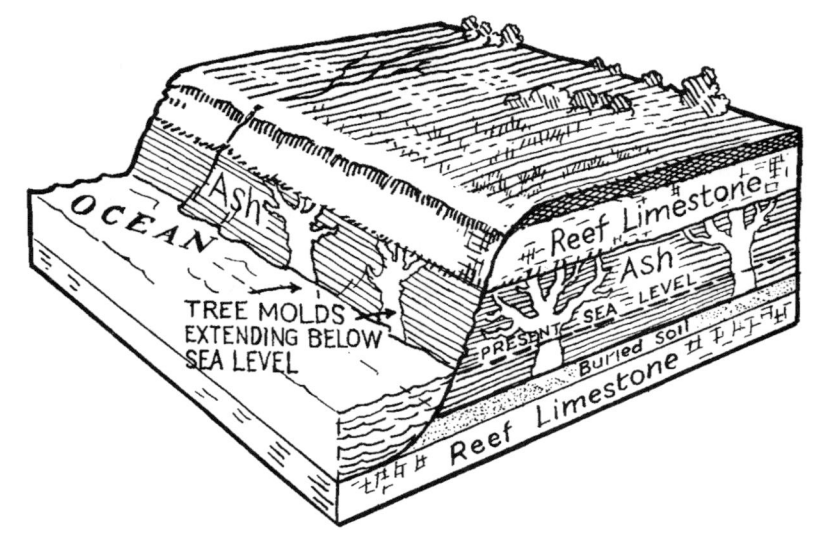

Fig. 1-3. Geologic cross-section of land in the Pearl Harbor area. (Stearns)

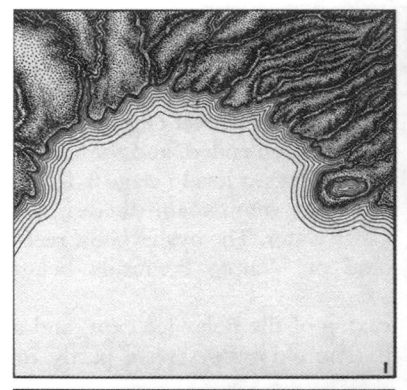

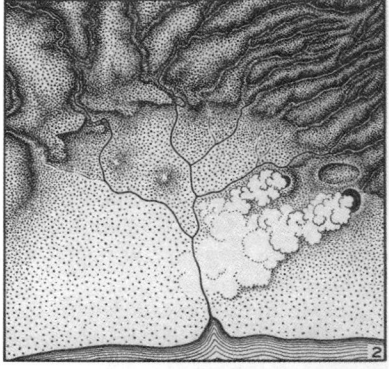

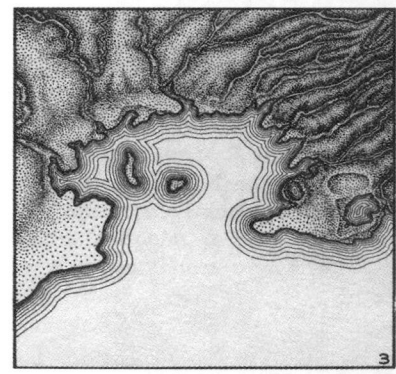

Fig. 1-4. Geologic history of the Pearl Harbor loch area. Top to bottom: (1) the sea was 95 feet higher than the present level; (2) the sea was 60 feet lower; (3) the sea was 25 feet higher; (4) present sea level.

"The south-east corner of the intersection of Farrington Highway and Depot Rd. was once selected to have a high-rise building. Pilings were driven into the ground and after a few strokes of the driving hammer, the piling would disappear with a 'swoosh' into the earth. Another would be placed atop the first piling's location and the process repeated until finally the project was abandoned as not being practical to support major buildings. The pilings that disappeared were said to have been found at the bottom of Pearl Harbor."
-Mike Mauricio

In an interview by Lani Nedbalek with "Cranky" Watanabe, Cranky relates how the swimming pool of the Waipahu District Park would continually crack because it was not built on ground capable of supporting something as massive as a swimming pool.

Lani also tells us that when the first building of Hawaii's Plantation Village (HPV) was built, the building began to shift. The shifting was so pronounced that you could take a round object like a ball and place it at one end of the building and it would swiftly roll to the other end. HPV officals wanted to keep the building as a unique attraction but city building inspectors would not allow it so it was torn down. The present building does not have any tilting problems as it is built on pilings sunk deep into the ground. To avoid flooding in the flood plain area in which it is built, the building sits quite high above the ground.

The majority of buildings in Waipahu are homes of one- or two-stories located on lots of about 7,500 square feet or less. Businesses occupy one- or two-story buildings along major roadways. In the past 15 to 20 years, the trend has been for strip malls and outlet malls to be built on outlying areas that were once sugar and pineapple lands.

Activity within the town of Waipahu is centered around Waipahu St., Depot Rd., and Farrington Hwy. Waipahu St. curves through the town in a general East-West direction. (Fig. 2-1)

Waipahu St. when it was called (Main) Government Rd., once curved northward around the mill of the Oahu Sugar Co. In 1899, by request from the Oahu Sugar Co. and agreement by the Interior Department of the Government of Hawaii, the roadway was curved southward around the mill and is now called Waipahu St. (Fig. 3-1)

Depot Rd. starts at Waipahu St. and runs down a slight hill running North-South towards the waters of Pearl Harbor. At the end of Depot Rd., a train depot was once located and for many in early Waipahu, this was the starting point for a trip into Honolulu. The older businesses and homes were located along Waipahu St. and Depot Rd.

"The area along Waipahu St. was called *shin-machi* [new town or street] and the area along Depot Rd. was called *hon-machi* [main town or street] by the Japanese community in Waipahu."
    -Masuye Akiyama

The many ethnic groups who immigrated to Waipahu gave way to the naming of various parts of Waipahu in transliterated words:

Donburo - The sugar mill communities were up on a slight hill or plateau; therefore, the other communities were transliterated to be "down below." Extending this, there is 'nishi-donburo' or 'west side down below' and 'higashi-donburo' or 'east side down below.'

Shoburo - That area at the end of Depot Rd. where Kapakahi Stream meets the waters of Pearl Harbor; the area was transliterated from "shore below." Shigemi Arakawa tells us that 'shoburo' might be more correctly "*shiofuro*" as the salt (*shio*) water [from the Pearl Harbor] area where baseball players took a bath (*furo*) after games.

"New Year's Day was a time when we went as a family to bathe in the 'shiofuro' area."
    -Goro Arakawa

"The Shio-Yu Teahouse, owned by Tomoichi Hamada, was located on the Waipio Peninsula in the 1930s. 'Shio-buro' and 'shio-yu' both translate to 'salt bath.'"
    -Shige Yoshitake

If "donburo" and "shoburo" seem like words coming from only the sugar-plantation town of Waipahu, at least "donburo" was not strange to one coming from Kohala, on the Big Island of Hawaii.

The Shio-Yu Teahouse was located slightly west of Camp 32 on the Waipio Peninsula.

Before sugar was planted on the Waipio Peninsula, rice paddies dominated the whole area.

"The 'r' in 'donburo' and 'shoburo' is pronounced as a rolled 'r'."
— Iris Yamaoka

"My ear tells me that 'donburo' should be spelled 'danburo' or 'dunburo'."
—Shige Yoshitake

The problem that led to this transliteration is that the Japanese do not have an 'l' in their language and therefore could not pronounce 'below.'

"I knew of 'donburo' and its meaning from the times when I grew up in Hawi. But 'shoburo' was entirely strange until I came here to HPV [Hawaii's Plantation Village]."
-Gail (Watanabe) Ifuku

[The community of Hawi in the Kohala District, on the Island of Hawaii, is on a mountain peak. Therefore, there would not be a "shore below" close by.]

The map (Fig. 3-5) shows businesses and landmarks from 1920 through about 2000. The growth of Waipahu was also changing quickly from decade-to-decade and even on a yearly basis.

What is interesting, however, is that early Waipahu supported many businesses that often duplicated products and services offered. It is estimated that in the 1920s, the population of Waipahu was about 4,000.

Robert C. Schmitt, writing in *Historical Statistics of Hawaii,* reports the population of Honolulu in 1900 as 39,306 and growing to 81,820 in 1920. Waipahu, as an outlying community was not considered separately until 1930. Schmitt's population report for 1930 through 1970, by decades, and comparing Honolulu and Waipahu, is shown in Table 1-1. Later sources provided 1980 and 1990 data. Population for all of Hawaii is also given for comparison purposes.

Table 1-1. Population by Decades

	1930	1940	1950	1960	1970	1980	1990
Honolulu	137,582	179,358	248,034	294,194	324,871	762,565	836,231
Hawaii	368,336	423,330	499,769	609,096	769,913	964,691	1,108,229
Waipahu	5,874	6,906	7,169	7,802	24,150	29,139	51,295

For this relatively low Waipahu population to have so many restaurants, grocery types of stores, laundries, theaters, and the like, is difficult to appreciate; but all of these apparently were able to generate enough income for their owners to subsist. The entrepreneurial spirit of the people of Waipahu gave much impetus to its growth.

Debra Miyashiro, librarian for the Department of Business, Economic Development and Tourism (DBED & T), State of Hawaii, helped us with many records. These show that in Waipahu there were 51 retail establishments in 1954. By

1992, this number had grown to 178. Retail establishments are considered as stores selling to the general public, i.e., food, apparel, furniture, drug stores, hardware, building materials, fuel, eating and drinking places, automotive and farm equipment dealers, and the like.

Farrington Hwy. runs East-West and in more of a straight line than Waipahu St. and was begun as the "Waianae-Waipahu Bypass highway" to more directly connect Honolulu to the further outlying western Oahu communities. After its completion in 1939, businesses sprang up along its way and continued the growth of Waipahu.

On the North-East portion of the intersection of Farrington Hwy. and Depot Rd., Raymond Sokugawa developed what might be called the first shopping center in Hawaii, the Aloha Shopping Center. It consisted of a series of stores connected to one another on a single street level (as a strip mall today might be described) featuring restaurants, drygoods, a gasoline station, etc.

Very Early Waipahu

Even before the early Hawaiians, much of the Hawaiian Islands was below the level of the ocean (see Fig. 1-4). In the Waipahu area, this is evidenced by a layer of seashells visible in a land cut of the area behind the Waipahu Cultural Garden Park. Shigemi Arakawa recalls that as a young man, in the area where Depot Rd. meets Pearl Harbor, on the Waipio Peninsula, there were caves in the coral that were used as burial sites. These are no longer visible and Shigemi cannot recall if they were old Hawaiian burial sites but definitely remembers that the caves had human remains.

The early Hawaiians have left parts of their civilization recorded in the form of petroglyphs. In Waipahu, there are two known sites shown in the map as *P. Heiau*s, sacred places of worship; they are known only from the memory of early scholars in Hawaiian history as there is no evidence of them existing today in Waipahu. These heiaus are shown in the map as H. These petroglyph and heiau sites are shown in Fig. 1-5.

Before discovery of Hawaii by the Western world, the early Hawaiians considered Waipahu to be the capital of Oahu. Royalty would often gather there especially relishing the fresh water gushing from artesian springs.

Some interesting tidbits about Hawaii's multi-ethnic population:

In 1884, there were about 18,000 Chinese in Hawaii.

In 1878, the Portuguese numbered about 500; in 1884, it was about 10,000; and in 1930, the figure rose to 27,600.

In 1900, the Japanese constituted about 40% of the Hawaii population; this was about 61,100 up from 116 in 1884.

Between 1900 and 1924, the Okinawan population grew by about 20,000 people.

In 1970, the State census showed that the 770,000 people were roughly comprised of the following percentages and ethnic backgrounds:

39.2%	Caucasian
28.3%	Japanese
12.4%	Filipino
9.3%	Hawaiian
6.8%	Chinese
1.3%	Korean
<1%	Black

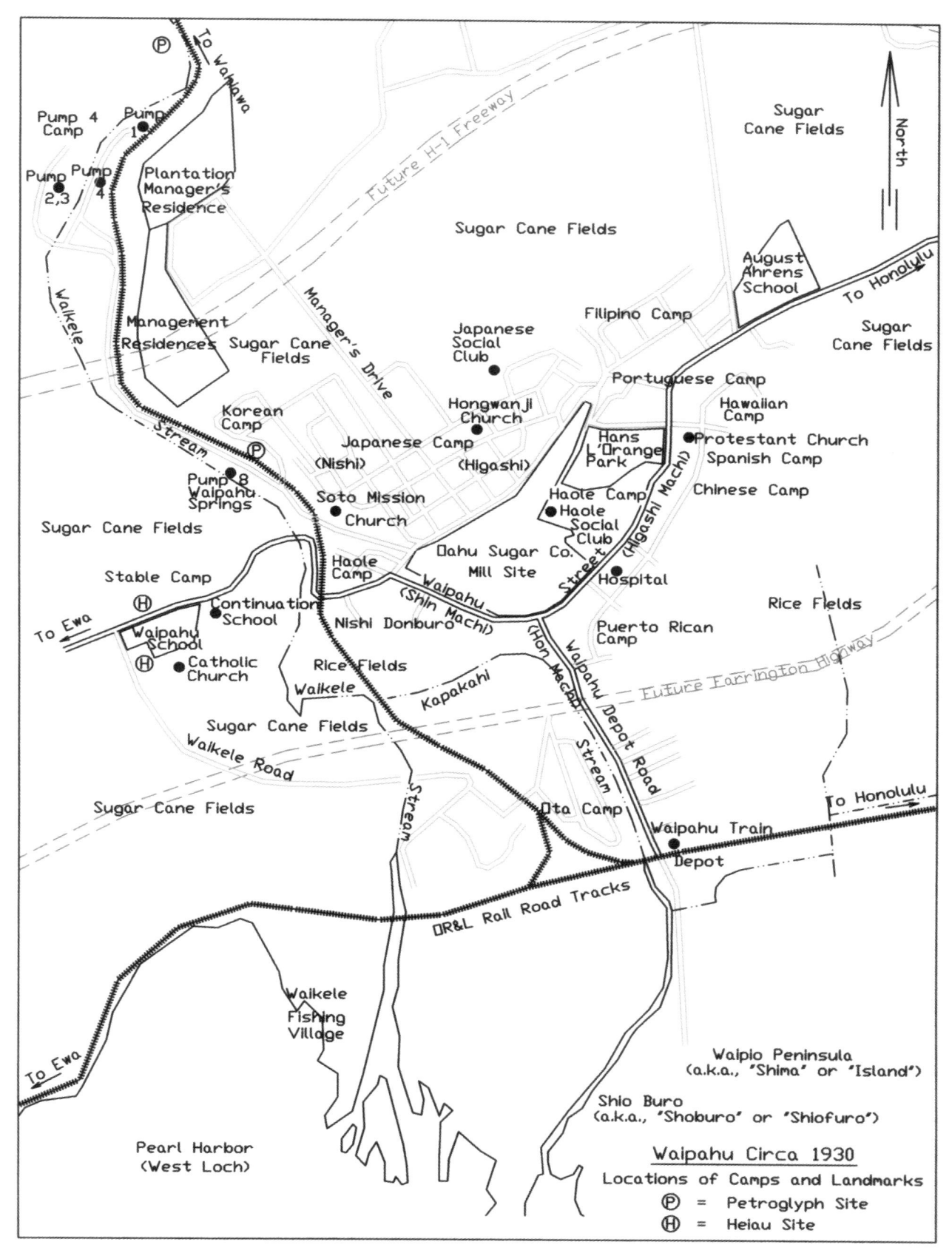

Fig. 1-5. Points of interest ca. 1930

The fresh water lent itself to the cultivation of *taro*. With poi from taro and fish from ponds built in the area adjacent to Pearl Harbor, the Hawaiians subsisted well.

Other products later grown in Waipahu having high fresh water dependence were watercress, water chestnuts, lotus root, rice, and burdock root. Except for watercress and rice, these other products did not attain enough high demand to make them prominent economic market goods. Watercress still exists today in the 'donburo' area adjacent to the Waipahu Cultural Garden Park and also across from August Ahrens Elementary School in the 'donburo' area of that part of Waipahu.

The Chinese were among the first immigrant groups to settle in Hawaii. They initially came to Hawaii to work on sugar plantations. In Waipahu, while there were hundreds working at the Oahu Sugar Co., many of the Chinese were already shop keepers, store owners, and farmers. They had been quick to recognize that the fresh waters in the 'donburo' areas could support the growing of rice, a staple from their old country.

"The Chinese blended well with the Hawaiians. It was a good relationship in that the Chinese worked hard for the Hawaiians, tending the taro fields and fish ponds, doing some cooking for them, and in general, being good immigrant visitors. The Hawaiians in return allowed the Chinese to use much of their lands. Much inter-marriage and familial bonding took place."
 - Douglas Chong

Records and photos of old Waipahu, together show vast areas of fish ponds that were later purchased from the Hawaiians by the Chinese and changed in usage to become rice paddies. Rice as an economic product did well in Waipahu but met its demise in the mid 1920s due to (1) competition from California rice, (2) loss by attrition of older Chinese who were the skilled rice growers, and (3) the increase in the Japanese population who preferred rice they were familiar with and as grown in their homeland.

After the Chinese, the Japanese were the next large immigrant group to settle in Waipahu. Closely following the Japanese in time were the Filipinos. Much of our story deals with the Japanese as they made up the largest portion of the population in the 20th century. And, the Japanese were an integral part of the

Barbara (Oyama) Kawakami relates to us the story she once heard about Queen Liliuokalani, who, on trips to her summer villa in Makaha, often stopped in Waipahu near the present Waipahu Cultural Garden Park, just to partake of the fine spring water.

Taro - *Colocasia esculenta*; the Hawaiian name is *kalo*. In the Ewa District, there were as many as 200 to 300 varieties of wet and dry land taro; kai-kea, kai-koi, haokea, and lehua were plentiful but kai-koi was the most flavorful and preferred by ancient Hawaiians.

The tuber root of the taro plant, more correctly called the corm, is boiled, peeled of its rough outer skin, and with water added, mashed to become poi, a bland and somewhat viscous paste.

Poi was the staple food for the Hawaiians.

Douglas Chong in *Ancestral Reflections*, shows as many as 30 rice paddies that the Chinese maintained in the old-time 'donburo' areas of Waipahu. This very definitive and well-researched book should be referred to for a more detailed history of the Chinese in Waipahu.

Oahu Sugar Co. during this period.

Immigrants as a whole

If one were to trace immigrant groups and their significant arrival dates in Hawaii, these would be as shown below.

Table 1-2. Immigrant Groups -
Arrival dates of significant groups

Chinese	1852
Japanese	1868
Portuguese	1878
Germans	1881
Scandinavians	1881 (Norwegians and some Swedish)
Okinawans	1900
Puerto Ricans	1900
Spanish	1900
Koreans	1903
Filipinos	1906

Dates shown are for immigrant groups arriving with purposeful immigration; i.e., not by accidental landing such as shipwrecks, navigational errors, etc.

A simplified scenario:
a) Planters need workers
b) They court country, X
c) Country X allows emigrants
d) Immigrants mis-treated or are poor workers
e) Planters court another country, Y
f) Country Y's workers are good workers
g) Many Country Y workers arrive
h) Hawaii now has too many workers from Country Y
i) Immigration from Country Y halted
j) Country Z courted
and on and on

See A Chronology for Waipahu at the end of Chapter 3. The first immigrant group, the Chinese, had the Chinese Exclusion Act; then the Japanese were restricted in immigration by the Gentlemen's Agreement and Japanese Exclusion Act.

Interspersed were strikes and general malcontent on the part of both planters and laborers.

The Chinese came because of over-crowding in China, failures of crops, and economy; the Japanese came because of a failing economy; the Portuguese came because of a failing economy; the list goes on and on. "The promised land," a future better than their present homeland, was generally the motive for immigrant groups to leave their home country.

Intertwined with the reason for each ethnic group immigration, are the views and politics of the planters (the various plantation owners) and the governments (both of Hawaii and the emigrating country). These would be trying to balance which ethnic groups would be courted to come to Hawaii, which ethnic groups were already in Hawaii and proving to be good ethnic additions, and the economics for all concerned.

"For many Japanese immigrants, the goal was to make money and go back to Japan. So when we went to Japanese School, our parents urged us to do well so that we could go back to Japan without having lost any of our Japanese language or culture."
-Henry Morisada

The people of Waipahu not only came directly from their home countries but from other islands in Hawaii. Some of those we were able to interview tell us their stories.

"I was born on Kauai and brought to Waipahu when I was two

years old. My father originally worked in Lihue [Kauai] but brought our then family of six kids to Waipahu and he worked for Oahu Sugar as a locomotive engineer.

My mother later told me how she carried me and when the ship from Kauai arrived at Honolulu Harbor, they would jump into the small rowboat that came up to the larger ship. That's because the larger ship never did go right up to the pier. She told me that some people missed the jump into the pitching rowboat and never came up! This was in the 1920s.

I told my mother later that if I had known about that, I would never have gone to Waipahu!"
                -Elsie (Fernandez) Moniz

"I left Waipahu in 1953 because I saw no future for me or the town. The people were nice but I couldn't see living there for the rest of my life."
                -Anonymous

"I grew up in Ota camp and when I was going to the University of Hawaii, I had a chance to be an exchange student in Santa Fe, New Mexico. It gave me an opportunity to see places other than Hawaii and I decided then that it was almost a 'now or never' kind of thing. It led to my meeting my husband, Bob, and eventually teaching in a Navajo school in the area of Four Corners*.

Later, my parents came up for a visit and they liked Albuquerque, New Mexico, so much that they bought a home there. Something they could never afford to do in Hawaii."
                -Myrna (Manuel) Tsinnajinnie

* Four Corners is the one place in the United States where the borders of four states (Utah, Colorado, New Mexico, and Arizona) meet at right angles to each other.

"I'm originally from Kauai. My first introduction to Waipahu was in 1956. I was a freshman at the University of Hawaii and was taking a ride as a passenger in a car taking a girl back to Waipahu after a party. The town seemed unwelcoming - dry and with no life. I decided then that Waipahu was not a place to live.

Six years later, after graduating and getting married, I settled into a house that was built on what was once cane lands [in Waipahu] and was teaching school at Barbers Point Naval Air Station.

After a few months, it felt like home. The butcher called me by my first name, Arakawas had everything we needed and the furniture/electronics store (Mid-Town Radio) gave us great deals.

In short, I settled into life in Waipahu. During the 1960s, Lin's Chop Suey and Country Inn were favorites of ours. In the 1970s, older stores were being torn down and replaced by newer structures and owners. The old families and friendly atmosphere disappeared.

I still think that Waipahu is a bedroom community with no common marketing of the community and little political clout in City and State Governments."
-Yoshiko (Tamashiro) Yamauchi

"I've always enjoyed visiting my daughter in Santa Barbara, California, but I still want to stay and live in Waipahu."
-Helen (Sato) Isono

The naming of Waipahu

Waipahu is the name of the spring located near Pump 8 of the Oahu Sugar Co. (see Fig. 1-5 and Back Cover). The spring is now capped but at one time gushed forth artesian water at the rate of 42.5 cubic feet per second! Please refer to the back cover for more information about this spring.

Early Hawaiians digging in the area discovered the spring gushing forth and named it *Wai-pahu* [*wai*-water; *pahu* - to burst, explode].

Legend also records how a woman lost her tapa anvil in a stream in Kahuku [at the northernmost tip of Oahu]. She looked far and wide and as she approached Waipahu, she heard the distinctive sound of her tapa anvil. The anvil had traveled the underground waterways and surfaced at the gushing spring of Waipahu. Another woman had found it and was using it. The tapa anvil was graciously returned to its righful owner and together they walked arm-in-arm across the Keonekuilimalaula-o-Ewa (the land of going arm-in-arm on the breadth of Ewa [plain]).

The spring was called Ka-puka-na-wai-o-Kahuku (outlet of water from Kahuku) at that time.

In a letter to the *Honolulu Star-Bulletin* newspaper in 1956, Simeon K. Nawaa writes in describing Ewa district:

"Note the absence of "Waipahu," [in a listing of areas] because it is not a tract of land, but only a spring located in Waikele. The Oahu Railway & Land Co. is the culprit responsible for misuse and confusion, when it built its station."

Legend records that the shark goddess Kaahupahau swam up from the sea of Puuloa [Pearl Harbor] to bathe in the fresh water of the gushing spring of Waipahu.

"The spring Waipahu created a natural swimming hole just because of all the water coming out. The water was clear and cold and the pond was quite deep. Surrounding the area were mango [*Mangifera indica*], rose apple [*Syzygium jambos*], and mountain apple [*Syzygium malaccense*] trees that we would swing from before dropping into the pond. There were rocks on one side of the pond."

-Lilly (Takushi) Tokuhara

Preludes to the Oahu Sugar Co.

In 1879, James Campbell hired California well-digger James Ashley to explore for subterranean water on his Honouliuli cattle ranch close to Waipahu in the Ewa District. Fresh water was found at a depth of 273 ft. demonstrating the feasibility of sinking more wells as needed to support agriculture.

Land that was arid and fit only for cattle grazing was now seen as having potential for agriculture. What was also needed was a transport system to connect the outlying west Oahu areas with the port of Honolulu. Enter Ben Dillingham.

Ben Dillingham put forth the idea of a railway system for west Oahu. The first train began operating on King Kalakaua's birthday, November 16, 1889, and eventually connected Honolulu with the outlying communities of Aiea, Pearl City, Waipahu, Ewa, Waianae, Waialua, and Kahuku.

This Oahu Railway & Land Co. had its stop in Waipahu at the end of Depot Rd. and it was called, appropriately, Waipahu Station.

Water had been found for agriculture, the Oahu Railway & Land Co. was in place, the Reciprocity Treaty of 1876 allowed for sugar to enter the United States duty-free. Ben Dillingham, therefore, began putting together plans for the Oahu Sugar Co., eventually incorporating it in 1897.

Mike Mauricio, writing in a column, *Sugar Legacy*, from the Hawaii's Plantation Village Newsletter, relates a possibly curious turn of events that might have happened.

"In 1889, plans were being drawn up for the new plantation which Dillingham wanted to name Oahu Sugar. Honouliuli

The prospectus of the Oahu Sugar Co. includes numerous references to artesian water coming out of the ground. Some powered rice mills and others were free-flowing, unharnessed outlets.

In the lowland areas of Pearl Harbor, cattle and horses were seen dipping their heads below the salt water and partaking of the fresh artesian water.

The many springs and some of their measured outputs led James Campbell to try his experimental bore to seek a greater and more steady source of water to support agriculture.

A marker denoting the site of the first artesian well in Hawaii can be found at the SW corner of the intersection of Ft. Weaver Rd. and Old Ft. Weaver Rd. going towards Ewa on Ft. Weaver Rd.

Fig. 1-6. First artesian well in Hawaii marker plaque.

"The original well is where a pump house is located a few hundred yards west of here (Honouliuli Shokai [store]) at the base of the mountains. It may have been capped earlier but it is still in use today."

-Wally Murata

The well flowed for 60 years after it was bored but was capped by the City & County government in 1939. The well was put back into use with the development of agriculture in the area.

When westerner Capt. James Cook, discovered Hawaii in 1778, sugarcane was already being cultivated by Hawaiians. The Hawaiians recognized that the stalks of cane yielded a sweet juice when chewed and had cane growing around their houses and in small patches.

The first successful sugar plantation was in Koloa, Kauai, in 1835.

was also considered but the board of directors finally settled on naming it Ewa Plantation. Imagine, there would be no Ewa if not for the plantation, for Ewa is the name of the district from Red Hill to Kahe Point. The lands themselves were situated on the ahupuaa of Honouliuli. If Dillingham had had his way, the plantation would have been named Oahu Sugar, and the area would still be known as Honouliuli. Seven years later when another plantation in Waikele would be built, he could have named it Ewa and maybe Waipahu, which is the name of a spring, would have been "Ewa." Looking at it from today's standpoint, Oahu Sugar would be in Ewa, while Ewa Plantation would be in Waipahu!

As things turned out, Honouliuli became a part of Ewa just as Waikele became a part of Waipahu while in actuality the formers are the land divisions and the latters are contrived names."

References - Chapter 1.

A History of Hawaii, Ralph Kuykendall, the MacMillan Co. New York, New York, 1926.

Waipahu Centennial Booklet, Mervyn Ah Tou, Edward Uemori, Michael Isobe, tri-chairs, Waipahu, Hawaii, 1997.

Hawaii's Sugar, Hawaii Sugar Planters' Association. Honolulu, Hawaii, 1985.

Waipahu: Its People and Heritage, P.O.S.E. Custom Publishers, Michael Mauricio, Ed., Waipahu, Hawaii, 1997.

Sugar Water, Carol Wilcox, University of Hawaii Press, Honolulu, Hawaii, 1997.

A History of Hawaii, Linda Menton and Eileen Tamura, Curriculum Research & Development Group, College of Education, University of Hawaii, Honolulu, Hawaii, 1989.

Waipahu, Lani Nedbalek, Wonderview Press, Wahiawa, Hawaii, 1984.

Historical Statistics of Hawaii, Robert C. Schmitt, University of Hawaii Press, Honolulu, Hawaii, 1977.

Ancestral Reflections, Douglas D. L. Chong, Waipahu Tsoong Nyee Society, Waipahu, Hawaii, 1998.

Whatever Happened to Hawaiian Locomotives, website of the Hawaiian Railway Society, Bob Paoa, 1998.

Japanese Immigrant Clothing in Hawaii 1885-1941, Barbara F. Kawakami, University of Hawaii Press, Honolulu, Hawaii, 1993.

Sugar Trains Pictorial, Jesse C. Conde, Glenwood Publishers, Felton, California, 1975.

Sites of Oahu, Elspeth P. Sterling and Catherine C. Summers, Bishop Museum Press, Honolulu, Hawaii, 1978.

The Peopling of Hawaii, Eleanor C. Nordyke, University of Hawaii Press, Honolulu, Hawaii, 1989.

Geology of the State of Hawaii, Harold T. Stearns, Pacific Books, publishers, Palo Alto, California, 2nd. ed., 1985.

History Makers of Hawaii, A. Grove Day, Mutual Publishing Co., Honolulu, Hawaii, 1984.

Traditional Hawaiian Uses of Plants, Isabella Aiona Abbott, Bishop Museum Press, Honolulu, Hawaii, 1992.

Early Hawaiian Life, Mahealani Pescaia, Dept. of Education, State of Hawaii, Honolulu, Hawaii, 1981.

Hawaiian Dictionary, Mary Kawena Pukui and Samuel Elbert, University of Hawaii Press, Honolulu, Hawaii, 1971.

A Pocket Guide to Hawaii's Trees and Shrubs, H. Douglas Pratt, Mutual Publishing, Honolulu, Hawaii, 2003.

The Oahu Mapbook, Phears Mapbooks, Honolulu, Hawaii, 2004.

Numerous documents, Department of Business, Economic Development and Tourism (DBED & T), State of Hawaii.

Numerous newsletters of Hawaii's Plantation Village.

-2- Oahu Sugar

...a horse ride and a broken leg...

The starting point of our story centers around the Oahu Sugar Co. Other landmarks, businesses, activities, and people are closely intertwined with the history of the Oahu Sugar Co. and we describe and locate them for reference from the sketch below.

Ben Dillingham, a native of Massachusetts, was first mate on a ship visiting Oahu in 1865. He broke his leg while on a horse ride and was left behind by his ship.

This turn of events led to the creation of the Oahu Railway & Land Co., the Oahu Sugar Co., and numerous other economic giants in the history of Hawaii.

Sugar cane, *saccharum officinarum,* was known by the Hawaiians as *ko*.

The initial, major stockholder of the Oahu Sugar Co. was H. Hackfeld and Co. Hackfeld and Co. eventually became American Factors, Ltd. (AMFAC). The officers of Oahu Sugar were Paul Isenberg, Pres., Ben Dillingham, 1st VP, Mark Robinson, 2nd VP, amd J.F. Hackfeld, Treas.

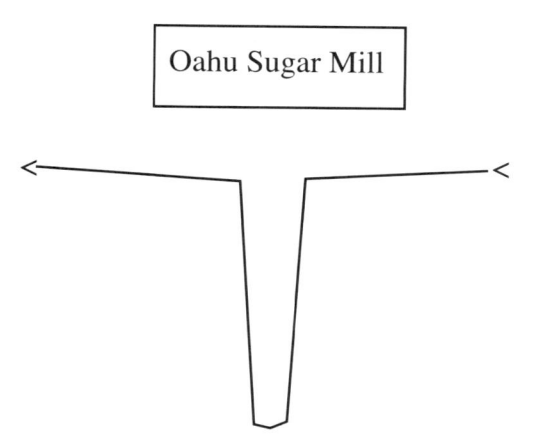

Fig. 2-1. A Trip through the town along Waipahu St., going East to West and detouring down Depot Rd.

The Oahu Sugar Co. was started by Benjamin Franklin Dillingham in 1897. The impact that the Oahu Sugar Co. made on the history of Waipahu is evidenced by the fact that the people of Waipahu celebrated their 100th Anniversary in 1997.

" *'Midst the waving tassels, stands Waipahu High.* That's the way our alma mater began. In high school, looking out through the window, I could see the canefields as they swayed back and forth."

-Anonymous 810

Some records indicate that the Oahu Sugar Mill site was once called Aualii and had crops of rice and bananas.

Legend recalls that the mill was on a plateau called Keone-kui-lima-lau-la-o-ewa (the land of going arm-in-arm on the breadth of Ewa).

August Ahrens, the first manager of the Oahu Sugar Co., skillfully laid out the plantation. In just two years he had wells drilled, purchased pumping machinery, built and equipped the mill, purchased horses, mules and pack animals, obtained seed cane and cultivation tools, employed a labor force and supervisory staff, and provided housing accommodations. This was the start of their first crop.

Oahu Sugar began with about 1,000 acres of land. The first crop, in 1899, yielded about 7,900 tons of sugar. Most of the sugar growing land was leased from the Bishop, the Ii, and the Robinson Estates. The mill and most of the sugar planted lands is on a plateau north of the town of Waipahu. This plateau is referred to as the Schofield plateau and sits atop a large aquifer. This aquifer is the source of many artesian wells in and around Waipahu and the source of well water for the cane that was grown on the Schofield plateau. Oahu Sugar's first office was located close to the spring Waipahu. Now capped, the spring was where Pump 8 got its artesian water.

Originally, the lands of Oahu Sugar were thought to be among the finest on the island for agriculture. In trying to clear the land, rocks and stones, some as large as houses and more properly called boulders, were encountered. They made for excellent building materials.

"From here [the courtyard of Waipahu Elementary School], you can see the walls of cleaved rock fronting all of those homes across Waipahu St. These are the originals from when the plantation first started. They go from here all the way back to where the Plantation Store building is located [eastern part of the Oahu Sugar mill]."
    -June (Saito) Tamashiro

"Don't forget that the stone walls were covered during parts of the summer months with the fragrant and beautiful night-blooming cereus [*hylocereus undatus*]."
    -Amy (Yasuda) Sakuma

"Later the plantation removed the night blooming cereus and planted some sort of ground cover; this was in the 1950s. The night blooming cereus was a good cover for the hilly land because it was like a cactus; with a lot of thorns and so it protected the hill from people trampling over the area and letting the hill eventually erode away."
    -Lilly (Takushi) Tokuhara and
    Judy (Yoshida) Hayashida

"Some parts of the hill below the mill were covered with grass. When the grass was watered, we kids used to take cardboard and use the hill to slide down to Waipahu St!"
    -James Serikaku

The mill site and land where most of the camps were located, some 70 acres, was held in fee-simple, purchased earlier from Mark Robinson.

In 1897, when Oahu Sugar started, there were 943 field workers:
44 Hawaiians
57 Portuguese
443 Japanese
399 Chinese

In 1925, there were 2,850 people on the payroll.

By 1930, there were 3,000 employees.

"Ridding ourselves of the tangled masses of lantana and mimosa were mere childs play compared to that which did not show on the surface-stones-big stones and close together, in fact stones as big as a house."
  August Ahrens, first
  manager of Oahu Sugar,
  1898

A bit dangerous as the bottom of the kids' ride abruptly ended at the top of the stone wall which was as much as six feet higher than Waipahu St!

At the head of Depot Rd. where it starts at Waipahu St., the stone wall has two cavities with curved ceilings. These housed the early volunteer fire department vehicles. [As this book is being written, these two cavities have been covered over with boards that serve as a place to post community notices.]

Mechanical advances in the fields and processing in the mill continued the growth of this sugar industry for years.

Sugar cane is a grass and as such requires much water. Surface water alone could not sustain Oahu Sugar. Along with artesian wells and man-made wells penetrating into the aquifer beneath those lands north of the mill of Oahu Sugar, production was maintained for a while. It became apparent that a good supply of water was necessary if Oahu Sugar was to continue its growth.

In 1895, the Hawaii Sugar Planters Association (HSPA) was started to coordinate efforts of planters and others concerned with agricultural production.

The HSPA changed its name to the Hawaii Agriculture Research Center (HARC) in 1996 to more completely reflect its role in Hawaii's agricultural community.

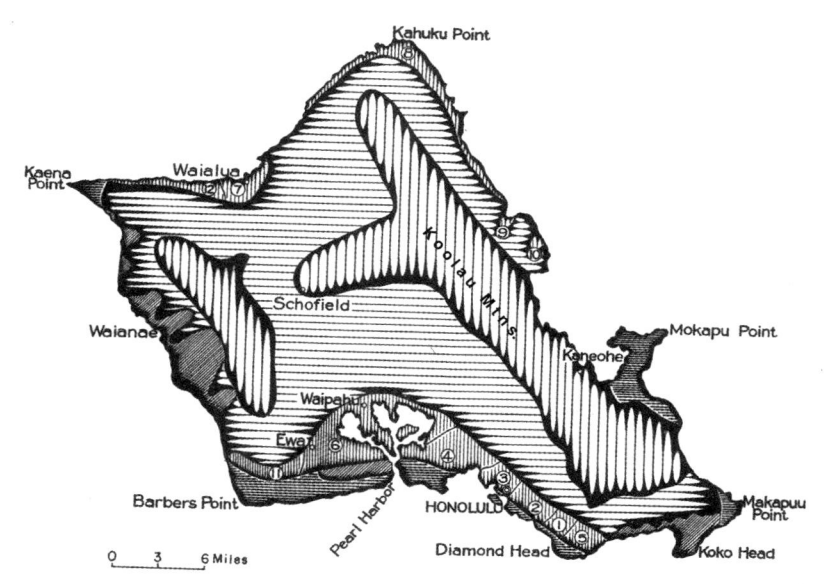

Fig. 2-2. Sources of ground water, from Stearns, the narrow vertical lines show artesian sources (the areas of Ewa and Waipahu around Pearl Harbor should be noted), the broad horizontal lines show basal non-artesian sources. Broad vertical lines show water contained in dikes that the Waiahole Water Co. went after in the Koolau Mountain range.

Securing water for irrigation was complicated by the fact that there are no large rivers on the island. And even if there were river sources, there are no suitable dam sites. Compounding this was the fact that the porous soil lets surface-water seep easily to ground water levels way below the surface.

In 1912, the Waiahole Water Co., a subsidiary of the Oahu Sugar Co., was formed for the express purpose of locating and transporting water to the cane lands of Oahu Sugar mainly from the Koolau mountain range. By 1916, water was being delivered by the Waiahole Water Co. at the rate of about 30 mgd (million gallons per day) providing only a portion of the water required for Oahu Sugar's many acres.

Groundwater from rain, wells drilled into the aquifer beneath the Schofield Plateau, and water from the Waiahole Water Co. all helped to give Oahu Sugar its needed 140 mgd average for its fields.

With additional water, larger crops were produced and the original 9-roller mill was expanded in 1903 to a 12-roller mill, the first in Hawaii. The mill was then further expanded to a 16-roller mill.

The Oahu Sugar Co., more properly called a plantation, consisted of the acres of cane grown, the sugar mill where stalks of cane were crushed and sugar juice was extracted, and partially refined sugar was prepared for export. The peripheral infrastructure were the workers and the town of Waipahu.

The people were located in clusters over parts of the plantation. By convenience, ethnic backgrounds, type of work done, or location of the clusters, these were referred to as "_____camp." There was Nishi (west) camp, Higashi (east) camp, Spanish camp, Stable camp, Pump 8, etc. Each camp could consist of one family or many families.

"There were many 'ethnic' camps but we all got along. Up until the early 1950s, you could leave your house doors unlocked because crime was almost non-existent."
          -Eddie Uemori

"When we went out, we would only use the screen door to close up the house. And that had only the screw-eye and hook type of lock since the door didn't have a spring to hold it closed. It was that safe."
          -Mel Bello

Where camp numbers were designated, these were because the

Waiahole Water Co. is a story by itself. Engineer Jorgen Jorgensen broke all records in America at that time for size and length of tunnel bores.

When completed in 1916, water was transported from the Koolau Mountain Range of Oahu to the Oahu Sugar Co. in Waipahu. The system was comprised of numerous tunnels and ditches.

The division between Nishi and Higashi Camps was Manager's Dr.

For many years, Manager's Dr. was the only paved road in the mill area!

Many other roads in the mill area were often sprayed over with oil to keep the dust down.

To get to the Waipahu Cultural Garden Park where Hawaii's Plantation Village (HPV) is located, find the intersection where Depot Rd. begins on Waipahu St. (there are several directions from which you can find your way here) on a road map.

Go west on Waipahu St., past Saiki Motors, and past another curve. The entrance to the park will be on your left.

Conceptualized in the 1960's, and dedicated in 1992, its 45 acres cover many aspects of plantation life in early Hawaii.

For the curious, the furo (bath) or furo-ba (bath house) had a firebox fired from outside the bath house that heated water contained in a four-sided redwood box inside the bath house. This redwood box generally had a copper bottom for better heat transfer from the concrete firebox to the water within the redwood box. And, the water could therefore not easily leak from the box. Inside the redwood box and over the copper sheeting, was a lattice of wood so that one wouldn't get burned by standing directly on the copper sheeting in the case of smaller furos.

camp was in that particular numbered field.

The fields of the Oahu Sugar Co. and their many camps are located on the map of Oahu as shown in Fig. 2-3. Hugh Morita generated this map from an original loaned to us by a donor who wishes to remain anonymous. The original map is said to be very accurate as aerial photos were used to validate much of the boundaries and camp locations.

Some typical house constructions within these camps are best seen at the Waipahu Cultural Garden Park. Cooking was done inside the houses in later years but earlier, there were common family cook-houses. Such was the case for toilet facilities; each camp had a common bath and toilet house. The bath accommodated male and females separately. Later in time, the houses had individual indoor toilet and bath facilities. The sewer system was a cesspool or, in some cases, sewer trenches.

"My grandparents recalled that in the 1920s, housing was primarily a long building with four families separated by walls that did not offer privacy because the separating walls did not fully go up to the roof. Cooking was done outdoors and the toilet facilities was another long building with holes in boards over a trench of running water. Bathing was in yet another building with a pool of warmed water separated by a wall for males and females. Because the wall was only above the water, kids could dive beneath the wall and go back and forth between the female and male sides! This *furo* box and the kitchen sink were both made of red wood. The kitchen sink faucet had a Bull-Durham® tobacco bag tied onto the outlet. They told me that this was to prevent fishes from coming through into our drinking water! But later, they told me that the bag was really to filter out particles of dirt."

-Rachel (Hiramoto) Fukuda

"During the 1930s we lived in a plantation duplex house (with 2 bedrooms and 1 living room). The walls were built of 1" x 12" lumber. Between the pieces of lumber there were 1/4" openings. To seal these openings from the outside, 1/4" x 2" lats were nailed. We would sometimes stick our fingers into the cracks and get stung by scorpions!

The bedrooms were small . . . about 10' x 10' and all seven of our family would sleep in one bedroom on the floor with a large *futon* [heavy blanket filled with cotton batting]. During the

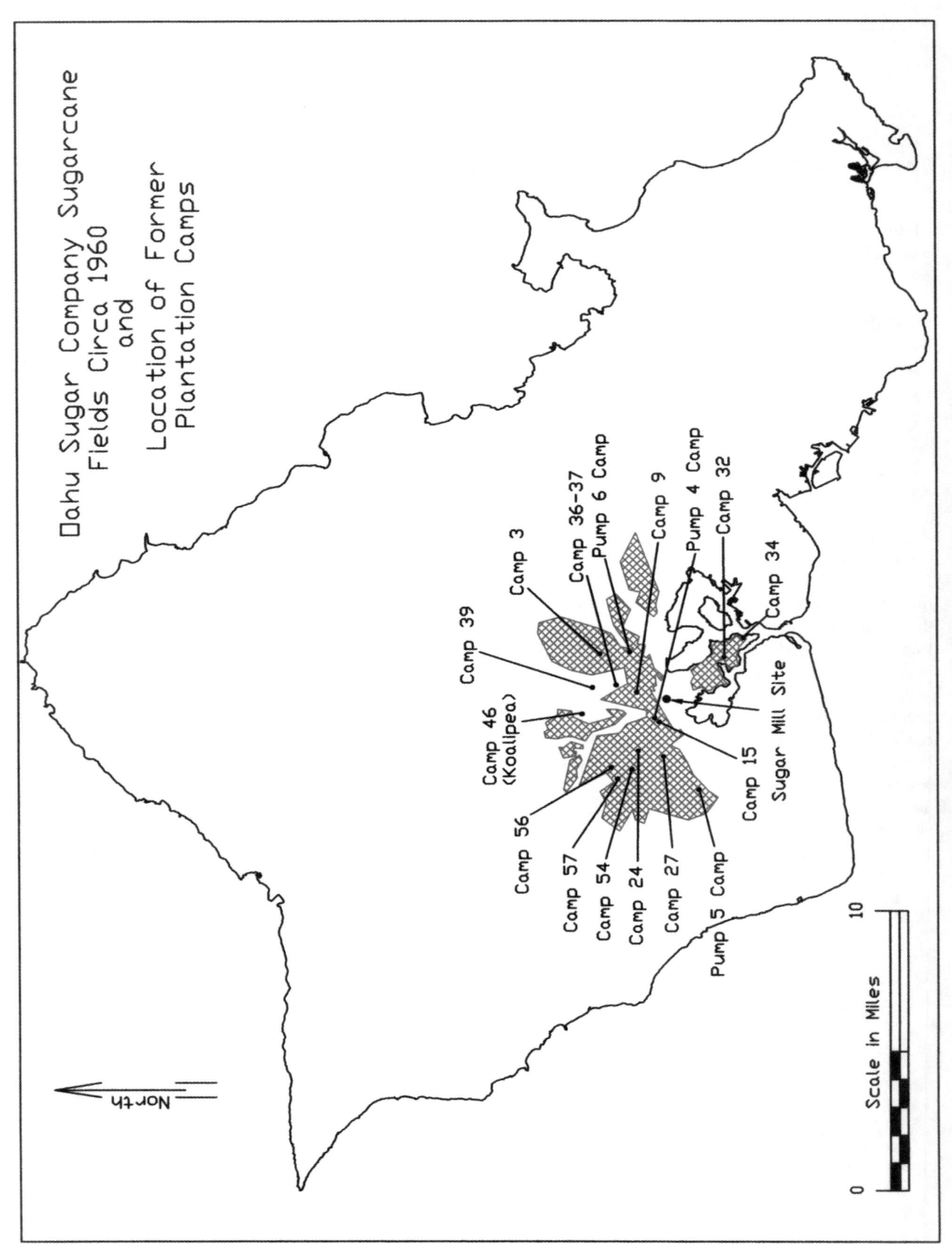

Fig. 2-3. Oahu Sugar Co. lands and camp locations ca. 1960.

summers, we would also use a mosquito net.

The kitchen was separated from the main house by about 15 feet and there was no covering between the house and the kitchen. The kitchen had a dirt floor and an open beam ceiling. There was a kerosene stove but no refrigeration device. Foods were kept in a "safe" [pronounced *say foo*] which was really a cabinet with several shelves and doors covered with screen to prevent flies from entering. At times there would be a large ham hanging from a wire in the middle of the kitchen. We used to cut pieces off the ham and cook it in a cast iron frying pan.

The mice scurrying about the beams at night when the lights were turned off were always a concern.

The toilet was about 100 feet away and made of wood. It had about 6 stalls and each stall was assigned to a family with the family name on the stall door so they had to keep their stall clean. The toilet seat was a piece of wood with a hole in it. There was running water under the toilet. I remembered that it really smelled. We used newspaper and other types of soft paper as toilet paper as we did not have any commercial types.

Kiawe [*prosopis pallida*] - aka algaroba, a tropical tree related to the mesquite.

Mr. Shinno, our neighbor, was a good carpenter and built a shack with a *furo* [bath] tub made of redwood. *Kiawe* wood was burned under the tub's concrete slab bottom for heating the water and we shared the furo with the Shinno family."
-Mitsuo Oshiro

"I remember visiting some of my friends in various camp areas, going to their bathrooms, and hearing the underground open-trench sewer lines. This would have been as late as the 1950s."
-Robert Castro

"The open trenches could have been U-shaped concrete channels about 12" wide and 12" deep with concrete coverings all buried just below the surface of the ground. This might explain how running water could be heard and yet the sewage was not seen."
-Hugh Morita

"We lived in Stable Camp and we didn't have a toilet in the house. There was a building outside that was our toilet. I hated it! It was always so smelly! It wasn't a cesspool, it was just a hole in the ground with the building over it that held, like, a toi-

let seat. When the hole in the ground got filled up, Oahu Sugar people came and moved the building over another hole they had dug. The first hole was just covered up ... maybe some lime was thrown in first."
                                     -Elsie (Fernandez) Moniz

Many a camp resident can remember that a night-time trip to the bathroom was not a simple trip "down a hallway," instead, it was a trip outdoors with a lantern.

This period might also have been when a famous mail-order catalog was in many an out-house not for reading but to be crumpled up and thus softened to be used as toilet paper?

"Toilet paper was cut-up pieces of newspaper crumpled up to make it soft. The better paper was the ones that would come as wrapping for oranges."
                                     -Herbert Harimoto

Toilet paper was invented in the U.S. in 1857 but it was not until the late 1880s that toilet paper on a roll was sold, marketed and accepted by the general public as ScotTissue.

DDT was invented in 1939.

And crumpled newspaper burned as a makeshift torch was a prerequisite to chase away cockroaches, centipedes, and scorpions!

"In the 1950s and 1960s, the Plantation used to fog or spray at dusk for mosquitoes. I think it was DDT and at that time, nobody knew how dangerous the chemical was and we kids would go running through the clouds of chemicals.

The mosquitoes were a real problem and we would have to sleep with a mosquito net over us or under the blanket."
                                     -Cornelio Nabarrete

Very early in the history of Waipahu and when Oahu Sugar was sending effluent from the mill and sewers donburo, there was an oxidation pond where the present-day Soccer Fields are located on the Waipio Peninsula.

Then, up until 1925, the sewer system took the waste from the camps and pumped it down from the mill site and parallel to Depot Rd. to an area on the Waipio Peninsula. (See the Waste Water Div. map.) Paralleling this sewer line was another pump line taking the mill effluent down to the same area where it was mixed in a reservoir with the sewer effluent and used to irrigate the sugar fields on the Waipio Peninsula.

"At first it was a pipe made from wood slats. Later the pipe was of metal, maybe cast iron(?), and you could hear the rocks tumbling in the pipe as the mill water came down Depot Rd."
-Mike Isobe

In 1956, the city took over the operation of the Waipahu pumping station. In 1982, sewage was diverted to the, by then, newly-built Honouliuli Waste Water Treatment Plant. By this time, processing included sewers from all of Waipahu as cesspool usage declined due to increased demand for frequent cesspool pumping. The map (Fig. 2-4) showing the sewer system of Waipahu comes to us as a courtesy of Jay Hamai of the City and County of Honolulu, Department of Design and Construction, Wastewater Division .

Clean water for Waipahu and Oahu Sugar Co. was provided primarily from artesian wells. Many, many pumps, each fed from several wells, gave those in Waipahu an almost unlimited supply of clean water.

"My father used to tell me that we paid Oahu Sugar Co. $1.00 per month for the water that we used. This could have been as recent as the 1950s."
-Robert Castro

Electricity was produced by Oahu Sugar Co. in such quantity that it could supply itself and still sell some to the Hawaiian Electric Co. In times when the mill was not producing enough electricity, it would purchase power from the Hawaiian Electric Co. [This was a common practice all over Hawaii where local utility companies would share their production resources with sugar mills.]

When sugar cane juice is extracted from the stalks of cane, one remaining product is bagasse. When dried, the sugar mills would use this as fuel for their boilers as an alternate energy source thereby reducing their dependence on oil to fire their boilers.

'The plantation gave everybody blocks of bagasse for use in their stoves and to heat bath water. These blocks were about 12" x 12" x 24" long. You would slice off a piece like you would slice bread and use the piece in the stove or water heating fireplace. You couldn't store the bagasse in the house because if it caught fire by itself [spontaneous combustion], the whole house

Electrification of Oahu Sugar began in 1912.

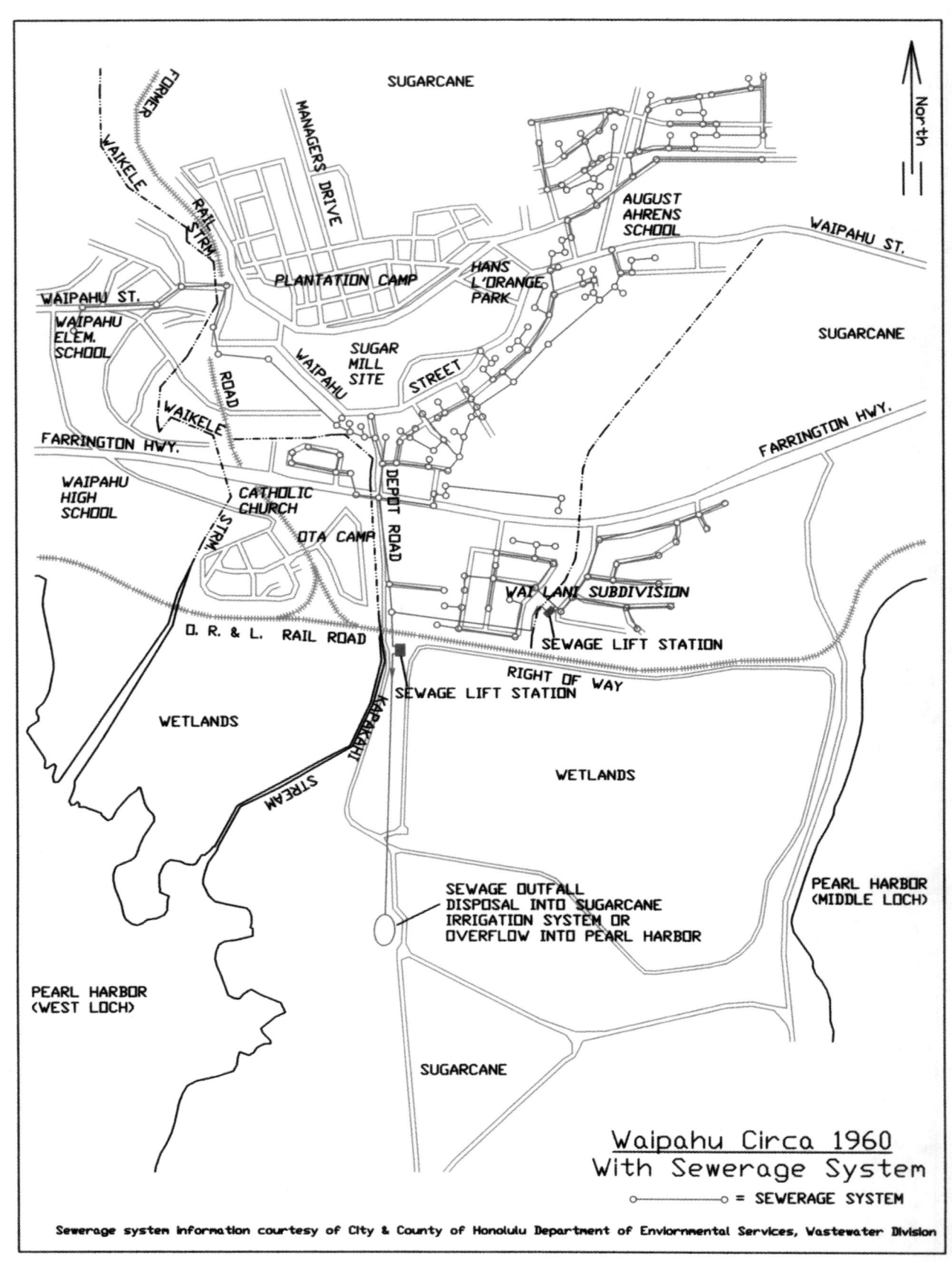

Fig. 2-4. Sewerage System, Waipahu ca. 1960.

could be burned down."
                              -Elsie (Fernandez) Moniz

Sometimes bagasse would just be taken from the mill and placed in heaps along the haul-cane roads to possibly be re-used in the fields.

"I remember seeing piles of bagasse on the roadside steaming! Decomposition was happening right there in front of me but at that time, I wasn't aware of ecology and re-use of materials."
                              -Robert Castro

Another by-product of bagasse was a fiber-board called canec. Crushed bagasse would be formed into tiles about 10" square by about 3/4" thick. These sometimes had a series of holes drilled in them thereby increasing the surface area for noise abatement. Canec was not particularly strong and so was used primarily as a ceiling tile.

Residents of some camps shared their memories of their camp life. In particular, Camp 46, Koalipea, was located closeby to present-day Mililani Town.

"The 'r' in koro is pronounced as a rolled 'r' as in previously noted pronunciations of donburo and shoburo."
        -Iris Yamaoka

'pea' in Hawaiian means pear or avocado!

"We used to call our camp 'koro pea.' Every family had an avocado tree. In those days, we only knew of these avocados as 'pears.' When these pear was about ripe, you would take the pear and shake it by your ear. If it was ripe, the seed would rattle, 'koro-koro' and hence our name for the camp.

On school days, the plantation used to send large trucks to pick up the kids and take them to school in Waipahu. The daily challenge would be to run up to the truck and be the first to throw your books into the cab (kinda like reserving your seat) where the driver was ... this was the best place because it had a padded seat and was protected from dust or rain. And the driver of the truck was generally Johnny Yasui, a famous boxer. So it was like being able to sit next to a celebrity."
                              -John Tasato

John Tasato shares a drawing he made of Koalipea, Camp 46. See Fig. 2-5. He points out the detail that can be seen between the old and new parts of the camp: outhouses vs. flush toilets within newer units. Note also chicken coops and vegetable gardens to supplement each family's needs; a pig pen to supple-

Koalipea - Camp #46

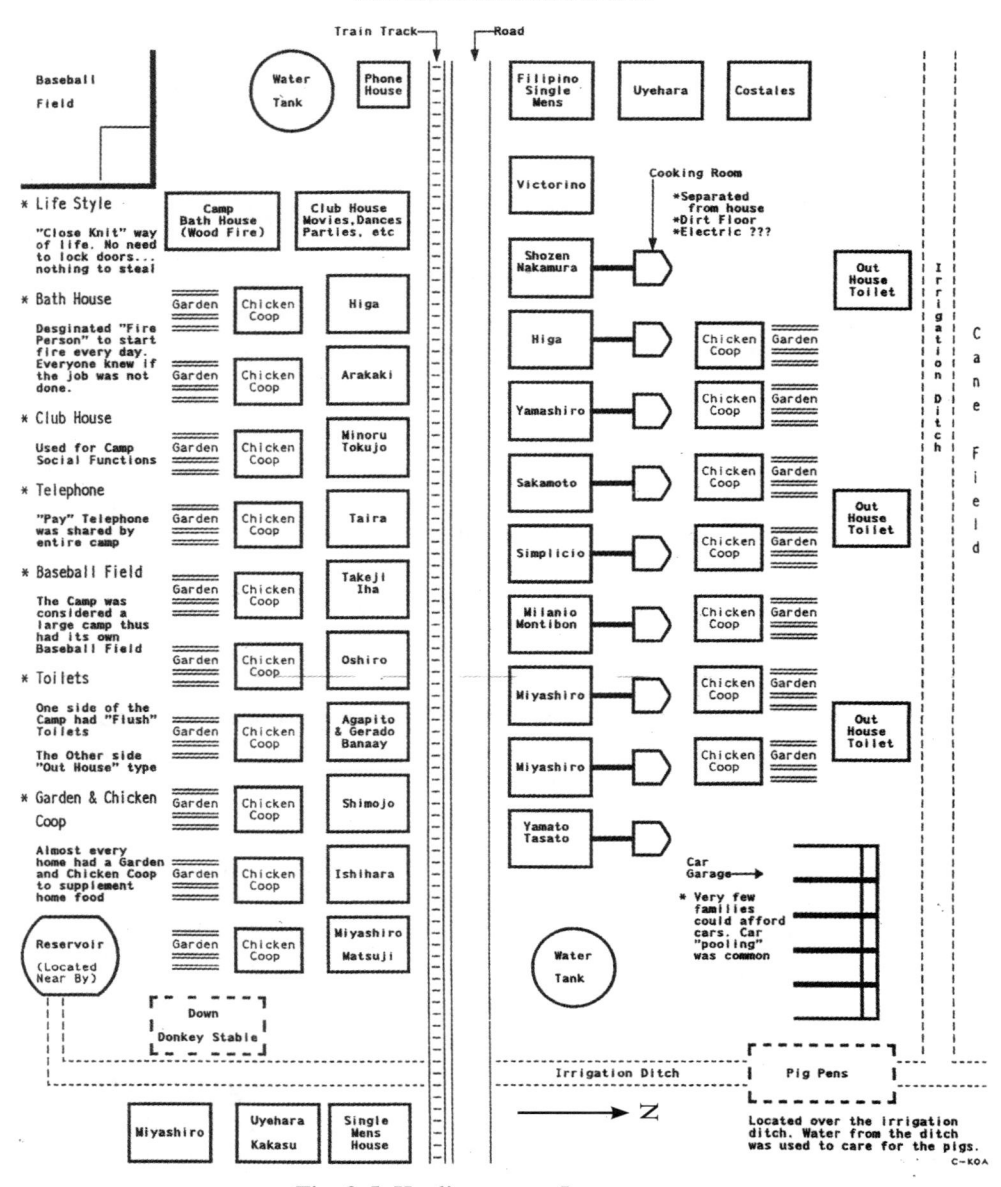

Fig. 2-5. Koalipea camp Layout.

Fig. 2-6. One view of Camp 46. Photo taken by Henry Taira and donated to Hawaii's Plantation Village.

30

ment income. And every home had an avocado tree!

The drawing is quite true in depiction in that the orderliness depicted is very close to the actual physical layout.

"The plantation gave us a field for athletic use at koro pea. We kids used it for football, baseball, everything. For basketball, the backboard for one end of the court was outside the 3rd base line of the baseball (field) layout. The other backboard was wa-a-a-y out in right field! Boy, did we get tired until we finally decided that only one backboard was gonna be used in our games!"
- Roy Tokujo

Work on the plantation was physically taxing. A typical day might start at 4AM when a wife might awake to prepare lunches for the day; her husband would get out to the fields and work for 8 hours till dusk, and return to camp for the evening meal, bathe, and retire. A woman needing to work might carry her young one on her back while working in the fields.

Kay Yamada writes about *Hole Hole Bushi* [ho-lay ho-lay boo-she]:

Japanese immigants sang about their frustrations and hopes, about their joys and dreams, while laboring under harsh conditions on the sugar plantations. One folk tune that survived the test of time was the Hole Hole Bushi. Some say it was based on the rice threshing song *To Usu Hiki Uta*, which was sung in Hiroshima, Japan. However, others say that other tunes were probably included in the basic melody and the song does not lead back to a specific Japanese tune.

Although some felt it was unworthy of much attention, the Hole Hole Bushi has evolved into a song which is greatly appreciated today because it realistically reflects the lives of early *isseis* [first generation in Hawaii]. It refers to the good and bad experiences of life and includes the pidgin language which evolved from the interaction between speakers of English and Hawaiian. "Hole Hole" refers to the work of stripping dried leaves from growing sugar cane stalks while "bushi" is the Japanese word for tune or melody. The immigrants added words, at will, to express their feelings. On the left below, are the verses in Japanese and pidgin and on the right, are the English translations.

Hole Hole Bushi

Yuko ka Meriken yo	Go on to America?
Kaero ka Nihon	Return to Japan?
Koko ga shian no	This is the problem
Hawaii koku	Here in Hawaii
Jyoyaku kiretara	When my contract is over
Wahine o yonde	Should I send for my wife
Yuko ka Hawaii no	And move on to Hamakua
Hamakua ni	Better on Hawaii?
Kane wa kachiken	My husband cuts the cane
Washa hore hore jya	I do the hole hole
Ase to namida no	By sweat and tears
Tomokasegi	We get by.
Hawaii Hawaii to	Wonderful Hawaii, or so I hear
Kite mirya Jigoku	One look and it seems like hell
Boshi ga Emma de	The manager's the devil and
Runa ga oni	His lunas are demons.
Tsuite kinasare	Keep up with me
Monku wa yamete	And stop your grumbling
Kuchi de hore hore	You can't do hole hole
Suru jya nashi	With your mouth!
Tsuite ikaryo ka	Why should I keep up
Omae no ato e	With someone like you?
Ore nya mashikin	You get the extra pay,
Aru jya nashi	not me!
Dekasegi wa kuru kuru	The laborers keep on coming
Hawaii wa tsumaru	Overflowing these Islands
Aino Nakayama	But it's only Inspector *Nakayama
Kane ga furu	Who rakes in the profits.
Asu wa koro koro yo	I'll be in court tomorrow
Mikka wa kimari	They'll give me three days for sure
Akai mofu	To have the red blanket
De karaboshi	In jail.
Hiza moto ni bakuchi	Gambling right under your nose
Ameya wa sakan nari	Whorehouses all over the place
Ome ni mienu ka	Can't see any of this, Consul **Ando?
Akuraki Ando	Staying in the dark?
Asu wa sande jya yo	Tomorrow is Sunday, right?
Asobi ni oide	Come over and visit.
Kane ga hanawai	My husband will be out watering the cane
Wasaha uchi ni	And I'll be home alone

What is shown here is one of many versions of the Hole Hole Bushi song.

*Joji Nakayama was an inspector in the immigration bureau in Hawaii. He worked with recruiter Robert Irwin to *reduce* the immigrants' contract wages from $15 to $12.50 per month. For his help, Irwin recommended bonuses and monthly supplementary pay from the immigrants' protection fund. By the end of his term, Nakayama was collecting a a salary of $6,000 a year, 40 times the salary of the ordinary Japanese plantation laborer. His salary exceeded the pay of any executive officer of the Hawaiian government outside of cabinet members.

**Consul Ando was Taro Ando, the first Consul General from Japan. He held the rank of Ambassador and arrived in Honolulu on Feb. 14, 1886.

Sanjugosen no	Why settle for 35 cents
Hole hole shiyo yori	Doing the hole hole all day
___-san to moi moi surya	When I can make a dollar
Akahi kala	Sleeping with that ___?

"My father told me that during the 1904 strike, when the *lunas* [overseers] were really mistreating the workers, the workers would run across Waipahu St. and ask my father to hide them in his grocery store (near where Tsumoto Store is today)."
-Harue (Hashimoto) Kanechika

Strikes at the Oahu Sugar Co.

1904
1905
1906
1909 *Great Japanese Strike
1920
1946 ****Paternalism ended
1958
1974
1979

*Yasutaro **Soga and Yokichi Tasaka, of the *Nippu Jiji* newspaper and Fred*** Makino and Motoyuki Negoro of the Higher Wage Association were imprisoned for agitating laborers to strike.

Affected were the Aiea, Ewa, Kahuku, Waialua, Waianae, and Waipahu (Oahu Sugar) Plantations.

The *Nippu Jiji* later became the *Hawaii Times* newspaper and Makino went on to found the *Hawaii Hochi* (which changed its name in 1942) to the *Hawaii Herald* and later still (in 1953), back to the *Hawaii Hochi* newspaper).

**In 1956, Soga received the Order of the Sacred Treasure from the government of Japan. Soga's pen name was Keiho Soga.
*** full legal name: Frederick Kinzaburo Makino Higgenbotham

****Rent-free housing, fuel and free medical benefits were no longer paid by the plantation.

In 1909, the Japanese sugar plantation workers struck for a 4-month period to finally arrive at a wage increase from $18 per month to $20 per month! Among issues were improvements in housing and sanitary conditions and an easing of racial discrimination of wages.

World War I (1914-1918) impacted many with double-digit inflation. The cost-of-living increased 40-50% since the start of the war. Of 45 commodities surveyed by a Japanese language paper, it was found that prices had risen from 40% to 207% with an average of 115%.

The monthly cost-of-living increased 42% for single men, 27% for couples, and 45% for couples with 2 children. It is in this time frame that living conditions must be viewed.

In 1920, another strike, this time initiated by Filipinos and joined by the Japanese, hit plantations in Aiea, Waialua, Ewa, Waimanalo, and Oahu Sugar in Waipahu. This was the first strike in which more than one racial group participated. While no specific terms were agreed upon by the workers, they cited their belief in the planters' sincerity during negotiations, surrendered and terminated the strike. The end of the strike brought an immediate rise in wages as well as improvements in working and living conditions.

For all their grueling work under taxing conditions, the Filipino field workers' meager wages of $0.77 per day were raised to $1.25 per day!

The growers were estimated to have lost $12 million dollars and labor lost about $200,000 during the 6-month strike period.

"My father earned $1 a day as a locomotive engineer. This was in the 1920s.

We had ten kids and I never went beyond the 8th grade. My mother stayed at home and took care of the kids. She didn't have side jobs or take in laundry or anything like that. My brothers went to work as soon as they were old enough. Mostly they worked for the Oahu Sugar Co. We girls stayed at home and helped with the family chores ... laundry, ironing, cooking. Our meals were very often soups with breads. Our family was so large and we couldn't even have chicken on the table except for very special times like Christmas or Easter. We had a lot of this Portuguese soup called *[Carne de] Vinha D'Alhos* . This was pork that was pickled for a few days in vinegar. We then made it into a soup."
     -Elsie (Fernandez) Moniz

Corum, in *Ethnic Foods of Hawaii*, describes this Portuguese dish as being cooked in a pot and not necessarily made into a soup.

Due to labor organization and a growth in world sugar prices, the sugar worker in Hawaii eventually became the highest paid sugar worker in the world.

"Paternalism was a good thing. But with the strike of 1946, this ended. I remember being in my father's car being driven to school (I went to Punahou) and we had to cross the picket line. The strikers beat on the car and I thought I was going to get killed! It wasn't really necessary but that's how strikes were; labor on one side and management on the other. And feelings extended to include management's family!"
     -Peter L'Orange

Each employee of Oahu Sugar received a house to live in rent-free, complete with firewood, fuel, and water. By the 1930s, garbage collection and street cleaning were in place. Additionally, the plantation rented buildings to tenants of various nationalities so they could have retail businesses on the side. This also gave plantation employees a wide variety of goods and services. There were barber shops, mid-wife services, noodle stands, laundries, and tofu makers to name a few.

"In the Higashi camp area, there was the Asao Store where I would purchase candy on my way home from August Ahrens School. There was a '*manju-ya*' that did transactions through what I think was their kitchen window. From there I could also get a 5¢ bag of cracked seed ... the best part was sucking on the brown paper bag after eating all the seed!

Manju-ya: sweet rice cake-store.

Konyaku: alimentary paste.

Manapua: Chinese steamed bun filled with meats or vegetables; aka char-siu bow.

Crackseed (or cracked seed) is preserved plum, generically whole or cracked, flavored with spices and primarily giving the seeds a salty-sweet flavor; from China.

One man sold peanut brittle and for 50¢ he would take a hammer and knock off a piece from the huge brittle he had. Another man had a puffed rice machine that for 25¢ and a cup of rice that my mother had given me, you could get puffed rice after a big 'bang!' from the machine. He would color the rice either red or green for us.

There were vendors that came around and sold home grown vegetables, *konyaku,* and *manapua*. A lot of these vendors carried their wares in baskets or cans hanging from a long, thick pole across their shoulders."
 -Anonymous

Traveling salesmen, *chumon-tori*, also made their rounds in the plantation camps.

"Families trusted the saleman's judgment regarding the goods that they sold. Some owned their own store, while others worked for various stores. I recall a salesman coming to our house to take orders. He sat on the front porch with his note pad while my mother gave him her order. A few days later, he delivered his items. These traveling salesmen brightened the lives of housewives with their stories and news.

Another traveling salesman was the medicine man. He would sell packets of medicine for various ailments and would dispense nostalgia about Japan along with the medicines."
 -Rachel (Hiramoto) Fukuda

"There was a Mr. Kikuchi who had a medicine distribution program. Each home had a pouch (package) that held several pills and medicines. When the items got low, Mr. Kikuchi would replace them and charge the family. There were red pills for headaches and sore teeth; and a black tar-looking substance was in a clam shell to be heated and spread on paper and applied to boils to suck up the infection and clean the boil out."
 -Zen Abe

"My grandfather, Suekichi Kikuchi, even went to the outside islands. He used to take my father along with him."
 -Karen (Kikuchi) Honke

The newsletters of Hawaii's Plantation Village give an interesting view of the economy as remembered by many interviewees.

Year	Cost of product/wage earning
1915	75¢ for 10-hour workday
1920	25¢ for a restaurant meal
1924	$1.25/day for 10-hour work day in pump department
1928	$1.05/day pulling weeds
	5¢ for a loaf of bread
	10¢ for picking a burlap bag of kiawe beans for sale to hog farmers
	1¢ for small brown paper bag of crackseed
1930	$1.00/day for 10-hour day as hapai-ko man
	5¢ for a block of tofu
	$2.00/month to have laundry done
	$2.50 for 100-lb. bag of rice
	$15.00 for a pig
1931	25¢ for a haircut
1932	$1.25/day for 12-hour field work
1936	$1.32/day for 12-hours field work
1937	$1.36/day for 12-hours work in fire room of mill
1944	2¢ for a cup of cocoa in a tin cup with a graham cracker in kindergarten
1946	$1.96/day for 8-hours; UNIONIZED
1948	$2.08/day ditto
1950	$3.36/day ditto
1960	$24/month house rent; 5-BR in Japanese camp
1981	$9.36/hour steam generator operator

Oahu Sugar instituted the use of the *bango* in 1905. The bango was a metal disc stamped with the number assigned to each worker (and hence his family) and worn from a cord around his neck. Some viewed this assignment of a number an indignity. As far as the plantation and the *lunas* [overseers] were concerned, it was far easier to remember each person by a number rather than some unfamiliar name (Watanabe, Arakawa, etc.). Different nationalities were recognized by the numerical sequence assigned. The bango also served as a means to issue pay as well as to pay for merchandise at the Plantation Store. (Other plantations later issued bangos in different shapes to reduce confusion.)

The American Institute of Economic Research has a website that gave us these comparative dollar values in cost-of-living. For the year 2000, and comparing $100 from a past year, the cost of living appears as in the following table.

$100 in 1920 is worth $ 861 in 2000
  1930   1031
  1940   1230
  1950   715
  1960   582
  1970   444
  1980   209
  1990   132
  2000   100

For 1950, a 10-cent movie ticket for a Saturday matinee would be about $0.72 in the year 2000 time frame.

Statistics can be used to tell many different stories. You can draw your own conclusions.

Bango - Japanese for number.

The Plantation Store (the most recent is a concrete structure on Waipahu St. diagonally across the street from the Waipahu Theater) carried everything a sugar worker might need. Here a worker could use his bango to pay for groceries, clothing, household items, etc., during a calendar month. When he got paid, what he owed at the Plantation Store would be first deducted from his monthly pay before he could have his money. Under certain circumstances this caused a worker to be continually indebted to the plantation; his monthly charges being greater than what he had earned.

Jabon - Japanese word for a large citrus fruit, aka pomelo.

"We [Arakawas of Waipahu] started the *jabon* system of charging goods. A plantation worker needing something would come into our store and take what he needed telling us 'eh, jabon this!' We would add the item(s) to his monthly credit list. I can't recall why the system started as using jabon to mean 'charge it!' "
       -Shigemi Arakawa

Harvesting of sugar cane was done in the early years (until about 1925) with pure manual labor. Leaves were trimmed off the stalks, and the stalks cut into convenient lengths so mules could haul the stalks to the mill for processing. Later in time, fields were burned to get rid of the leaves, the stalks holding the sugar juice were hacked with large knives similar to a machete but with a broader blade and called (of course) a cane knife.

"In the early 1930s, I got about 75¢ a day as a 12 year-old picking up cane after the *hapai-ko* (carry cane) trucks."
       -Lillian (Oshiro) Oshiro

"In the early 1940s, an eleven-year old could only work in the fields clearing the irrigation ditches. At 12, you could work in the fields."
       -Eddie Uemori

"Summers (1940s to early 1950s) for 16-year-olds could be spent working in the pineapple fields. If you were fortunate enough, you could get a job in the pineapple factory (in Honolulu) because field work was hot, dusty, and very tiring.

In a way, this factory work was a good thing because we kids from the country could mix with the city kids."
       -Mel Bello

"When cane was harvested, everyone had to plan around the soot generated from the burning cane fields. If the wind was from the direction of the burning fields, you could be sure that any laundry hanging outside would get particles of soot. Trying to brush these off would only cause the laundry to have black smudges!"
- Myrna (Manuel) Tsinnajinnie

Burning of cane fields was a step-saving method of removing leaves; only the stalks that held the sugar juices were left after a field burn to be harvested and taken to the mill.

"When it was harvest time, they (canefields) were burned. What an awesome sight that was!"
-Anonymous 810

"I remember that summers were especially sooty, dusty, noisy and smelly as the Oahu Sugar mill was in operation 24 hours a day. The fields were burned and the mill seemed extremely noisy unloading the cane at night."
-Bernice (Tamura) Hamai

"I can still remember the very sweet smell of the burning cane; and then the hapai-ko trucks going by to take the cane to the mill."
-June (Saito) Tamashiro

Contests between sugar plantations would be held to judge which plantation had the more efficient field crews. Cutting the cane and loading the stalks onto special cane hauling wagons was referred to as hapai-ko work. Eventually, harvesting was done mechanically but for many years, field work was simply accomplished by the grueling power of man and mule. Later, cranes were used to pick up the stalks and trucks and the railroad were used to do the hauling to the mill.

"When the Plantation was using trucks to haul the harvested cane to the mill, they would go slowly past our houses. We could pull off a stalk or two and break it in enough places that we could chew off the outer skin and get after the insides! The cane was so sweet and we would spit out the fibrous part. It was like cleaning your teeth with a sweet brush!"
-Jane (Mitsumoto) Matsunaga

In the mill, sugar stalks were fed by conveyor to be crushed by huge rollers turning in tandem. The crushed sugar cane yielded the sweet sugar juices as a first step in processing. In 1903, the Oahu Sugar Co. installed the first 12-roller crushing mill in the

Fig. 2-7. Locomotive #7, Puuloa.

Territory of Hawaii.

"As I remember, when we were in our high school years, in the late 1950s, we had an excursion to visit Oahu Sugar. We toured the sugar mill and the smell in the mill was terrible! That is the bad memory. The good memory is that the sugar mill personnel gave us little cloth bags filled with brown, un-refined sugar as a memento of our visit."
        -George Arita

"I remember that Oahu Sugar used to give the visiting kids brown sugar that had been pressed into the shape of a scoop of ice cream on a cone. It wasn't a large cone but it was yummy."
        -Robert Castro

After the sugar extraction process, the railroad hauled the raw sugar to the connection point at the Oahu Railway depot (Waipahu Station) at the end of Depot Rd. From Waipahu Station, the sugar was transported to Honolulu Harbor for export.

Oahu Sugar owned nine locomotives at one point. Of these, #7, named *Puuloa*, and bearing Serial No. 19741, remains today as a memento of sugar mill times on the grounds of the Waipahu Cultural Garden Park. Puuloa is a 0-6-2T type of engine that burned Bunker C fuel in its later years after being converted from the earlier, more expensive, coal.

Elsie (Fernandez) Moniz remembers the locomotives and their engineers. Along wih information from *Sugar Trains Pictorial* by Jesse C. Conde, the sidebar lists all the locomotives and their engineers of the Oahu Sugar Co. ca. 1920.

The Waipahu Hongwanji is located near the plantation camps and close to the mill. Its start goes back to 1898 when a dedicated minister, The Rev. Yemyo Imamura, would ride his horse all the way from Honolulu to minister to his parishioners in Waipahu. In 1902, the first temple was dedicated and the grounds have been home to the Mission since 1910. The present Mission structure was rebuilt in 1952.

"I attended the Waipahu Hongwanji Mission [Church] every Sunday. Although we understood the basic tenets of Buddhism, our understanding of the finer points were not developed because only Japanese was spoken by the *bonsan* [minister]

Puuloa was #7 because it was the seventh locomotive acquired by Oahu Sugar. It was originally Honolulu Plantation's No. 4 and went to Oahu Sugar in 1947. Built in 1901 by the Baldwin Locomotive Works on the mainland, Puuloa is actually the second No.7, the first being scrapped earlier. Sugar locomotives were not noted for speed but instead for great power. Puuloa's center driving wheels are flangeless and therefore could negotiate 24° curves on a 3% grade.

Locomotive	Engineer
#1 - Waipahu	Joe Carvalho
#2 - Waipio	Manuel Carvalho
#3 - Waikele	George Castro
#4 - Waiawa	Manuel Fernandez (Elsie's Dad)
#5 - Waikakalaua	John Silva
#6 - Koalipea	Charlie Alfonso
#7 - Puuloa	Manuel Silva
#8 - Hoaeae	Raymond Moniz
#9 - Waikane	?

This Waipahu Hongwanji is also referred to by many as Higashi [east] Church.

During the Tokugawa Era of Japan, Tokugawa Shogun decided that the Hongwanji religion was becoming too large and powerful.

He therefore split it into two: Nishi (west) and Higashi (east). The Nishi Hongwanji is the part that eventually came to Hawaii and settled in the Higashi part of Waipahu!

during the services. It did however, keep us in line.

In the 1930s, after attending English school, we attended Japanese language school for six days per week, one hour per day, at the Waipahu Hongwanji Mission through grade eight."
-Mitsuo Oshiro

"I think that the fees for the Japanese school was $2.25 for the family's first child, $1.75 for the second child, and $0.75 for the third child. This was a monthly fee."
-Lillian (Oshiro) Oshiro

Oahu Sugar was the figurehead father of Waipahu. Occasions such as Christmas was a time for the Oahu Sugar Co. to make sure that the children of Waipahu were given a treat.

"Through the 1930s and 1940s, children growing up in Waipahu awaited in anticipation, the coming of Christmas. It was such a rare treat for us to receive the brown goodie bags that were given each year by the Oahu Sugar Company. All the children were gathered in the sugar warehouse at the mill. The bags of sugar were all cleared out and in this large hall Santa Claus came and gave each child a paper sack of goodies. The sack held an apple, an orange, hard candy and nuts. For me and many of my friends, it was the first time that we were given a bag of treats at Christmas-time by anyone."
- Shige Yoshitake by way of
Marlene (Okada) Hirata

"Oahu Sugar always played Christmas carols over their loudspeakers at night."
-Bernice (Tamura) Hamai

At another time, the season was still there and remembered by another slightly differently.

"Christmas was a time that was very festive and Depot Rd. was colorfully decorated. I lived on Waipahu St. and I recall anxiously waiting for Santa who would come riding by on a firetruck."
-Anita Ishibashi by way of
Marlene (Okada) Hirata

"I remember walking from August Ahrens [Elementary] School to the ball park (which is now Hans L'Orange Park) with my

Hibari Misora, born Kazue Kato, began her singing career at age 11. She was born on May 29, 1937, and died on June 24, 1989. She is thought of as having brought Japan through the trauma, devastation, and recovery from WWII with her singing style.

classmates to await Santa's trip through the town passing out brown goodie bags. It was the highlight of the holiday season for me each year. When I received my precious brown bag of goodies which always held a shiny red apple, an orange, nuts and uniquely colored hard candy, I did my familiar holiday ritual of blowing air into the brown bag, shaking it up and slowly sniffing and relishing the "special smell of Christmas." Although each of us have our own plantation memories at different places and times, Santa never forgot to deliver our brown bag of treats. We were always delighted when we opened up our bags because in them were the anticipated familiar items from Christmas to Christmas. These were the simple but heartwarming holiday joys of Christmas for the children of Waipahu."

- Marlene (Okada) Hirata

Several told us about movies held at the Oahu Sugar Co. It was a weekly event popular with kids.

"I think our parents paid about $5 a month for movies. They were held in the Higashi Camp area. I remember seeing the Takarazuka Girls [a Japanese troupe from Japan] and Hibari Misora."

-Bernice (Tamura) Hamai

"Saturday nights were when we kids got to see movies at the Plantation. During the day, we would place our *goza* [straw] mats in front of the screen (sort of reserving our space) and when it got dark, the movies would be started. The films were generally Japanese movies in black and white."

-Anonymous 810

The Shako Club was the Waipahu Japanese Social Club. Shako in Japanese means social. Another version was 'Sho-sho' Club because the Japanese had a difficult time pronouncing "social."

"These outdoor movies were shown on the wide lawn at the Japanese Social Club [Shako Club] which was located in Higashi Camp across the road from the Hongwanji Church. Movies were shown mostly on a monthly basis. The screen, when not in use, was rolled up under a roof for protection from the rain. The structure was also equipped with draw curtains, dressing room, and a *hanamichi* [side platform] used by actors to go onto the stage for live performances."

-Shige Yoshitake

"The Shako Club brought people together."

-Rachel (Hiramoto) Fukuda

"There were amateur nights when the people could participate in singing and dancing contests and win small prizes. I think these were arranged by Mr. Ichiro Konno of the [Nippu Jiji] newspaper that eventually became the Hawaii Times. Mr. Konno was even able to arrange a guest appearance by Hibari Misora, the famous Japanese singer. I remember Mr. Konno as being a very distinguished-looking man with white hair."
                                    -Lilly (Takushi) Tokuhara

When Oahu Sugar closed in 1995, it had contributed dollars to the Hawaiian economy, given people livelihoods in the sugar industry over many years, produced entrepeneurs by choice or necessity, contributed to the technological advances of the sugar industry, and given Waipahu an identity.

The influence of Oahu Sugar permeated through the entire town of Waipahu. For clarity, the area donburo of the plateau that had the mill and most of the mill camps is described in the following chapters.

This would be those areas along Waipahu St. and include Depot Rd. and Farrington Hwy.

In 1898 Suessmann & Wurmser (S & W) purchased 8000 acres of land that included present-day Hickam Air Force Base, the Honolulu International Airport, parts of Pearl Harbor, Halawa Heights, Aiea, and Pearl City. This became the Honolulu Sugar Plantation. In 1935, then owner C. Brewer relinquished much of its land to the Federal Government. Honolulu Plantation started refining sugar in 1906 in Aiea. This is also where the most recent HSPA (HARC) facility is located.

In 1947, Oahu Sugar purchased Honolulu Plantation (aka Aiea Plantation).

In 1960, Oahu Sugar produced an all-time high of 75,000 tons of raw sugar from 11,400 acres of land.

In 1970, Ewa Plantation merged with Oahu Sugar.

In 1971, Oahu Sugar produced 121, 750 tons of sugar from 10,124 acres of land.

The planation managers of Oahu Sugar are remembered:

August Ahrens	1897-1904
E.K. Bull	1904-1919
J.B. Thompson	1919-1923
Ernest W. Greene	1923-1937
Hans L'Orange	1937-1957
C.E.S. Burns Jr.	1957-1964
Karl Berg	1965-1965
John Humme	1965-1976
David Ballie	1976-1978
Garvie Hall	1978-1979
William Balfour Jr.	1979-1980
David Ballie	1980-1982
William Balfour Jr.	1982-1995

Oahu Sugar Production Tidbits

In 1899, the first harvest yielded 7892 tons of sugar from 1050 acres of planted land. August Ahrens, the first manager of Oahu Sugar, had estimated in his first annual report that the yield would be between 5,500 to 6,000 tons of sugar.

In 1917, Oahu Sugar reaped 37,210 tons of raw cane.

In 1928, Oahu Sugar broke a world record by producing 12.02 tons of sugar per acre.

In 1937, Oahu Sugar harvested 76,888 tons of raw cane.

In 1947, Oahu Sugar acquired Honolulu Plantation (aka Aiea Sugar) thus adding 3,000 acres of sugar acreage.

In 1949, 80,160 tons yield were harvested; this was a yield of 11.60 tons per acre of planted land,

In 1960, 75,000 tons of raw sugar here harvested from 11,400 acres of planted land.

In 1970, Oahu Sugar merged with Ewa Plantation; this yielded another 60,000 tons of sugar annually. Oahu Sugar was now the second largest sugar plantation in Hawaii and the third largest in the U.S.

In 1982, Oahu Sugar had 55 square miles of property; 15,488 acres were cultivated. The sugar crop yielded 93,217 tons of sugar. (All of Hawaii's plantations had 204,749 acres and yielded 982,913 tons of sugar.) Oahu Sugar used 115 million gallons of water per day. (By comparison, the City of Honolulu used half this amount.)

Oahu Sugar consumed 300 pounds of Nitrogen fertilizer, 225 pounds of P[hosphorus] fertilizer, and 400 pounds of Potassium fertilizer per acre.

Sugar Facts

• Sugar cane has a juicy and fibrous stalk that is enclosed with a rind or skin. The fibrous stalk holds the sweet juices and has a grain parallel to the length of the stalk. Chewing or otherwise crushing the stalk releases the juices but the remaining fibrous matter cannot be eaten.

• Sugar cane "seed" are really lengths of preferred (known high sugar yield) cane stalks about 18" long with nodes (or nodules). The seed cane stalks are laid in furrows on the ground and covered with a thin layer of dirt. From the nodes, roots appear down into the ground and new stalks and leaves appear upward. Where cane has been harvested and the stalks with roots are still in the ground, the new cane plants are called "ratoon" crops.

• The process whereby sugar is produced in the plant, starts with photosynthesis where the sun's energy is converted to carbohydrate energy; chlorophyl from the plant uses this energy to combine water with carbon dioxide to form sucrose, a form of sugar. The sucrose goes to the stalk for storage by the plant and for further plant growth. The sugar stored in the stalk is what is harvested and processed to produce brown sugar and molasses.

• Stalks of mature cane can grow to about 30 feet tall and from 1" to 2" in diameter. The color of the stalks vary from light green to yellow to even a dark purple depending on the species. The tapered leaves coming out from the nodal areas may be as wide as 2" and 36" long with a central spine. The leaves are light green in color and have sharp edges.

• Sugar cane requires about two years from seeding to harvest.

• One ton of water is needed to produce one pound of sugar.

• "Harvesting" in the cane industry consists of burning the fields of cane to remove leaves and dead plant matter. The stalks that contain the sugar have high moisture content (and hence do not burn). These are gathered after the fire and taken to the mill, washed to remove dirt, and crushed to extract the sugar cane juice.

• The retrieved dirt is returned to the fields and the remains of the cane stalks is called bagasse. This bagasse had secondary uses 1) as a fuel for burning in the mill boilers and 2) as an insulating and sound abatement board for use in home construction.

References - Chapter 2.

J. W. Coulter, pamphlet, undated

Unpublished manuscript, Kay M. Yamada

Plants in Hawaiian Medicine, Beatrice A. Krauss, Bess Press, Honolulu, Hawaii, 2001.

Oahu's Hidden History, William H. Dorrance, Mutual Publishing, Honolulu, Hawaii, 1998

Ethnic Foods of Hawaii, Ann Kondo Corum, Bess Press, Honolulu, Hawaii, 2000.

Japanese Immigrant Clothing in Hawaii 1885-1941, Barbara O. Kawakami, University of Hawaii Press, Honolulu, Hawaii, 1993.

Whatever Happened to Hawaiian Locomotives, website of the Hawaiian Railway Society, Bob Paoa, 1998.

Sugar Trains Pictorial, Jesse C. Conde', Glenwood Publishers, Felton, CA. 1975.

Extraordinary Origins of Everyday Things, Charles Panati, Harper and Row, New York, New York, 1987.

Geology of the State of Hawaii, Harold T. Stearns, Pacific Books, publishers, Palo Alto, California, 2nd. ed., 1985.

Newsletters and archival records of the Oahu Sugar Co.

Numerous newsletters of Hawaii's Plantation Village.

Numerous documents, Department of Design & Construction, Wastewater Division, City & County of Honolulu.

Numerous documents, Board of Water Supply, City & County of Honolulu.

Sugar Water, Carol Wilcox, University of Hawaii Press, Honolulu, Hawaii, 1997.

Numerous brochures and pamphlets, HSPA.

Website *quixium.com*, 2005.

Sites of Oahu, Elspeth P. Sterling and Catherine C. Summers, Bishop Museum Press, Honolulu, Hawaii, 1978.

-3- Along Waipahu St. and down Depot Rd.

*. . . the road curved this way and
then that way . . .*

A trip through the town
After Annexation in 1898, Hawaii began to grow in population, (mostly immigrants), and the economy began to boom. Oahu Sugar was the center around which the town of Waipahu grew.

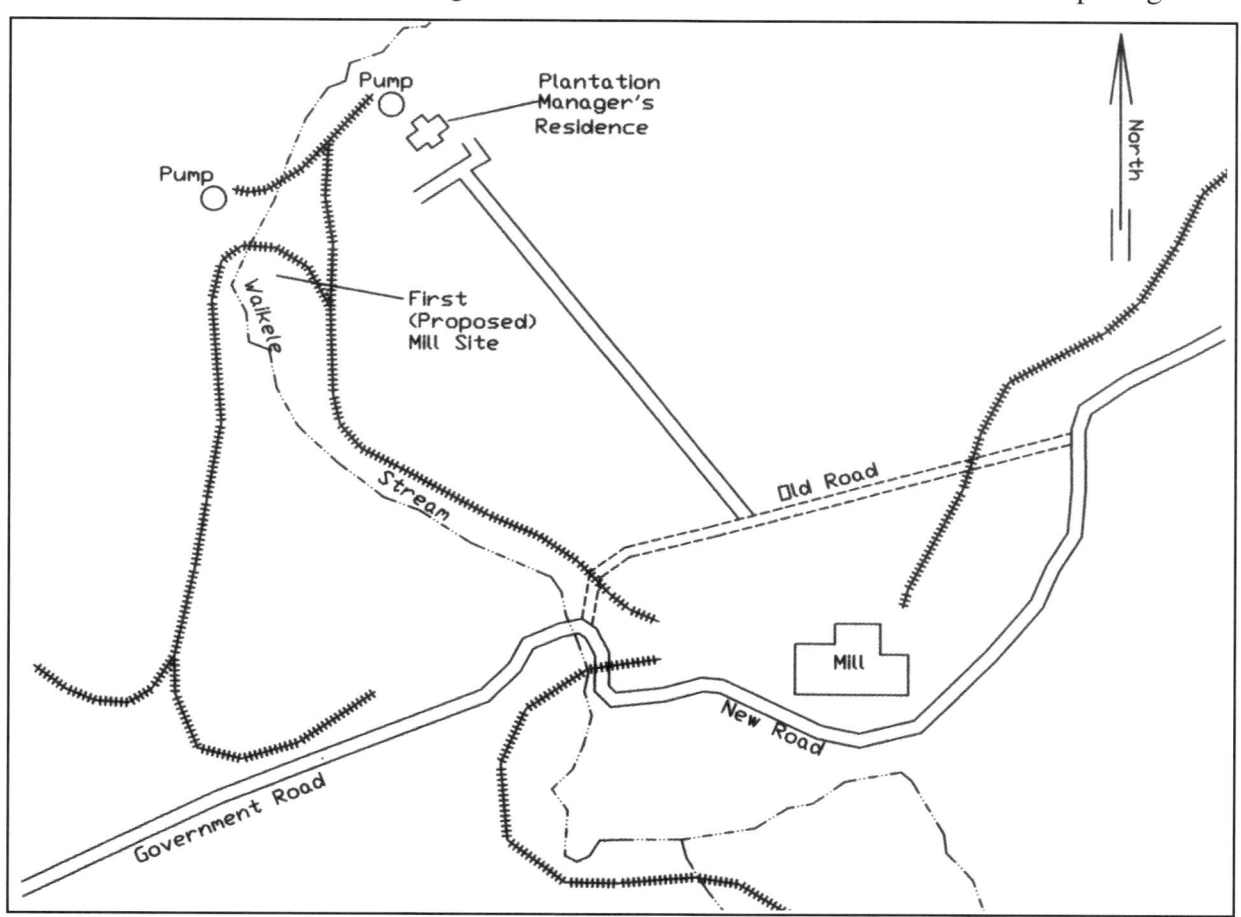

Fig. 3-1. The new pathway for Waipahu St.

"August Ahrens was a chemist in Germany before he came to Hawaii to be the manager of Waianae Plantation. He resigned to be Oahu Sugar's first manager."
- Anonymous

When Oahu Sugar was started, Main Government Rd. curved north around the mill. August Ahrens requested that the road pathway be changed to go south of the mill and with approval from the government of Hawaii, the road pathway was changed. This is the present Waipahu St. (map from Nedbalek-*Waipahu*)

Credit should be given to those visionaries who saw that they could make a life for themselves and their families in the town around Oahu Sugar.

From the 1900s there were drygoods stores, restaurants, meat markets, produce markets, theaters, soda fountain stores, watch repair stores, photography studios, etc. In many cases there were duplicates as in the case of restaurants. All made a living for their owners. The ethnicity of Waipahu can be seen from various statistical reports and the names of the various businesses.

Some major structures or businesses along Waipahu St., Depot Rd. and Farrington Hwy. and their diversity can be seen by way of old maps. Hugh Morita consolidated information from many people and produced Fig. 3-5. This map covers places and stores of note from about 1900 through 2000 and the reader should refer to the text for the locations of these establishments and their impact in the history of Waipahu.

In 1920, it is estimated by some that the population of Waipahu was about 4,000 people. This would have made Waipahu the second-most populous city in Hawaii next to Honolulu (see Chap. 1)

Along Waipahu St.
At the eastern end of Waipahu St. is August Ahrens Elementary School. The school was built in 1924 and is named after the first manager of the Oahu Sugar Co.

Lulu Corbly was a principal at this school and at the time, corporal punishment was allowed. Many have commented that if you received punishment at the school,

"then you must have done something very wrong...then you received another punishment from your parents when you got home."
                            -Anonymous

Lulu Corbly taught at Waipahu Elementary School and probably learned to use a water hose for punishment from the principal there, Alice Carter. When Lulu Corbly went to August Ahrens Elementary School as principal, some of the boys had figured out how to evade a waterhose spanking.

"Some of the boys would run to Nabarrete Store and get note-

The principals of August Ahrens Elementary School are remembered:

Maud Lowell Tucker	1924-1927
Elizabeth L. Heen	1928-1941
Lulu Corbly	1942-1958
Gladys Hashimoto	1958-1961
Isami Kurasaki	1961-1977
(1971-1972 he exchanged positions with Ned Doty from Phoenix, AZ)	
Dickie Hamasaki	1977-1987
Richard Lee	1980-1989
Art Ouye	1989-1991
Anthony Chun	1991-1993
Roger Bellinger	1993-1994
Florentina Smith	1995-present

pads. Before a boy went in to get his waterhose spanking, he would stuff the notepads inside his pants in the buttock area. On getting the spanking, he would scream and yell and even cry if his acting was good. Then he would go out and pass the notepads to the next incoming boy."
-Marlene (Okada) Hirata

"I remember teaching there and Lulu Corbly was going to punish a frail Filipino girl with a rubber hose. I told Lulu Corbly that 'if you hit that girl with the rubber hose, I will report you [to higher education officials].' Lulu looked at me and saw the determination on my face and did not hit the girl.

And do you know that Lulu Corbly and I became good friends after that incident?"
-Diana (Hirotsu) Herrst

But there must have been good being done there.

"If I had to give credit to important people in my life in Waipahu, it would be to Lulu Corbly, Clarence Dyson [principal of Waipahu High School] and Janet B. Faye [English teacher and advisor of the College Club at Waipahu High School]. They encouraged me and my classmates to go on and seek higher education.

See Chapter 9 for another story about Janet Faye.

Janet Faye considered the top ten students of the graduating class and took it upon herself to make sure that these students were able to get a higher education. And generally, she would try to find scholarships such that the students could go to an Ivy-League school on the East Coast."
-Mel Bello

Mel's parents owned Bello Store across from August Ahrens Elementary School. Mel went on to attend the University of Notre Dame and majored in Chemical Engineering. He was the first recipient of a scholarship from the HSPA. Eventually, he served as editor of the book, *Spacecraft Thermal Control Handbook*.

Crackseed (or cracked seed) is preserved plum, generically whole or cracked, flavored with spices and primarily giving the seeds a salty-sweet flavor; from China.

Such accomplishments for a young man from Waipahu!

"Bello Store had a variety of items: grocery, household dry goods and items from the Philippines, etc. Next door was a [crackseed] store owned by a Japanese [Shinsato] family. Sometimes we used to go there after school and buy a little bag

of crackseed as an after-school treat. The fun part was sucking the small brown bag after we had eaten the seeds because we didn't want to waste even a small bit of the preserved seeds!"
-Myrna (Manuel) Tsinnajinnie

"We, as teachers, were cognizant of the fact that many of our incoming students did not know English. We encouraged their parents to keep their kids talking their 'home' language. Pidgin was something they should not to be concerned about; we teachers would take care of teaching the children English. We felt that as long as the students could communicate, eventually, we could teach them English.

I especially enjoyed teaching my kindergarteners [at August Ahrens Elementary School]. One boy, "S" came from one of the many immigrant families settling in Waipahu. He was especially bright and while speaking only his native Filipino when he came into my class, he learned English quickly. I can only imagine how his parents would have been telling him that this [Hawaii] was his new home and he should try very hard to learn all that he could. "S's" life must have been 'Filipino at home with parents' and 'English while at school.' Towards the latter part of the school year, another Filipino boy entered my class. This boy would not talk. So I asked "S" to please help me and talk to the new boy in Ilocano ... or anything, so the new boy would talk. I told "S" that if we could get the new boy to talk, we can eventually help him to learn English. "S" looked at me and said. 'I cannot, I English now.'"
-Mary Ann (Sato) Saito

August Ahrens School was also known as an English Standard School. There was no kindergarten and grades 2 and 3 were known as "receiving" grades for the English Standard grades. About one-half to two -thirds of grades 1 through 4 were regular grades and the rest were of the higher English Standard classes. Being selected for the English Standard grades meant that a student could skip a grade. Grades 5 through 8 were covered by Waipahu Elementary School.

The multi-ethnic make-up of Waipahu meant testing of "English Standards" could be done very qualitatively by simple questioning of a student, parental employment status, ethnic background, etc.

"I was asked to recognize a thread and a thimble. This test was to determine if I should be placed in an English Standard class."
-Bernice (Tamura) Hamai

"When I started at August Ahrens and throughout my elementa-

ry school years, there were quite a few teachers from the mainland [continental U.S.] and I think that they helped to open my mind up to the world that was outside of Waipahu and Hawaii."
-Jeannette (Goya) Johnson

August Ahrens Elementary School celebrated its 50th birthday during the 1974-1975 school year with a special assembly and a parade down Waipahu St. At one time, August Ahrens Elementary School was the largest elementary school in Hawaii with over 2,200 students in grades K-6!

"Across Waipahu St. from August Ahrens Elementary School on the road leading donburo was the Uyehara Hospital until about 1948. Then it became the Kokubun Sewing School; this was until 1959."
-Francis Kokubun

Further along on this road, still going donburo, is a 2-acre plot of watercress farmed by Al Watanabe. Still fed by artesian wells but non-productive at this time due to parasite and insect problems, Al hopes that various agricultural groups/agents can one day help him to eliminate the problems so he can return to successfully farming watercress.

Back-tracking a bit, across Waipahu St. from August Ahrens Elementary School and going west was a Johnson Pool Hall, then the Shinsato Store and then the Bello Store. Still further west is Nabarrete Store. Originally started by his father, Cornelio Nabarrete still runs the store primarily as a neighborhood convenience store with essentials for families immediately around him. Cornelio remembers that before his father bought the store, it was owned by a Yago family, and before that, a Kaneshiro family owned the store.

In the Spanish camp area, there is a short little lane called Ii Place. The Ii name is prominent in the history of Waipahu and Hawaii. Papa Ii was a general under Kamehameha I. He received some 18,000 acres from the ruler in an ahupuaa going from the area behind Schofield Barracks down to Pearl Harbor. Parts of this ahupuaa make up the town of Waipahu.

Going west on Waipahu St. where it intersects with Paiwa St., some of the old-time stores are Tsumoto, Nii Superette, Kiso Store (today a concrete products store but previously a general merchandise store).

"Before the Tsumoto Store it was the Oahu Shokai [store] run by the Yoshii family and before that, the Yoshidas ran a grocery store that made deliveries of their groceries out of the back of their truck."
-Lilly (Takushi) Tokuhara

"My uncle used to tell me that my grandmother (his mother) was illiterate and so whenever she extended credit to someone, she would draw that person's face as a record since she didn't know how to write the name!"
    -Judy (Yoshida) Hayashida

In this area, referred to as Spanish Camp, the Okadas had a saimin stand.

"In the Spanish camp area, there was a watercress farm owned by the Oshiro family. We used to take a jar of mayonnaise, a loaf of bread, a bag of Kool-Aid ®, and a pitcher down to the watercress farm. We made watercress sandwiches and had Kool-Aid to drink using water from the artesian wells feeding the watercress. We just enjoyed the quiet and peaceful area, lounging around under shade trees."
    -Marlene (Okada) Hirata

"Donburo from Spanish camp, there was a Kaneshiro *tofu-ya*. I can still remember going there to watch them make the tofu and I can still remember the smell of the place. It wasn't a large place but it was always steamy, hot and humid. My mother used to send me there to get *okara*."
    -Hazel (Nakamoto) Sumile

For more information about tofu and okara, see Chapter 8.

Tofu-ya is the store where tofu is made and/or sold

"My father, Sanra Goya, had a slaughterhouse for pigs in the Spanish camp area. (His piggery was on the Waipio Peninsula.) He would slaughter the pigs and deliver pork to two small stores for sale.

My mother had an icebox on the open back of her car and park the car on the roadside. The icebox was filled with pieces of pork and she could sell you what you wanted or trim it down to a size you wanted."
    -Jeannette (Goya) Johnson

Across the stores is Hans L'Orange Park. Named after the most revered, loved, and respected manager of Oahu Sugar, the 7-acre sports facility has fields for baseball and football and is used for community gatherings.

It was originally the Oahu Sugar Co. athletic field but in 1972, it was dedicated as the Hans L'Orange Park and put under the auspices of the Parks & Recreation Dept. of the City and County of Honolulu.

Kawano's department store had appliances such as refrigerators, stoves, radio, and phonographs. Their soda fountain was known for the green river drink.

The Waipahu Hospital was built in 1918.

"For a small town like Waipahu, there were 3 other hospitals:

Tamura Hospital in Ota Camp,

Uesato Hospital close to the Waipahu Theater,

Uyehara Hospital near August Ahrens School and on the same street going down to Watanabe Watercress Farm,

The Plantation Hospital served only employees [of Oahu Sugar] and their dependents for free. The Japanese hospitals were very small in size, but the doctors served the community well."
 -Anonymous

At the northwest corner of Mokuola and Waipahu Sts. is the Filipino Community Center, Inc. More commonly called the FilCom Center, it is across the street from the site of the old Waipahu Hospital. The FilCom Center opened in June, 2002, and seeks to serve as a center to preserve the culture, arts, and history of the Filipino people in Hawaii. In 2006, the Filipinos will celebrate 100 years of their presence in Hawaii.

Next door to the FilCom Center is the old Plantation Store building; it was built in 1918 to the serve the employees of the Oahu Sugar Co. Directly across the street was the first department store started by Kazuyuki Kawano. The two-story building housed the department store as well as a Chinese restaurant and a taxi stand. On the second floor was a beauty parlor, the Aoyama [Blue Mountain] Photo studio, Dentist Stanley Yanase's office, etc.

"The taxi stand was on the left side of Kawano Store [as you faced the store]. Some of the taxi drivers were Mitsugo Nitta, a Mr. Abe, Masanobu Kokubun, a Mr. Nakagawa, a Mr. Iboshi, a Mr. Watanabe, and a Mr. Hashimoto. The taxis were of the 8-passenger size and their Honolulu stand was in the Aala area."
 -Bernice (Tamura) Hamai

"In the 1930s to the 1940s, taxi rides into Honolulu were about 35¢ to 40¢ one way. Not too many people had cars."
 -Henry Morisada

The whole left side of the theater has been covered over such that the window openings and places where the PO Boxes were, is not visible at this writing.

"Taxi rides into Honolulu used to be about 50¢. I think that this was in the 1950s. There was another taxi stand next door to the Bank of Hawaii building. Those taxis ran only in Waipahu."
 -Lillian (Oshiro) Oshiro

The next building over, going west, is the Waipahu Theater. The Waipahu Theater was built on Waipahu St. in 1931. The building also held the first U.S. Post Office in Waipahu. If you face the theater, on the left side, window-like openings can be seen. These once served as the postal service windows.

"On the left side of the theater and in back side of the postal service windows, were post office boxes. In those days, the mail was put in boxes such that one box held the mail for the named box holder as well as for some of the neighbors living immediately around him."
 -Amy (Yasuda) Sakuma

For the kids in the late 1940s, Saturday movies at the theater were 9-cents.

"I remember it was 9-cents because when we didn't have money and wanted to see movies, we used to hang around outside the theater and ask for the one penny change from the other kids who had a dime. Nine pennies of change later we had *our* nine cents and so could buy the ticket to go in and see the movies!"
 -Thayer Nakamoto

"Featured movies were of Hopalong Cassidy®, Roy Rogers®, and Gene Autry®. There was also Andy Panda®, Flash Gordon®, and Batman® in chapters. They had kids games, mostly dart throwing is what we remember, and the prizes were comics.

Junior Mints®, Big Hunk® and the Look® candy bars were sold. This was about 1947."
 -Lilly (Takushi) Tokuhara and
 Judy (Yoshida) Hayashida

"While in grade school, my dad gave me a monthly allowance of 10 cents to spend on anything my heart desired. In addition, I received another 10 cents from a brother, who lived and worked in another town and who came home for visits once a month. One can't imagine how elated and grateful I felt to have this extra money.

I spent the first 10 cents by attending a Saturday matinee at the Waipahu Theater. Admission was 9 cents and 1 cent was for candy. The other 10 cents I saved for later.

I often wondered if others were as fortunate as me."
 -Anonymous

"Shirley Temple, the child movie star, came to Waipahu Theater in the 1930s. There was such a huge crowd and I felt like I was going to be crushed."
 -Jane (Kimura) Arita

This visit to Waipahu is recalled by another.

"When Shirley Temple visited Waipahu, she was taken to

For the curious, Shirley Temple was born on April 23, 1928. Her career began at about age three and her popularity waned at about 1939.

the Manager's house at Oahu Sugar. When word got out that Shirley Temple was in town, it seemed like the whole town of Waipahu was up at the Manager's house! The people chanted 'Shir-ley, Shir-ley, Shir-ley Tem-ple.'"
-Sumiko (Nakamura) Oshiro

Hibari Misora, the famous Japanese movie actress is also remembered to have visited the Waipahu Theater.

Connected to the Waipahu Theater building was the old Fire House. This can be recognized today by what remains of the arched doorways. (This firehouse came into existence later than the one with stone archways [now covered over] in the stonewall of Oahu Sugar at the top of Depot Rd. where it meets Waipahu St.)

Hanaoka Fountain was located next to this fire station. It is remembered by some as being a narrow but deep store.

"When you went into the store, along the right wall was the fountain, about 30 feet long, and across that, on the left wall, were racks of comics."
-Cornelio Nabarrete

"The back room had pinball machines and only adults could go back there; but you could hear the machines from the front part of the store."
-June (Saito) Tamashiro

Downstairs, soda water was bottled under the brand of Waipahu Soda Works.

Next door to the Hanaoka Fountain was the Sing York Kee Market selling fresh meat as well as other general store items.

"There was a store called Wong's Grill in the area and for 5¢ you could get a paper cone filled with chow fun [flat noodles, soft but pan fried]. Plain [no vegetables or meats] but with a few drops of shoyu [soy sauce]. So *ono* [delicious]! I think this was in the 1940s."
-Jane (Mitsumoto) Matsunaga

There were other Chinese stores and restaurants and the next building over housed the Pang Kui Store, one of the longest active merchants along Waipahu St., on half of the first floor.

The other half of the first floor was the Kawano Music Store. Upstairs was the office of Dr. Thomas Ohara, the second dentist to have a practice in Waipahu.

Continuing west on Waipahu St., the Tawata Saimin Stand is remembered as pioneering the fried saimin dish. The corner where Depot Rd. begins from Waipahu St. now is a parking lot for a neighborhood bar.

Beginning a detour down Depot Rd.
This corner is the site of the former Bank of Hawaii building, now gone but it is still used as a cornerstone benchmark in describing locations around the center of town.

Fig. 3-2. The old Bank of Hawaii Bldg at the corner of Waipahu St. and Depot Rd.

The old Bank of Hawaii (BoH) building was built on June 30, 1916, and was the first branch office of the Bank of Hawaii. It had an estimated 1,000 sq. feet of floor area. The branch was relocated to its present location at the corner of Depot Rd. and Farrington Hwy. on June 8, 1955, and has 4,406 sq. feet of floor area.

This information and photo of the first BoH building (and the newest BoH building - see Chap. 5) was provided by the Archives of the Bank of Hawaii and we are able to use the materials through the efforts of Margot L. Baist, Corporate Communications, Bank of Hawaii.

Old-timers use this corner to describe locations as "on the Bank of Hawaii building side" or "from the old Bank of Hawaii, if you went along Waipahu St. towards ...."

Across Depot Rd. at this intersection was the Henry Kam building.

"They would paint the building and then throw sand on it

before the paint dried. The building would then look like it was built of concrete."

-Shigemi Arakawa

A drawing at the end of this chapter shows many businesses recalled from memory by some old-time residents of Waipahu. Many businesses are no longer in existence and some have changed ownership and the nature of their business. Taking a short detour and going south on Depot Rd., Arakawas of Waipahu was located on the eastern side of Depot Rd.

Arakawas of Waipahu is a very special story. Much has been written about this store and family and we treat this very special part of Waipahu in Chapter 9. The most remembered presence in the 20th century is its store on Depot Rd. but before then they were on Waipahu St. and moved to Depot Rd. where they even ventured into the hotel and taxi business. Their largest department store on Depot Rd., before they closed, was once the site of the Magoon Theater that at one time showed black and white movies. The theater eventually became a roller skating rink in the 1920s. Then the roller skating rink area eventually housed the hardware and garden departments of the most recent Arakawas store.

A bit south of the most recent Arakawas department store was located the Miyamoto Saimin Stand and Cornelio Nabarrete remembers:

Originally, saimin was only flour noodles in a broth made from dried shrimp and seaweed. Today, saimin delicacies have many types of added meats, vegetables, and eggs. Shiro's Saimin Haven in Waimalu immediately comes to mind for a very wide variety of excellent noodle dishes. (See also Chap. 4)

"I used to go to the area around Depot Rd. [quite a ways from his home] and cut back through a little lane that had Arakawa's Dept. Store. There was a very small *saimin* [noodles in soup] stand. It was so small that I think only 3 or maybe 4 people could sit there at one time. I can't remember the old Japanese woman's name [Setsuko; aka Set-chan] that ran the saimin stand. One day I ordered a bowl of saimin. It was only 5 or 10-cents for a big bowl and always very *ono*. I asked for the fork that she usually gave me but this time she said that I would have to use chopsticks! Or, if I was gonna eat the saimin, I would have to learn how to use the chopsticks. I took a *long* time to eat that bowl of saimin! But I learned how to use chopsticks!"

-Cornelio Nabarrete

Cornelio Nabarrete is Filipino and his family probably never used chopsticks at home when he was a youngster.

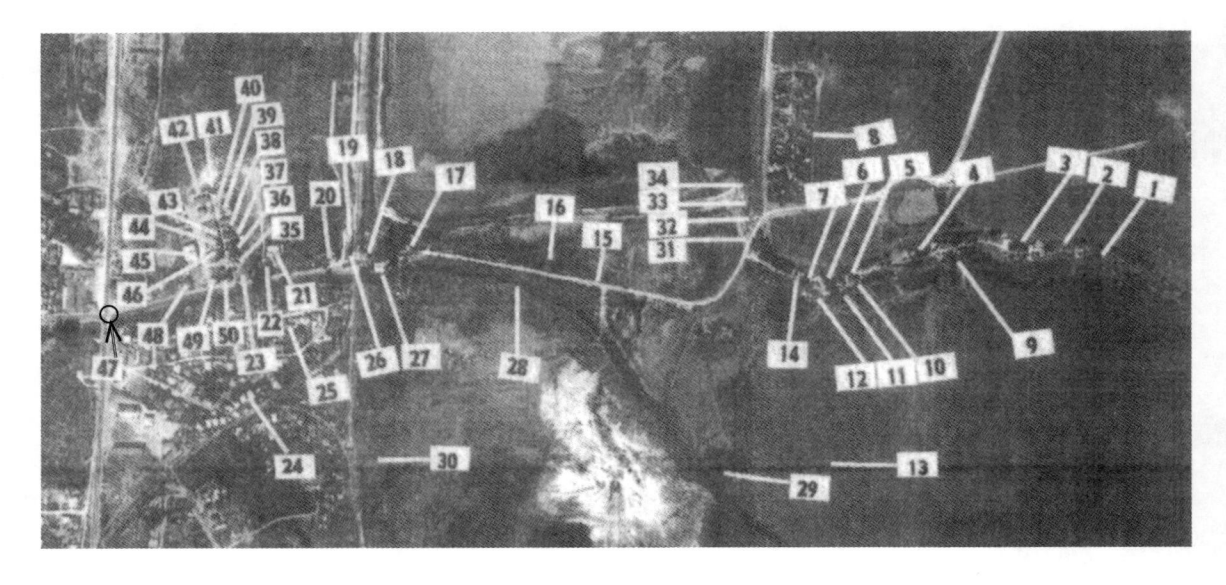

Fig. 3-3. Aerial photo of Shoburo (primarily along Depot Rd. , south of Farrington Hwy.) ca. 1952.

Legend for Aerial Photo of Shoburo ca. 1952.

1. Miles Yoshihiro
2. Tomoyoshi Watanabe
3. Pak To Pang, Jim Pang
4. Minoru Ueno
5. Hamada Main Tea House
6. Shinso Hamada
7. Mill Worker Residence
8. Camp 32, Oahu Sugar Co.
9. Ueno Aku Boat
10. Hamada Small Tea House
11. Hamada Salt Bath House
12. Joe Auyong
13. Large Fish Pond
14. Auyong Rice Mill
15. Harry Pang, Ali Yong Pang, Sambo Pang
16. John Costales, Josephine Costales, Rudy Costales
17. Sewer Pump House
18. Sonny Wong Store
19. Oahu Railway Warehouse
20. Kim Loy Kam Store (Sonny Liu)
21. Yabuki (Henry Morisada)
22. Tora Ishikawa
23. Eugene Yoshioka
24. Oahu Railway Section Camp
25. Kenneth "Mamo" Kuniyoshi
26. Oahu Railway Depot Station
27. Isaburo Isobe, Auto Repair
28. Kapakahi Stream
29. Sumida Fish Pond
30. Johnny Mau
31. Bobby Wong
32. Haruo Shigeta
33. Yasuo Arakaki
34. Summer Pang
35. Joe Pang
36. Matthew Lee
37. Albert "Hiro" Arakawa
38. Douglas "Kabo" Mukai
39. Timothy Wong
40. Richard "Toki" Kozuma - Harry Kikuchi
41. Wilfred Abe - Ruth Oshiro
42. Shigemi Arakawa
43. Takemi Arakawa
44. Sei Kaneshiro - Horace Taba
45. Arakawa Warehouse
46. Zempan Arakawa - Goro Arakawa
47. Farrington Highway - Depot Rd.
48. Walter Asari - Wally Higashi
49. Kazuo Arakawa
50. Rodney "Jun" Arakawa

Fig. 3-4. The Pedal Pushers cycling club ca. 1935.

"Waipahuans must have loved saimin! There were quite a few saimin stands. I can remember Shiroma Saimin Stand in Higashi [camp], Miyamura in Nishi [camp], Tawata and Afuso in Machi, Okada in Spanish Camp, Miyamoto Saimin Stand next to Shintaku Store and Matsumoto Store in Nishi donburo.

We used to take pots for take-out orders. What a treat that was!

Shiroma later took over Afuso and in the 1940s, Horiuchi bought out Matsumoto.

I believe every establishment had their own noodle making machine. My favorite was the saimin that Mr. Horiuchi made. He had the knack of curling it somehow."
-Anonymous

Across the road from Arakawas was the Waipahu Bicycle and Sporting Goods Store.

This was originally started by "Buster" Takayesu's father, Giyei Takayesu, and came to occupy the T. Ota Store on Waipahu St. This store was home to the *Pedal Pushers* cycling club of the 1920s. When Giyei turned the store over to his son, Gisei (Buster), it eventually became another pillar of business in Waipahu on Depot Rd. The store, today, has a two-sided carved wooden sign that shows the starting date of 1923 hanging above the front door in the building that Buster built in 1953.

Buster, with his son Ben, later also started the McCully Bicycle and Sporting Goods shop in the McCully area of Honolulu.

"I remember that Buster used to sell us a [bamboo] fishing pole with a hook, line, and a sinker for 10¢ so we could go fishing around Waipahu streams and Pearl Harbor if we ventured that far."
-Henry Morisada

"My parents had a restaurant near here on Depot Rd. In the 1920s, full meals were only 25¢; for this, you could get miso [fermented soybean paste] soup, tsukemono [pickled vegetables], fried fish, and rice."
-Rachael (Iwao) Harada

Closeby was Nobuo and Sasayo Ishihara's candy store. They

were the first to produce a famous island frozen sweet. This was shaved ice with ice cream. And another treat was a deep fried doughnut that was filled with *an* (paste of crushed red beans and sugar). There would be lines down the street on some mornings before the store opened its doors for the 5¢ fluffy and soft treat.

"Mr. Ishihara would sing Japanese songs while he was making *senbei*. They also sold water lilies imported from Japan. I think the Japanese put the flowers on the altars at their homes and at the church."
                                        -Bernice (Tamura) Hamai

Senbei - a Japanese sweet rice cracker coming in many shapes, sizes and flavors. Light and crisp in nature, it is served with tea or eaten from the bag as a snack treat.

The Ishihara family name continues in the history of Waipahu.

Later in time is the well-known George Dean Photo Studio. Owned by **George** Kurisu and Hideo **Dean** Ishihara, they were pioneers in the taking of photos for school annuals and classes.

Related to Hideo is the Ishiharaya senbei factory on Depot Rd. beyond Farrington Hwy. Originally owned by Hideo's brother and sister-in-law, Mitsuo and Etsuko, the factory is now run by Hideo's son, Ira. The senbei is known far and wide in the Hawaiian Islands (and beyond in some cases) for its exquisite flavor and high quality of production.

Going further south on Depot Rd. is the Isobe Repair Shop. The repair shop caters to repairs of trucks and autos and sits on land where the original Oahu Railway and Land Co. (OR & L) had its train depot, Waipahu Station. In fact, Masa and Mike Isobe tell us that the office of the Isobe Repair Shop is where the OR & L turntable used to be where locomotives were turned end-for-end as needed for a different direction of travel.

In 1931, train fare from Honolulu to Waipahu was $0.40 and in 1940, the fare was $0.30; these were for 2nd class fares. First class fares were a bit higher. Passenger operations ceased on Sept. 1, 1940.

OR & L shut down completely in 1947.

The Isobes had their family home across Depot Rd. at this location and where today, the still-standing steel railroad bridge crosses Kapakahi Stream as a memento of OR & L's presence in the history of Waipahu.

Just beyond where the steel bridge is located, Kapakahi Stream meets the waters of Pearl Harbor. But going even further south on Depot Rd. and onto the Waipio Peninsula were the now-covered caves in coral that were there when Shigemi Arakawa was a young man. He remembers these caves as having human remains but cannot say with any certainty whether they were

Hawaiian burial sites.

Today, the area has been bull-dozed over and covered with all types of modern-day trash and debris from construction remains. Mangrove vegetation now covers the shoreline areas around Waipio Peninsula.

"The [water] area, called the Pouhala Marsh, is home to the Hawaiian Black Necked Stilt Bird that is today on the National Register of Endangered Species."
                                        -Darrlyn Bunda

"In the 1940s and 1950s, we used to go down there and rope railroad ties together to use as a raft. We used to use long poles and push ourselves around. Sometimes we could catch bull-frogs."
                                        -Cornelio Nabarrete

The Waipio Peninsula was initially rice paddies then became sugar cane lands with two plantation camps.

"My father had a piggery there but he used to slaughter pigs in the Spanish camp area and distribute them to two little shops for sale. This would have been in the 1930s.

There was a mullet [*Mugil cephalus* and/or *Neomyxus leuciscus*] pond in the area (owned by the Uyeno family) and rice paddies where the Police training facility is today."
                                        -Jeannette (Goya) Johnson

Of course, later in time, fields of sugar gave way to military uses during WWII.

A contributor (who wishes to remain anonymous) allowed us to use the aerial photo, Fig. 3-3. This display, with locator numbers and legend, shows some of the landmarks we describe and more in some cases; e.g. the rice mill (#14) that supported the rice industry of years long past. In navigating through the photo, start at #47 (highlighted with **O**), which is the intersection of Farrington Hwy. and Depot Rd.

Sites of Oahu, locates Lepau, a dwelling place of Hawaiian Alii [royalty] in ancient Hawaii, on an eastern point of the Waipio Peninsula on the Middle Loch side of Pearl Harbor. Near the tip of the peninsula towards the mouth of Pearl Harbor was

"Scow," an area that old-timers remember as the area where boats [scows] left to go to Ford's Island [Ford Island] since Oahu Sugar had sugar cane growing on the island at one time.

See Chapter 6 for some of the history of Ford Island.

"There used to be sea horses, about 3" to 4" long [or high] on the West Loch side of the Waipio Peninsula."
-Ron Ichiyama

"The *China Clipper* and similar types of sea planes could often be seen taking aff and landing in the [Middle] Loch of Pearl Harbor off Pearl City. The best view was from where the Ted Makalena Golf Course is today."
-Zen Abe

At one time (as late as the 1950s), Kapakahi Stream was a beautiful, clear stream that was home to *funa* and *koi*. Their presence is probably due to families living in the donburo area where Hawaii's Plantation Village is today. These families were raising funa and koi. With the many floods that plagued the area, the fishes probably found their way into the stream as a new home. The funa are remembered as varying in size from 8" to 12" in length and red or orange in color. The koi, were mostly black and as large as 24" to 30" in length!

"Funa is the Asian name for the common goldfish (*Carassius auratus*). It was brought from China as a possible food source in the late 1800's. The goldfish is in the same minnow family (*Cyprinidae*) as the carp. Carp [koi] have a more slender body and has one barbel (slender thread-like whisker) on each side of the mouth. The goldfish has a deeper body and no barbels. The carp can get large, about 4 feet, whereas the goldfish can get to 16-18 inches. In my opinion both are not good to eat."
-George Arita

"I think it was the Mikami family that was raising the kingyo [goldfish] in concrete pots."
-Goro Arakawa

"My parents had a pond that had a half-dozen or so koi. These were solid red or black as I remember."
-Diana (Hirotsu) Herrst

"You could see the bottom of Kapakahi Stream from between the railroad ties and tracks of the steel bridge near the train depot; the water was so clear and deep!"
-Ed Yamada

Today the Kapakahi Stream is covered on both banks by overgrown grasses and litter of modern-day civilization pollute the stream. The beautiful fishes are gone and replaced instead by old tires, cans, bottles, and the like. The stream, not very deep, no longer allows its bottom to be seen due to the pollution of mankind.

"One sweep with a scoop net from the stream would give you a bucket full of *opai* [these opai were good as bait for larger fish and could even be salted and fried for a meal!][opai - freshwater shrimp]."
-Zen Abe

Reversing the travel direction and going north from the Isobe's repair shop, Kapakahi Stream parallels Depot Rd. and crosses

The Big-Way Supermarket was jointly owned by Haruto 'Windy' Shintaku and Takeshi Yokono; a merger of Shintaku Store and Yokono Store.

As we go to press, the Waipahu Community Association acquired the Big-Way Supermarket site and is planning to integrate it into plans for rejuvenating the whole of the Kapakahi Stream banks with pathways going all the way to Hawaii's Plantation Village.

Darrlyn Bunda, Executive Director of the Waipahu Community Association, wants the Festival Market, as it will be known, to feature foods (fresh vegeatables, fruits, and seafoods), preparation methods, and arts & crafts from the many ethnic groups that make up Waipahu's diverse cultural background.

under Farrington Hwy. being briefly visible north of Farrington Hwy. and then goes underground (actually covered over by civilization to make a large parking area).

In the 1930s, there was a narrow wooden bridge across Kapakahi Stream that allowed one car at a time to cross the stream. It later collapsed but by then Farrington Hwy. was completed (1939). Later in time, the site was home to the Jizo San statue. Still going northward, the stream is behind the buildings that had the George Dean Photo Studio and Waipahu Bicycle and Sporting Goods as well as a few other stores.

The stream then meanders in a northwesterly direction (in front of the former Big-Way Supermarket) and can be seen emerging behind the Saiki Motors Shop on Waipahu St. From there it heads west in the donburo area where the Waipahu Cultural Garden Park and Hawaii's Plantation Village is today, and from where the stream starts with its artesian well and basaltic leak sources from the aquifer beneath the Schofield plateau.

Before the Flood Control Project of the 1930s, this donburo area would continually be flooded in times of heavy rains as it was the pathway of the Waikele Stream. With the diversion of Waikele Stream to directly feed into Pearl Harbor, the donburo area was made usable. Kapakahi Stream has maintained its integrity to this day as only a small outlet of water into Pearl Harbor; the water source being a balsaltic leak (mainly in the area of HPV) from the Schofield aquifer.

"I think there was an Ige family in the donburo area and they tied their house to the railroad tracks so it wouldn't get swept away when floods were expected."
                                            -Ken Kimura

In 1954, even with the Flood Control Project intact, a violent rainstorm sent up-rooted trees down Waikele Stream. These trees jammed across the upright pillars of the concrete bridge of Waipahu St. and again, the donburo was flooded causing much destruction and financial ruin.

Where the Waipahu Cultural Garden Park is today, stores that were there in 1954, such as the Horiuchi Store, were so decimated by this particular flood that they forever closed their doors.

"When the area would flood, we kids had a grand time playing in the flood waters on our parents' farm but they had the chore of cleaning up and settling back into a normal life. Lots of farm animals (pigs and chickens) were washed away ... to say nothing of the planted crops that were destroyed."
                              -Diana (Hirotsu) Herrst

"We used to see the cows, pigs, and mules stuck in the mud. Literally stuck in mud; the mud was so deep that their entire legs were not able to move to let them get out of their predicament."
                              -Lilly (Takushi) Tokuhara

"A lot of the piggeries were so devastated that they moved to the Diamond Head area of Honolulu."
                              -John Tasato

The road leading into the parking lot in front of the Big-Way Supermarket is located just as it was in the early 1920s and 1930s. The paved parking lot area (unpaved at that time) had the old Tin Can Theater owned by the Matsuo family. (Mr. and Mrs. Seiichi Matsuo also had the Nippon Gekijo [theater] in the Aala area of Honolulu.) While the Waipahu theater had wooden walls, the roof was made of *totan* [corrugated sheetmetal].

"The kids used to throw pebbles on the roof to annoy the movie-goers. And maybe that's how it got the name of Tin Can Theater. The place could hold about 2 or 3 hundred people and usually showed silent Japanese movies in black and white. A *benshi* would accompany the movie and spoke the parts of male, female and children with low, high, and child-like voices. I think movies were 25¢ in the 1920s. Once in a while we might have a traveling troupe of maybe 15 live actors."
                              -Shiro Matsuo

Some remember the theater as the Mikami family theater as the Mikami family might have been the custodians of the theater for the Matsuos.

"We used to play in the area (in the late 1940s) and there was a large concrete slab that we used to call 'cement.' I wonder if that was where the theater was located."
                              -Arlene (Kobashigawa)
                               Kuniyoshi

The Marigold Bar was originally the Plantation Dispensary, then it became the Community Center and during WWII, a USO Center.

Going north on Depot Rd. and then west on Waipahu St., numerous small businesses were located and their nature changed with the years. Of note is what used to be the Marigold Bar. Originally, in 1898, it was a dispensary for the Oahu Sugar Co.

After being used for the USO, the building became home to the Waipahu Community Church that was originally started by The Reverend Hiro Higuchi. A new church was built on a promise made by members of the 442nd Regimental Combat Team when Reverend Higuchi served as Chaplain of the 4-4-2 during WWII. Its members promised to help him build a church on their return. Initially, only a social hall was built and later, in 1950, the church became a reality and today is located on Mokuola St.; a combination of the Waipahu Evangelical Church and the Waipahu Community Church. It is known as the Waipahu United Church of Christ. The new sanctuary building was built next to the first church which is now used for Sunday School as well as for other purposes.

"When I was a grade schooler at August Ahrens Elementary School, I remember that the Rev. Hiro Higuchi would gather (about 10 of) us in a grassy area of the school grounds and preach the Christian religion. He gave each of us a small Bible and I was thrilled with it as the Buddhist religion (as I knew it) did not have anything in writing that I could understand. So I took the Bible home and told my mother that I wanted to become a Christian. My mother admonished me, 'we are Buddhists' and that was the end of that!

I remember the Rev. Higuchi as a strong, out-going man."
　　　　　　　　　　　　-Bernice (Tamura) Hamai

"The store that your grandfather had was located slightly to the Waianae [west] side of where Saiki Motors is today. As you look at Saiki Motors, there is a driveway on the left leading down the hill toward the stream.

On the left side of the driveway is a tamarind tree. Sometime in the 1920s I was going to cut a piece from it to make a cutting board but was told by everybody that it was bad luck to damage that tree in any way. With that kind of 'protection' it's not surprising that the tree is still there today!"
　　　　　　　　　　　　-Hideo Ishihara

Tamarind - *Tamarindus indica*; sweet-sour fruit in seed pods; used to make drinks, sauces, jams, syrups.

"When we were kids, we used to pick the fallen tamarind fruit

off the ground. Only the ripe ones would fall down even if we threw rocks up into the tree. This was about 1935. I'm surprised that the tree is still there today!"
                              -Masuye Akiyama

Down this driveway and on the left is a concrete pad that Goro Arakawa tells us that his mother told him that the Arakawa's very first store was at that location.

From this Waipahu St. area, old-timers recall that there were many, many businesses. A drawing at the end of this chapter shows the many stores that had frontages on Waipahu St. (and stilt-type supports for the back end of the stores). Quite often, these stores held the living quarters of the store owners in the rear. And donburo were gardens and farms.

"There was the Serikaku Garage on Waipahu St. [before this was relocated to Farrington Hwy.] and next to that was the *Charm School of Fashion* where Mrs. Alice Nitta taught the Kimata method of drafting patterns for clothes. I used to go there for summer classes.

Behind the school and below were lowlands with some taro planted."
                              -Bernice (Tamura) Hamai

"The Chinese had a temple in this area and the roof looked like it was held up by miniature carved elephants. We kids used to say that we had to bite our finger if we pointed at the temple; otherwise we would get bad luck."
                              -Ron Ichiyama

This was the Chinese Kwan Dai Temple. About a lot west of this point was a Chinese School and then the Tsoong Nyee Society Hall. The Hall has been rebuilt in just about the same location it was long ago, in Hawaii's Plantation Village (HPV), a part of the Waipahu Cultural Garden Park.

The park and HPV is more fully described in Chapter 9.

Leaving the exit gate of HPV, on the right is a bridge that crosses the old railroad tracks. But taking Waipahu St. straight ahead, the road will take a turn to the left. At this point, if one could continue straight ahead, a steel gate controls access to the Spring Waipahu (see the back cover for details about this spring).

Then a second bridge crosses over Waikele Stream.

"We used to dive off the bridge into Waikele Stream and use it like a swimming hole. It was dammed up just past the bridge so the water was about 8' deep! This was when we were elementary school kids at Waipahu Elementary School ... about 1950.

The water was really cold."
-Darryl Tupinio

"Every summer, using rocks and California grass [*Brachiaria mutica*] from the banks of Waikele Stream, we used to build a dam and raise the water level so we could dive in; the water was so cool and fresh we could just dive down and take a gulp of water to quench out thirst. Pineapple trucks from the fields of Kunia and Wahiawa used to pass on the street (before Farrington Hwy. was built) [therefore before 1939] and we used to climb on these slow-moving trucks and toss down some pines. I think the truck drivers knew about this but didn't care. We had fresh pineapple a lot of times!"
-Zen Abe

Up the hill from this point, on the left side of the road is located Waipahu Elementary School. It was originally called the Waipahu Grammer School and was started in September, 1899, by the Oahu Sugar Co.

"This monkeypod (*Samanea saman*) tree has a background traceable to the beginning of the school so it's over a hundred years old. It's a stately looking tree and gives a nice shade to the courtyard, don't you think?"
-June (Saito) Tamashiro

In 1932, part of Waipahu Elementary was used by the Continuation School, a school to further the education of Oahu Sugar Co. workers beyond elementary school. Classes were held in the afternoon and well into the evening. With the outbreak of WWII, the school was discontinued in 1941 when it sustained heavy damage due to bombing and the loss of students volunteering to the war effort.

Waipahu Elementary School also housed Waipahu Intermediate

The principals of Waipahu Elementary School are remembered:

Mary Ross	1899-1904
Sophie Overend	1904-1916
Alice Carter	1916-1938
Lillian Fennell	1938-1961
Domingo Los Banos	1961-1962
Thomas Osakoda	1962-1969
Georgiana Oshio	1969-1985
Linda Chung	1985-1987
William Wong	1988-1992
Bruce Naguwa	1992-1996
Mamo Carreira	1996-2003
Keith Hayashi	2003-present

Alma Mater
On the leeward side of Oahu
Stands Waipahu Elementary School
Knowledge gained with guidance and love,
We honor with loyalty
Waipahu Elementary School,
Remember forever and treasure too
Waipahu Elementary School,
With colors bright gold and blue

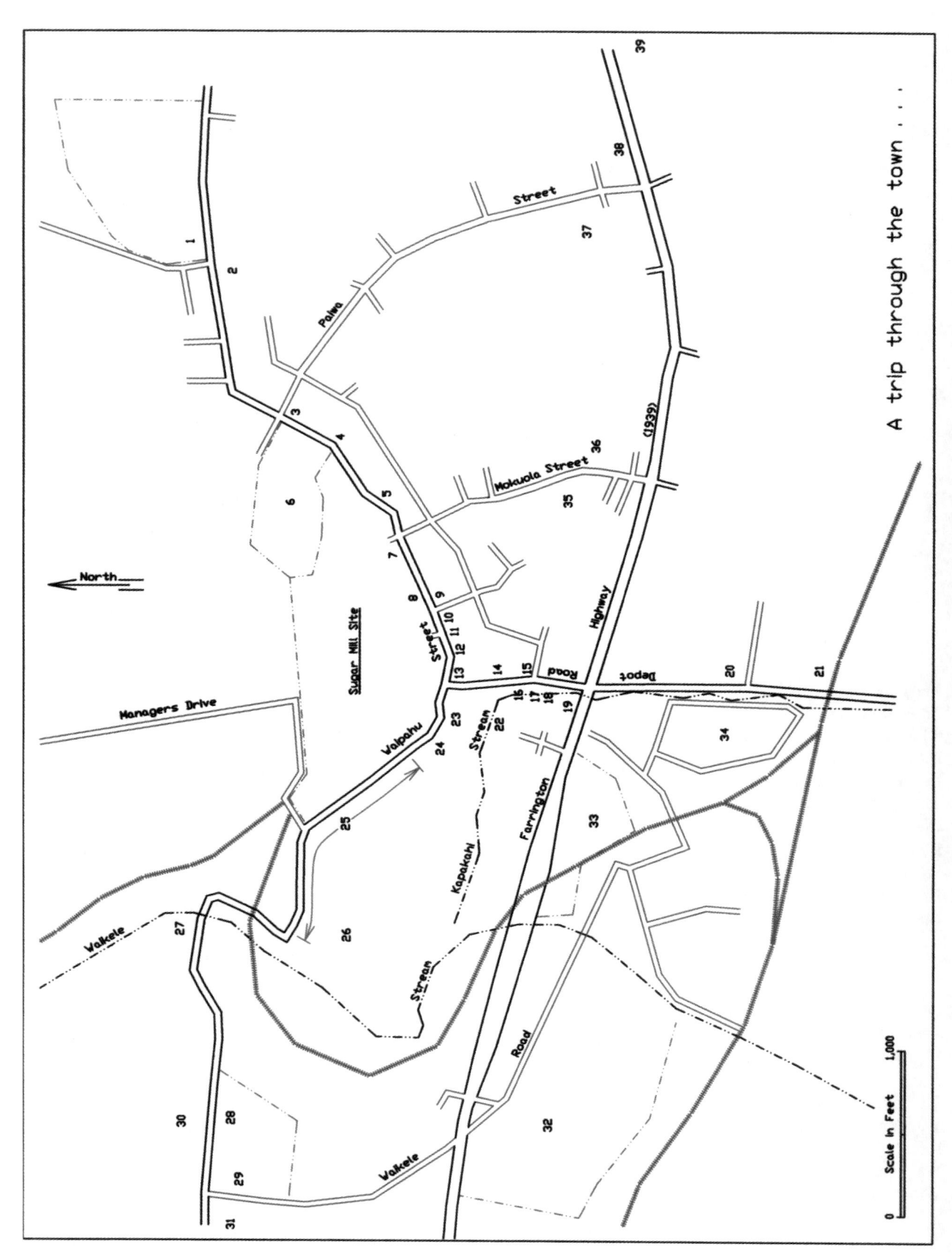

Fig. 3-5. A trip through the town with significant locations.

Legend for A Trip through the Town . . .

These entities, some old, some new, or some long gone, are referred to in the text and the locations shown should give the reader a better picture of Waipahu.

1	August Ahrens Elementary School	21	Isobe Repair Shop
2	Nabarrete Store	22	Tin Can Theater
3	Tsumoto Store	23	Marigold Bar
4	Nii Superette	24	Saiki Motors
5	Kiso Store	25	Numerous stores on stilt type supports
6	Hans L'Orange Park	26	Hawaii's Plantation Village in Waipahu Cultural Garden Park
7	FilCom Center		
8	Old Plantation Store	27	Waikele Stream Bridge
9	Kawano Store	28	Waipahu Elementary School
10	Waipahu Theater	29	Old graveyard
11	Old Fire Station	30	Former Stable camp
12	Hanaoka Fountain/Sing York Kee Mkt./ Pang Kui Store/Tawata Saimin Stand	31	Soto Zen Shu Church
		32	Waipahu Intermediate and old Waipahu High School
13	Old Bank of Hawaii		
14	Arakawas of Waipahu	33	St. Joseph Church
15	Miyamoto Saimin Stand	34	Ota camp
16	Waipahu Bicycle & Sporting Goods	35	Waipahu United Church of Christ
17	Ishihara Candy Store	36	Waipahu Civic Center
18	George Dean Photo Studio	37	Waipahu District Park
19	New (present) Bank of Hawaii	38	KAHU Radio Station
20	Ishiharaya Senbei	39	New Waipahu High School

and High School until 1939 when the physical plant of these upper level schools was completed (see Chap. 5).

"Alice Carter was the principal when I was going to Waipahu Elementary School. The most dreaded thing was the waterhose punishment she gave out. The waterhose was green on the outside, maybe a foot long and about about an inch in diameter and had a 1/4" wall thickness.

If you had done something very wrong, pulling weeds or other such punishments were mild compared to the open palm that Alice Carter required you to present to get a whack from the hose!"
-Charles Ishikawa

"We had planted avocado trees on the school grounds and when they finally gave fruit, we would try to pick them. Mrs. Carter's husband would tell us that we couldn't pick those fruit and even if we told him that we were the ones that originally planted the trees and so should be allowed to pick the fruit. He wouldn't listen and told Mrs. Carter! The result was that we each got 20 whacks on the butt with the rubber hose!"
-Pete Behasa

"Mrs. Carter used to hate it when we kids used to talk in Japanese around her. Of course, it was a convenient way for us kids to talk around her and not have her know what we were discussing!"
-Diana (Hirotsu) Herrst

Ruth Hawk was a teacher at Waipahu Elementary School. With her husband they set the school's 50th Anniversary song, *Waipahu! Waipahu!* to the music of *Piha Kanalima Makahiki [Full 50 Celebration]*. (Her husband, Leonard "Red" Hawk, in 1928, wrote and composed *May Day is Lei Day in Hawaii*, the centerpiece song of all May Day programs in Hawaii.)

In 1860, St. Joseph's Rectory was built on the corner of Waipahu and Waikele Sts. Closeby was the church's graveyard. Parts of this graveyard exist today, a neighbor of Waipahu Elementary School. In 1902 the church was rebuilt and later still, on land donated by the Oahu Sugar Co., the present church was built (in 1936) and dedicated on March 16, 1941, as St. Joseph Church. This is the church on Farrington Hwy.

May Day is Lei Day in Hawaii

Land of the flowers
Of flowery bowers
In her gay dress she appears
A sweet happy maid
May her dress never fade
As she carries this day thru the years

Chorus:

May Day is Lei Day in Hawaii
Garlands of flowers everywhere
All of the colors in the rainbow
Maidens with blossoms in their hair
Flowers that mean we should be happy
Throwing aside our load of care
Oh! May Day is Lei Day in Hawaii
Lei Day is Happy out there

"After the present church was built, the old one had to be demolished. Rather than tearing it down, it was set afire and used by the fire department for fire-fighting practice."
-James Serikaku

Across Waipahu St. from Waipahu Elementary School was Stable Camp, the center for the mules and horses that provided early transportation and power in the fields of sugar.

"They called Stable camp the 'Beverly Hills of Waipahu.' There was a manure pit. We would bring manure home in burlap bags and use the manure in our vegetable gardens."
-Zen Abe

"I remember that Oahu Sugar also kept bison [American plains buffalo] in the Stable camp area. I don't know if it was an experiment but I do remember trying to chase the strays out of our vegetable gardens. They were huge! And they really were buffalos as I confirmed later when I went to the mainland [continental U.S.]."
-Ronald Ichiyama

"Yes, these were not water buffalo with the long horns. They had short horns and a large hump on their backs."
-Darryl Tupinio

Returning to Waipahu St. and crossing Waikele St. is the Soto-Zen Shu church that was originally located on the grounds of the Oahu Sugar Co. mill on the Nishi (west) side of Manager's Dr. It was started in 1903 and The Reverend Senei Kawahara was the priest. Its first temple was built near the mill in 1905 and was rebuilt in 1949. The present church was located at its present site in the 1960s and was built under the guidance of Gijo Ozawa who was the priest from 1951 to 1974.

A popular pronunciation of Soto was sometimes Sodo.

"The parking lot used to be [one] cemetery of the Oahu Sugar Co. before it was relocated to Mililani."
-Kenichi Watanabe

The parking lot houses the Jizo San statue that used to be at the intersection of Farrington Hwy. and Depot Rd. This memorial is for two children that perished during one of the floods plaguing the donburo area. It offers prayer for these two children and hopes that such an event will never occur again.

Fig. 3-6. Jizo-san Statue.

A bit away from the central part of Waipahu town is the Hawaii Okinawa Center. The idea of an Okinawan Center was first conceptualized by the Governor of Okinawa, the Honorable Junji Nishime in 1980. Individuals, businesses, and the governments of Hawaii and Okinawa gave much support to its construction.

The Hawaii Okinawa Center is in the area bounded by Kamehameha Hwy., Ka Uka Blvd. and Ukee St. in the Waipio-Gentry region of Waipahu.

Fig. 3-7. The Okinawan Center's main building.

The major parts of the center were completed in 1990; this was 90 years after the first Okinawan immigrants came to Hawaii.

The Center was built to honor the sacrifices and courage of these first immigrants and is dedicated to the preservation, promotion, and perpetuation of the Okinawan culture. Located on 2.5 acres of land, the Albert T. and Wallace T. Teruya Pavilion and the Yeiko and Kameko Higa Office Building house facilities for performing arts, banquets, a museum and archives storage, and administrative offices. The landscaping and architecture of the center blends new and old in a tasteful, tranquil, and elegant style.

In 2005, the Serikaku Chaya (teahouse) will be added thus completing the original master plan. The addition will serve as a place for members to meet and have fellowship. It was made possible by a donation from the James Serikaku family in memory of parents Shigeru and Soyo Serikaku.

Shigeru Serikaku's accomplishments in Hawaii's aviation history is described in Chapter 9.

A Chronology for Waipahu
The world, the nation, Hawaii, Waipahu, and Oahu Sugar - happenings of interest.

1776 - American Revolutionary War
1778 - Capt. James Cook discovers Hawaii
1820 - Missionaries arrive
1835 - First successful sugar plantation; Koloa, Kauai
1842 - US recognizes Kingdom of Hawaii
1848 - Great Mahele
1850 - Masters and Servants Act; foundation of contract labor in Hawaii
1852 - First Chinese recruited sugar workers arrive in Hawaii
1868 - First Japanese (Gannen-mono*) arrive in Hawaii; (unsuccessful immigration)
   *Gannen-mono - people of the first year of the Meiji Era
1874 - David Kalakaua becomes Hawaii's last King; composes *Hawaii Ponoi*
1876 - Reciprocity Treaty between US and Hawaii; sugar enters US duty free
1878 - Portuguese arrive in Hawaii; Liliuokalani composes *Aloha Oe*
1879 - James Campbell, in Ewa, arranges to drill the first artesian well on Oahu
1881 - Scandinavians (mostly Norwegian and some Swedish) and Germans arrive in Hawaii
1882 - Chinese Exclusion Act; Planter's Labor & Supply Co. founded (basis of later HSPA)
1885 - Japanese (Kanyaku Imin*) arrive; (successful immigration) *first government contract workers
1887 - Pearl Harbor leased by US from the government of Hawaii
1888 - OR & L started by Ben Dillingham
1890 - McKinley Tariff discriminates against Hawaiian sugar
1891 - Liliuokalani proclaimed Queen
1894 - Republic of Hawaii established; Wilson-Gorman Tariff Act repeals the McKinley Tariff Act of 1890; reinstates tariff on foreign sugar; Hawaii regains advantage for its sugar
1895 - Hawaii Sugar Planters Association (HSPA) founded
1897 - Oahu Sugar started; Waipahu "born"
1898 - Hawaii annexed to US
1899 - Waipahu (Elementary) School opens with 125 students; first crop from 1050 acres yields 7892 tons of sugar
1900 - Okinawans, Spanish, Puerto Ricans arrive in Hawaii; Organic Act negates contract labor system (as a result of Hawaii being annexed) and becomes the basis of the laws of the Territory of Hawaii
1901 - Hongwanji Mission established
1902 - St. Joseph Church established
1903 - Soto Zen Mission established; Koreans arrive in Hawaii; first 12-roller crushing mill in Hawaii
1904 - Leaf hopper damages much cane crop
1906 - Filipinos arrive in Hawaii; Japanese strike to get 95¢ up from 85¢ per ton of harvested cane
1907 - Fuel oil replaces coal for locomotives
1908 - Gentlemen's Agreement; restricts Japanese immigration; City & County of Honolulu formed
1909 - Pearl Harbor Naval Shipyard construction started; Great Japanese Strike
1912 - Electrification of Oahu Sugar begins; Waiahole Water Co. formed by Oahu Sugar
1913 - Serikaku builds and flies the first airplane in Hawaii
1914 - Paul A.G. Messchaert invents a special groove for increasing output from sugar crusher rolls
1915 - Nishi Japanese School opened in camp area
1916 - Waiahole Aqueduct completed

1917 - Oahu Sugar stops growing cane on Ford's Island; mill and power plant is re-built; now a 14-roller mill
1918 - Waipahu Hospital and Plantation Store built
1920 - Filipinos strike; joined by Spanish, Portuguese, Chinese, Japanese; Lahaina disease (root infection) destroys much of cane crop
1923 - Gasoline field equipment introduced at Oahu Sugar; Athletic Field completed
1924 - August Ahrens Elementary School opens; Japanese Exclusion Act (prohibits further Japanese immigration)
1925 - H109 variety replaces Lahaina variety of sugar; first crop loaded entirely by machinery
1926 - Sewers system begun; Ewa and Oahu Sugar Cos. joined by rail
1928 - Lei Day in Hawaii is started on May 1; electrification of pumps started; supplemented by Hawaiian Electric
1930 - Steam tractors replaced by gasoline tractors; garbage collection, street cleaning in place by Oahu Sugar
1931 - No fuel oil burned; Depression; all power generated by burning bagasse; Fire Station and Waipahu Theater built
1932 - Continuation School started
1934 - Jones-Costigan Act (Agricultural Adjustment Act) limits sugar production; Tydings-McDuffie Independence Act limits Filipino immigration
1935 - Oahu Sugar plants Irish potatoes as a result of the Jones-Costigan Act.
1936 - Hoosar Mill case eliminates Jones-Costigan Act; 8-hour workday for mill operation at Oahu Sugar implemented
1938 - Waipahu High School opens
1939 - Completed: Waipahu Flood Control Project, Waipahu High School, Farrington Highway
1940 - 32-8560 variety of sugar replaces H109
1941 - WW II begins; U.S. Army and Navy take over 2414 acres of Oahu Sugar Co. lands for defense
1942 - Several hundred Japanese interned at Honouliuli Internment camp; students at Waipahu High School harvest 2,937,461 lbs. of potatoes; cane cleaning plant added; generators expanded to 10,000 KW capacity
1943 - Yields of sugar lowest in history due to war
1945 - WW II ends; 1933 variety replaces 32-8560 cane on lower elevations
1946 - ILWU strikes all plantations; end of paternalistic system; workers now pay own rent, medical and fuel
1947 - Oahu Sugar acquires Honolulu Sugar (aka Aiea Plantation); adds 3000 acres of cane land; stops using OR & L, instead uses trucks for hauling
1948 - Voluntary Juvenile Officers started in Waipahu
1949 - Oahu Sugar reports 80,160 tons of sugar or 11.60 tons per acre of planted land; cane washing plant expanded to handle over 200 tons per hour
1950 - United Airlines Stratocruiser "Waipahu" is christened at Honolulu Airport; Internal Security Act eliminates English literacy requirements for immigrants
1951 - Airplanes used to fertilize sugar; 44-3098 variety replaces 1933 variety
1952 Immigration and Nationality Act; im migrants allowed to acquire citizenship and petition families from homeland to come to U.S.
1953 - High grade centrifuge is installed
1954 - Big Flood of donburo; 2915 variety of cane is planted on higher elevations
1955 - Waipahu Hospital is discontinued
1959 - Hawaii becomes a State; Oahu Sugar has a harvest of 102.73 tons of cane per acre and 13.64 tons of sugar per acre
1960 - Oahu Sugar records 75,000 tons of raw sugar from 11,400 acres of planted fields; new steam generator installed at Oahu Sugar; added power plant

increases capacity to 16,500 KW
1961 - Oahu Sugar becomes a wholly owned subsidiary of AMFAC (American Factors - successor to H. Hackfeld & Co.)
1962 - Waipahu Shopping Plaza opens
1965 - Westgate Shopping Center opens; Immigration and Nationality Act; abolishes all national quotas for immigration
1969 - Waipahu High School moves to the east end of Waipahu; physical plant now becomes Waipahu Intermediate School
1970 - Oahu Sugar acquires Ewa Sugar
1971 - H-1 Freeway goes through Oahu Sugar land
1972 - Waipahu Cultural Garden Park groundbreaking; athletic field at Oahu Sugar is dedicated as Hans L'Orange Park
1988 - Waipahu Town Center established
1992 - Waikele Shopping Center opens; Waipahu Cultural Garden Park dedicated
1995 - Oahu Sugar closes; Arakawas of Waipahu closes
1996 - Waipahu Civic Center opens
1997 - Waipahu celebrates its Centennial

Presented herewith is a list of native rulers of Hawaii. The most recent are mentioned in the history of Waipahu.

Native Rulers of Hawaii

Name	Born	Ascended	Died
Kamehameha I (Kamehameha the Great)	c.1737	1795	May 8, 1819
Kamehameha II (Liholiho)	1797	May 20, 1819	July 14, 1824
Kamehameha III (Kauikeaouli)	Aug. 11, 1813	June 6, 1825	Dec. 15, 1854
Kamehameha IV (Alexander Liholiho)	Feb. 9, 1834	Dec. 15, 1854	Nov. 30, 1863
Kamehameha V (Lot Kamehameha)	Dec. 11, 1830	Nov. 30, 1863	Dec. 11, 1872
William C. Lunalilo	Jan. 31, 1832	Jan. 8, 1873	Feb. 3, 1874
David Kalakaua	Nov. 16, 1836	Feb. 12, 1874	Jan. 20, 1891
Lydia Liliuokalani	Sept. 2, 1838	Jan. 29, 1891	Nov. 11, 1917

Liliuokalani was deposed and the Kingdom of Hawaii came to an end on January 17, 1893. In 1894 the Republic of Hawaii was established.

To continue the rulers of Hawaii, the following is presented to complete the picture of Hawaii through the end of the 20th century.

Provisional Government

Name	Term began	Term ended
Sanford B. Dole	Jan. 17, 1893	July 4, 1894

President of the Republic of Hawaii

Name	Term began	Term ended
Sanford B. Dole	July 4, 1894	June 14, 1900

Governors of the Territory of Hawaii

Name	Appointed by President	Term ended
Sanford B. Dole	McKinley	Nov. 23, 1903
George R. Carter	T. Roosevelt	Aug. 15, 1907
Walter F. Frear	T. Roosevelt	Nov. 29, 1913
Lucius E. Pinkham	Wilson	June 22, 1918
Charles J. McCarthy	Wilson	July 5, 1921
Wallace R. Farrington	Harding	July 5, 1925
(second term)	Coolidge	July 5, 1929
Lawrence M. Judd	Hoover	March 1, 1934
Joseph B. Poindexteer	F.D. Roosevelt	April 2, 1938
(second term)	F.D. Roosevelt	Aug. 24, 1942
Ingram M. Stainback	F.D. Roosevelt	Aug. 24, 1946
(second term)	Truman	April 30, 1951
Oren E. Long	Truman	Feb. 28, 1953
Samuel Wilder King	Eisenhower	Sept. 2, 1957
William F. Quinn	Eisenhower	Aug. 21, 1959

Governors of the State of Hawaii

Name	Term began	Term ended
William F. Quinn	August, 1959	1962
John A. Burns	1962	1974
George R. Ariyoshi	1974	1986
John D. Waihee III	1986	1994
Benjamin J. Cayetano	1994	2002
Linda Lingle	2002	Present

References - Chapter 3.

A Pocket Guide to Hawaii's Tree and Shrubs, H. Douglas Pratt, Mutual Publishing, Honolulu, Hawaii, 2003.

Hawaii's Native & Exotic Freshwater Animals, Mike N. Yamamoto and Annette W. Tagawa, Mutual Publishing, Honolulu, Hawaii, 2000.

Numerous newsletters of Hawaii's Plantation Village.

History Makers of Hawaii, A. Grove Day, Mutual Publishing of Honolulu, Honolulu, Hawaii, 1984.

A History of Hawaii, Ralph S. Kuykendall, The MacMillan Co., New York, New York, 1926.

Shore Fishes of Hawaii, John E. Randall, University of Hawaii Press, Honolulu, Hawaii, 1999.

Website of the *Hawaii United Okinawa Association,* 2004.

HUOA Breaks ground for "Serikaku Chaya," The Hawaii Herald, Aug. 19, 2005.

Waipahu, Lani Nedbalek, Wonderview Press, Wahiawa, Hawaii, 1997.

Sites of Oahu, Elspeth P. Sterling and Catherine C. Summers, Bishop Museum Press, Honolulu, Hawaii, 1978.

Ancestral Reflections, Douglas D. L. Chong, Waipahu Tsoong Nyee Society, Waipahu, Hawaii, 1998.

Newsletters and archival records of the Oahu Sugar Co.

St. Joseph Church, Waipahu, Celebrates Fifty Years of Service, Lynn Nalani Oamilda, un-dated.

Website *shirleytempledolls.com*, 2004.

-4- Some culture we retain to this day

. . . we brought this and we brought that . . .

The various immigrant groups coming to Hawaii brought many items and customs that are still a part of the culture of Hawaii today.

The need to communicate between various nationalities led to the derivation of pidgin [English] not only in Waipahu but all over the Hawaiian Islands. Pidgin was a combination of English, Hawaiian, Chinese, Portuguese, Japanese, or whatever language that was most colorful and appropriate to the need. On the sugar plantations, one example is the description of a special road. What might have been a "cane hauling road" was changed in pidgin to "haul cane road." The meaning was still there and it required less syllables and effort to speak! Maps today still have "haul cane road" as names.

Mike Mauricio, writing in the HPV *Plantation Village News*, writes a bit more.

"Pidgin arose out of a necessity to communicate and no matter how maligned it was back in the academic circles, it was an integral part of plantation society. Pidgin is supposed to be a Chinese slur of the English [British] word 'business' from back in the days when the English made regular stops at Chinese ports.

In Hawaii's case, most of the words pertaining to field work were Hawaiian and perhaps Hawaiian should be considered the 'lingua franca' of the plantations. [The] Japanese language figures heavily in pidgin also because their vowel sounds are nearly identical to Hawaiian and the other nationalities found it easy to associate the two; at least phonetically.

In Japanese, there are past, present and future tenses for the word 'to do something.' Shimasu is a future tense, 'shimashita' is past and the present tense is 'shiteimasu,' shortened to 'shite' and pronounced 'shtay.' My grandfather would say 'come shtay' or sometimes 'shtay come' or 'go shtay' or sometimes 'shtay come, shtay go.' "

"Pidgin is very uniquely 'Hawaiian.' And intonations in speech patterns from people growing up in Hawaii is very unique and different from other speech patterns in the U.S. You can always recognize people that grew up in Hawaii by the way that they talk."
-Mary Ann (Sato) Saito

"Pidgin is how you learn and communicate with other nationalities."
-Harue (Hashimoto) Kanechika

Hawaii's Plantation Village at the Waipahu Cultural Garden Park has been collecting and displaying many of the various ethnic groups' foods, clothing, tools, music, household appliances, children's toys, all sorts of living necessities, and even a custom or two.

We highlight only a portion of some of the ethnic groups and what they brought with them to Hawaii. Many of the things that we describe were in place in the 1800s and 1900s, and some are still a part of our culture today in the 2000s.

Portuguese. Coming from the Azores and the Island of Madeira, the Portuguese brought with them the *braguinha* or *machete de braga*. This is the forerunner to the current *ukulele* [jumping flea in Hawaiian].

They also brought with them bread-making skills that today are most evident in *pao doce* or sweet bread.

"I remember that our neighbor used to share bread she baked in her backyard *forno*. This was dome-like in shape and a smaller version of an igloo, with a door opening and a small opening at the top to allow smoke to escape. A fire would heat up the entire oven and when the oven was hot enough, the ashes would be scraped out and the bread dough would be placed inside to be baked by the heat from the oven. I think the oven was built of clay or dirt or something like that.

A loaf of bread would sometimes have a whole egg imbedded in the dough and when it was baked, the egg was cooked along with it. When a bunch of kids were given a whole loaf, none of it made it back to our homes ... we ate it all by the time we got home!"
-Ron Ichiyama

Pronouncing ukulele properly:

The 'u's are pronounced as the 'o's in 'moon'; NOT 'you.' And the 'le' is pronounced 'lay.'

So the pronunciation becomes 'oo koo lay lay.'

"Every Saturday morning, one of the women who owned the oven just outside the yard of our Japanese neighbor, fired up the oven and with a long-handled wooden paddle, inserted the rounded bread dough onto the metal shelf inside the oven. The aroma wafting through the air was a signal for all of us kids to rally around the oven.

When the bread came out, the woman would slice up the first loaf, butter the slices and hand each of us a slice. To this day, I am convinced that it was the best bread I've ever tasted. Portuguese women are masters at their bread making and I am truly blessed for having had this experience."
-Anonymous

Malasadas (solid doughnuts) are often credited to the Portuguese as having come with them from their home country. We are told that when some Portuguese women were preparing their breads, one batch of dough did not rise properly. Someone took a handful of this dough and tossed it into a nearby pot of hot oil. *Viola*! Hot malasadas! Later sugared for more flavor and this is what we know of today!

Chinese. Probably most significant from this ethnic group is Chinese cooking and food. Whether it be the Cantonese, Peking, or later introduced Szechwan styles, Chinese restaurants abound in and around Hawaii today. The popularity of these restaurants demonstrate how well the foods are liked and are therefore a common part of our society today.

Mildred (Seu) Kam, who settled in Waipahu in 1954, shares the names of somes spices important in Chinese cooking and their English counterpart names.

Chinese name	American name
Bat kock	Star anise
Bung tong	Sugar crystals
Chin yee	Fungus
Chung choy	Preserved dried turnips
Dau see	Salted black soybeans
Doong goo	Dried mushrooms
Fu chuk	Dried soybean curd (pkg.)
Fu chuk pin	Dried soybean curd sheets
Gum choy	Dried lily flower
Hau gau	Oyster sauce

Hoisin jeong	Vegetable sauce
Hoong jo	Dried red dates
Hong yun	Chinese almonds
Jee ma	Sesame seeds
Jee ma yau	Sesame seed oil
Kwo pee	Dried tangerine peel
Kwong yau gee	Dried scallops
Me gee soo	Monosodium glutamate
Nam yui	Red bean sauce
Ng heong fan	Five-spice powder
See yau	Soy sauce
Sup gum geong	Chinese pickles
Wong tong	Chinese brown sugar
Yee chee	Shark's fin
Yin wo	Bird's nest
Yuen see jeong	Bean sauce

(Your best source for many of these spices is an Asian food supermarket or Chinatown.)

Her husband, Albert, especially likes Gau yuk [pot roast pork] and she shares that recipe with us.

Gau yuk is sometimes written and pronounced as Kau yuk.

2 lb. pork belly
Boil until a chopstick will easily pierce the meat
Put in running water until cold and pat dry
Rub soy sauce on skin and fry on low fire until brown
Cool, cut into chucks
Put salt, five-spice seasoning, and sugar
Add a little food coloring [#5 red was the favorite but its use is banned today; consequently, the dish is served brown and is no longer a colorful red]
Place into bowl with Irish potatoes (or taro) and steam until soft

A favorite Chinese food today is dim sum (aka manapua). A dumpling or bun of rice flour filled with combinations of meat, vegetables, pork, or seafood and baked or steamed. The dim sum has undergone many modifications and today is sold in Chinatown, bakeries, Chinese markets, and wherever there is a need for a hearty snack food.

Tofu (bean curd) has its origins in ancient China but the Japanese-made versions are quite popular in Hawaii. See the sidebar in Chapter 8 for a short description of the tofu-making process.

The Chinese also brought with them the celebration of their New Year (typically in early February). Today the celebration is held primarily in the Chinatown area of Honolulu. A main feature consists of a Lion Dance with accompanying firecrackers. The very colorful dance is today perpetuated by many Chinese societies. The dancers make up a string of humans under a simulated Lion's head with a dragon-like body undulating to drum rhythms as they go from (mostly) business to business, blessing each for the coming New Year. Of course, specialty foods come with the celebratory season.

"You can find candied fruits and vegetables at almost all times of the year today but I always associated these with the Chinese New Year. Carrots, pineapple, coconut, squash, and burdock root were some that had a thick coating of sugar as well as being permeated with the sugar. Sweet, juicy, and yummy!"
-Mike Yamamoto

Filipino. In the history of Waipahu (and Hawaii), the Filipinos were initially the 3rd largest immigrant group. An interesting custom that Filipinos brought with them is *caobou-caobou* Or, as Hawaii would call it, cowboy-cowboy. The connotation is that cowboys would lasso and thereby capture their prey. Caobou-caobou describes how a Filipino man would capture an already (in most cases) married woman and take her for his wife.

"In reality, the suitor would give the woman he was trying to court, flowers, gifts, and show her flashy items like cars and clothing, and try to entice her to run away with him. As far as I know, nothing came of these encounters."
-Pete Behasa

"My legal, given name is Mercedes. I was a very sickly girl and so when I was about 5 years old, my parents determined that evil spirits were causing me to be sick. I was taken outside in the yard and a passerby would see me and give me another name: 'Oh, who is this? Let's call her Edith!' This was to confuse the evil spirits who then wouldn't be able to recognize me and make me sick. (All this was a planned thing.) So the name I got as a result of this passerby seeing me was 'Edith' and I've used this name ever since. I think this was an Ilocano custom."
-Edith (Correa) Valdriz

"The Marungay (horseradish) tree was very popular with the Filipino families. In fact, if you saw a Marungay tree in a yard, you could be pretty sure that a Filipino family lived there."
                    -Myrna (Manuel) Tsinnajinnie

As with all immigrant groups, foods remain with us today as a characteristic of the Filipinos. But the Filipino foods show their historic backgrounds of Spanish and Asian influences. Corum's book, *Ethnic Foods of Hawaii*, gives a good overview of many ethnic foods.

Clothing such as the barong tagalog, a lacy dress shirt, is still very evident with the Filipino males at events such as parties and weddings.

Japanese. The Japanese introduced their type of rice (somewhat sticky and not fluffy as the Chinese rice) to us and with it, sushi. Noodles called saimin in many forms and presentations are a regular part of today's Hawaii. (See sidebar in Chap. 3.)

The bon-odori remains with us today as a celebration to memorialize the dead. But in many instances, it is a social event during the summer months. Typical clothing of Japanese kimonos worn at bon-odoris also carry forth to our day.

In the *o-bon* season one activity was the bon dance held in the evening and outdoors. The Bon Odori [dance] is to memorialize the dead.

Bon is celebrated in Japan in mid-July. But in Hawaii, the season is spread out from mid-June through August to allow each Buddhist group (and other organizations) to put on this event. The event has become a social as well as a fund-raising event.

"I was about 9 years old and would spend some summer weekends with grandpa and grandma in Waipahu. I remember that on one occasion, we went to a local *o-bon* festival at the Waipahu Hongwanji near the sugar mill. This was the traditional celebration to memorialize the dead. There would be a large area about 100' in diameter with a *yagura* [a four columned tower] about 25 feet in height constructed of massive timbers tilting towards each other as they pointed upwards. Part way up was a platform which held the *taiko* [large drum] beat upon with stout drumsticks by the drummers.

One of the Matsuo descendents from the Tin Can Theater owners in an earlier chapter, is Shiro Matsuo, the founder of *Shiro's Saimin Haven*.

Shiro Matsuo was officially declared Hawaii's Statesman of Good Will as Manuela Boy, on Aug. 20, 2003, by Governor Linda Lingle.

As a colorful, muti-faceted and multi-talented individual, he shares a poem he wrote appropos to early Waipahuans and immigrants in general.

    A Tribute to the Issei*
[*First Generation from Japan]
As I daily watch the obituaries
I am saddened at the diminishing
   personalities
Of a brave band of pioneers.
Surely they had no peers.
They came from a land far away
To make their stake in Hawaii Nei.
'Tis almost the end of an exciting
   and challenging era.
I want to give them the loudest
   'Hurrah!'
They worked diligently and
   faithfully
For a dollar a day
Didn't falter or weaken come what
   may.
They taught us to love, be loyal and
   respect this nation.
They saw to it that we were clothed
   and given an education.
What we are, what we do,
What we have today
We owe them in many a way.
In my memories I will always
   remember
This priceless treasure,
As I meditate in my solitude
Deeply and humbly I pray in
   gratitude
'Til the end of my time I say
Thank you, thank you in every way.

Those who wanted to dance would form concentric circles around the tower and dance to the music of the taiko and singers/chanters. They would dance singularly and not hold one another or otherwise be grouped. All would be dressed in traditional Japanese clothing.

There would be lines (similar to clotheslines) from strategic locations outside the area leading radially inward to the tower. On these lines would be clothes-pinned paper notices, announcements, and brightly colored banners. Grandpa Tatsuichi Ota pointed out one paper that was noting his donation to the Hongwanji temple.

I also remember that one particular dancer was exceedingly attractive. She stood out because of her delicate beauty, very graceful dancing, and the fact that she was Portuguese! Everyone around me commented that she was an exceptional part of the Waipahu community. Only as we compile this book, have I found that her last name was probably Mundon."
- Michael Yamamoto

"I remember one very popular dance as the 'Tanko Bushi' — the coal miner's dance."
-Anonymous 810

"We went to many bon-odoris at many different Hongwanji temples. As I remember, each Hongwanji had a color of its own. When a dancer from another place came to the dance, he or she was given a small, white *tenugui* [towel] stenciled with the name of the particular Hongwanji he had come to dance at, and these were neatly folded length-wise, placed around the back of the neck and crossed in front above the upper chest and tucked into the *kimono* [Japanese straight-cut garment like a tunic with long sleeves].

The yagura had a platform or stage about halfway up the four column post structure that held taiko drummers and the singers, and above that was a simple roof that was sometimes pointed at the top. Dancing around the yagura was first clockwise for one dance (song) and with the next dance, the dancing would go in the counter-clockwise direction. About once every hour a small band or orchestra would play a live dance number. Otherwise, the taiko drummer and vocalist provided musical accompaniment for the dancers.

Traditional wear was most evident with the older folks. Ornate kimonos with *obis* [wide sashes] and white *tabi* [heavy cotton socks that enclosed the big toe singularly and apart from the other toes that were enclosed as one]. Tabi footwear might be the standard wear for these older folks. Of course, women's wear was more ornate than men's wear. Quite often the ornate kimonos might be of brightly colored silk. The younger folks, in *yukata* [lightweight cotton] kimonos, would not be as traditionally dressed and might use zoris [slippers of straw or rubber] or *geta*s [wooden clogs] as footwear."
- Dennis Togo

"The coming of the New Year was a big time for all of us. Families were busy getting ready for this event. This meant pounding the rice to make *mochi* (rice cakes). This involved neighbors getting together to make them. From early morning our mothers started to cook the 'mochi-gome' (mochi rice) on a makeshift stove using firewood. When the cooking was done, the men took over, and using a large mortar and pestle [generally so large that the pestle was really a large wooden mallet swung overhead into the stone mortar][in Japanese, the mortar was an *usu*, and the pestle a *kine*], they pounded the rice in rhythmic motion. It was quite a sight to see.

Then the mochi was ready to be formed into round, domed dumplings; some stuffed with sweet red bean paste, others without fillings. We helped with this part. On New Year's morning, the plain mochi and vegetables were made into "ozoni," a traditional soup that brought good luck, good health and good fortune [for the coming year]. This soup was eaten the first thing in the morning.

After breakfast, my father would give the children (4 of us) monetary gifts. Since my brother was the oldest, he got the most money while I got the smallest amount since I was the youngest. That was all right. I was still happy to receive it. The monetary gift increased each year, and we looked forward to this each year.

I can still recall and cherish this particular experience that happened with the coming of the New Year."
-Anonymous 810

Celebrations of the New Year and mochi-making, especially during the New Year, are still with us. But mochi as a snack, a

From *Ethnic Foods of Hawaii*:

Mochi has symbolic meaning. To the Japanese it stands for longevity. Also, mochi, sounding like the Japanese word for wealthy (kane = the root word for "wealth" ; kane-mochi = rich person) symbolizes wealth and prosperity. The traditional New Years's Day breakfast for Japanese families consists of ozoni, a clear soup with mochi and vegetables in it. Ozoni may include in it konbu (seaweed), daikon (white radish), mizuna (a mild green leafy vegetable), and sometimes cuttlefish. But it always includes mochi.

present given as a gift, and an offering to deceased relatives in memorium are also a part of Hawaii's Japanese culture.

As with the Chinese, Japanese restaurants abound in and around Hawaii. Other ethnic groups have been able to assimilate themselves with Japanese cooking and quite a few Japanese restaurants today are in reality owned by other than Japanese people. However, the food presentations are still superb.

Domingo Los Banos led us to the following story. It has been condensed and the fuller story can be examined in *Dendo*, cited in the References of this chapter.

Doshisha Theological School in Kyoto, Japan, was founded in 1875. Doshisha translates to 'institute for students with the same ideals.' The school is a result of a missionary educated at the Philips Academy at Andover, Amherst College, and the Andover Theological Seminary in Massachusetts, going to Kyoto and starting the Christian school in 1874.

Robert Irwin, Hawaiian Consul in Japan, wanted to have a Japanese clergy in Hawaii to work with the immigrants. Shinichi Aoki, a student at Doshisha, was selected at the last minute to accompany the first immigrant group to Hawaii. Aoki arrived in 1885, and immediately held a Christian service at the Immigration Depot in Honolulu. This was the first event in the opening of the way for Japanese immigrants to become Christians.

Consul General Taro Ando and his wife, though not Christians themselves, saw the need to improve the moral lives of the Japanese. They took up the cause of uplifting the lives of Japanese in Hawaii thus reducing the drinking, gambling and public menace types of behavior that immigrants had come to exhibit. Consul Ando and his wife founded the Japanese Mutual Assistance Association (aka the Benevolent Society) and in 1889, formed the Invalid Home for Japanese. This home later became the Kuakini Hospital and Home, then the Kuakini Hospital, and today is the Kuakini Medical Center.

Koreans. This immigrant group first came to Hawaii in 1903 to work on the sugar plantations.

Most people today connect kim chee [spicy hot, fermented vegetables with lots of garlic] with Koreans. Today, kim chee is made with many, many types of vegetables and is served with the family meal, as a side dish to a plate lunch, and sometimes even as part of celebratory dinners.

Their other foods are today also a part of Hawaii's culture though not as widely appreciated as Hawaiian, Chinese or Japanese foods. Again, see Corum's book.

This hard-working group of immigrants instilled in their children the importance of education and the drive to be good, productive citizens.

The importance of children in the Korean culture is evidenced by *Baek-il*, or 100th day celebration of a child's birth. Foods (mostly rice cakes) such as baekseogi (for longevity, representing cleanliness and freshness), susupo-tteok (to prohibit bad things), injeolmi (for patience), and songpyeon (for thought), make up the four types of food in the celebration.

The *Tol* or *Chut-tol* is the big celebration for the child's first birthday. The child is dressed in elaborate clothing and an assortment of rice cakes along with symbolic items such as yarn, money, books, etc., are put in front of the child. Whatever the child selects is taken as an indication of the child's future.

Puerto Ricans. The Puerto Ricans first came in 1900 from a Caribbean island home that resembled Hawaii in many ways.

Climate was most comparable and taro in Hawaii was like their dry land taro yautia; bananas were like the Chinese and Hawaiian types. They also grew sugar cane, coffee, and rice back in their island home.

However, their small numbers have not impacted today's Hawaiian culture as have other ethnic groups. Their island nation was originally settled by Taino Indians, African slaves, and the Spaniards thus giving Puerto Ricans a multi-ethnic background.

Blase Camacho Souza, guest writer for the *Plantation Village News*, gives a good insight to Puerto Ricans lives with a description of terms:

Arroz blanco - white rice
Arroz con gandule - rice with pigeon peas
Batey - hard-packed dirt area around the house

Kim Chee (just one of many versions):

3 large won bok (aka celery cabbage, makina, Napa cabbage)
1c. Hawaiian salt (coarse or rock salt)
1 large bowl of water

Sauce:
1 t. MSG
3 T. sugar
1 T. ginger, chopped fine
1 T. garlic, chopped fine
3 stalks green onion, minced
2 t. paprika
1T. cayenne
1½T. salt
1c. water

Cut cabbage cross-wise into 1½-inch pieces. Let sit for a few hours in salted water. Drain and squeeze out excess water.

Pour sauce over cabbage, mix well, store in jars, refrigerate for a few days.

Jean Chur in
Cookbook I -
Hawaii's Plantation
Village

Bomba - improvised verse
Cafe con leche - coffee with milk
Chorizo - sausage
Cuatrista - cuatro player
Cuatro - a 4 or 5 double-stringed instrument
Danza - a dance of Spanish origin
Decima - a ten-line rhymed verse
Guaracha - an old Spanish dance
Guiro - an instrument made from a long gourd
Jibaro - countrymen of the highlands of Puerto Rico
Las Navidadas - Christmas holidays
Lechon asado - roast pig
Mazurca - a dance of Polish origin
Morcillas - blood sausage
Pan - bread
Pan dulce - sweet bread
Paseo - promenade
Plena - Puerto Rico's coastal plain folkloric music
Polca - a European dance, adapted by the Spanish
Pollo guisado - chicken stew
Seis - a folk dance and its music
Seis bombeao - seis music with improvised verse
Seis con decima - seis (music) with decima (verse)
Vals - Puerto Rican waltz
Viandas - root vegetables (taro, dasheen, yucca, etc.)

The Spanish influence in Puerto Rico's history is evident with Navidad (Christmas) and Ano Nuevo (New Year), part of their celebrations.

If you made a roster of people in Hawaii's history and tried to attach a particular ethnic group to a person, you would be hard-pressed to do so. What may appear to be from an "X" ethnic group might really be from a "Y" ethnic group. And many people in today's Hawaii have ethnic backgrounds with "X-Y-Z-A-B-C" and you would call these people "cosmopolitan." Of course, a person might look like "X" but on query, he might tell you 'I'm "Y" but with a little bit of "B" from my mother's side.'

The point being: Hawaii's ethnic make-up is like the mongrel dog . . . in Hawaii, a *poi* dog . . . all mixed up!

Taking this a bit further, the customs, clothing, and food of today's Hawaii is a mixture or blend of many races.

References - Chapter 4.

Dendo, Mary Ishii Kuramoto, Nuuanu Congregational Church, Honolulu, Hawaii, 1986.

Numerous newsletters of Hawaii's Plantation Village.

Docent Manual, Hawaii's Plantation Village, 2003.

Ethnic Foods of Hawaii, Ann Kondo Corum, Bess Press, Honolulu, Hawaii, 2000.

Hawaii's Plantation Cookbook, The Original, Friends of Waipahu Cultural Garden Park, Waipahu, Hawaii, 1983.

-5- Along Farrington Highway

. . . a connector highway, a by-pass highway . . .

The principals of Waipahu High School are remembered:

Dallas C. McLaren - 1938-1942
Clarence B. Dyson - 1942-1953
Alton V. Armstrong- 1953-1969
Gordon Kushimaejo-1969-1974
Milton Shishido - 1974-1997
Patricia Pedersen - 1997- present

Alma Mater
'Midst the waving tassels stands
  Waipahu High
Breezes from the mountains, sweep
  across the sky;
Let us pledge our love to Alma
  Mater
Keep the precepts without fail
In loving praise, our voices raise
Waipahu, our high school
Our Alma Mater, Hail!

All Hail Waipahu, Hail Waipahu
Hail, Hail, Hail!

The high and intermediate school was located on the grounds of Waipahu Elementary School because even if the government of Hawaii had mandated the creation of the high school, the physical plant was not immediately ready. When it was completed in 1939, this physical plant was where the current Waipahu Intermediate School is located. The first graduating class of Waipahu High School was in 1941.

Loko Hanaloa, another large fishpond, was located in the middle of the Waipio Peninsula and had an area of about 195 acres.

In and around Pearl Harbor, the ancient Hawaiians had as many as 27 fishponds. Today, many have been filled in or otherwise lost.

Farrington Hwy. runs east-west through the town of Waipahu. Originally conceived as a means to by-pass the business and residential parts of the town, its main function was to connect Honolulu with the western-most areas of Oahu.

At the eastern-most part of Farrington Hwy. that is a part of Waipahu, is located Waipahu High School. Originally, Waipahu High and Intermediate School was located where the present-day Waipahu Intermediate School is located (at the western edge of Waipahu). The separation between the high school and the intermediate school was made in 1969.

Waipahu High and Intermediate School was founded in 1938 and originally had students from Aiea, Pearl City, Waipahu, Ewa, Nanakuli, and Waianae because in those early days there was no other high school in west Oahu. This fact is the main cohesive force behind the group of people meeting at the Marukai Store in Torrance, California.

These people presently meet on the 2nd Wednesday of each month at the store and enjoy lunch and each others' company recalling events and episodes in history from the recent past and from long ago. The group has a diverse make-up but they all went to Waipahu High School ... this is the common thread that holds them together!

Somewhat hidden behind Waipahu High School is the Ted Makalena Golf Course and the Waipio Soccer Complex. This area, which was covered over and later came to house these athletic sites, was once part of *Loko Eo*, an ancient Hawaiian fishpond. Loko Eo is estimated to have been about 137 acres in size. After being a fishpond, the site became rice paddies and later still, the area held an oxidation pond for the Oahu Sugar mill effluent.

"Going further west and on the northern side of Farrington

Hwy. was the old **KAHU** radio Station. This area is now a subdivision of homes."

-Roy Higa

In the 1950's KAHU radio was AM 940 with country-western music. In 1988, it became KDEO FM 102.7 and continued through the 1990's.

The KAHU radio tower is remembered as sitting amidst a field of marsh grasses. This large expanse of the donburo area was home to mainly rice fields and taro patches in the early 1900s because there were so many artesian wells feeding the area. Today, the wells are capped and the area is instead a field of homes.

"I was trying to develop the area with a four-story apartment building. We started with pilings that were driven into the ground. After a few hits, the pilings would disappear into the ground!"

-Alaric Sokugawa

Going further west is the Waipahu District Park on Paiwa St. Facilities there include an average size gymnasium, baseball fields, tennis courts, basketball and volleyball courts. The presence of artesian wells cannot be fully ignored. The swimming pool built on "spongy" land" (see Chap. 1) was demolished and a new pool rebuilt on the site in 1992. Pilings were sunk into the ground and the current pool was built on these pilings. Buildings in the complex are built slightly above the normal ground level to avoid flooding. There appear to be spots in the surrounding grassy areas where artesian water keeps constant puddles of water.

At the corner of Mokuola St. and Farrington Hwy. the Waipahu Civic Center houses the Waipahu Public Library, community meeting facilities, District Court Systems Branch, Social Services Offices, unemployment offices, and public health offices to name a few. Closeby is a terminus for buses.

"Going west along Farrington Hwy. and across from the Jack-in-the-Box®, was located the Wai Lani Inn. It was one of the better restaurants (by country standards anyway) for the Waipahu/Ewa area. It was a landmark up until the 1960s. Today the restaurant is no longer there and has been replaced by a 7-11® Store. I know the Wai Lani Inn was owned by Matsuko Okada [Mrs. Hideo "Major" Okada]."

-Roy Higa

Still going further west on Farrington Hwy. are a series of strip malls. Of interest is the northeastern corner of the intersection of Farrington Hwy. and Depot Rd. In the mid 1940s, Raymond Sokugawa began the mall there that could properly be called the first shopping center in Hawaii, the Aloha Shopping Center. He was able to secure tenants such that there was a service station (later to be Charley's Service Station), a supermarket (Country Market), a florist (Country Florist), a beauty parlor, (Pauline's) dress shop, (Beta) Shoes, a jewelry store, Oahu Finance, and other various and sundry stores.

Continuing along Farrington Hwy. past newer strip malls, Depot Rd. and Kapakahi Stream are crossed and heading west, on the northern side, is the present-day Bank of Hawaii (that was on the corner of Depot Rd. and Waipahu St. long ago).

Fig. 5-1. The new Bank of Hawaii building at the northwest corner intersection of Farrington Hwy. and Depot Rd.

Then Mid-Town Radio and other stores are located.

A service station owned by the Nakamoto family was located slightly west of the Mid-Town Radio building.

"Our parents named the service station 'Nakamotor' Service. This was in the 1940s to 1950s."
                                        -Tyler and Thayer Nakamoto

Across Farrington Hwy. is Pahu St., a road leading towards Ota Camp and the West loch of Pearl Harbor.

At the southwest corner of Depot Rd. and Farrington Hwy. Shigeru Serikaku had his service station (relocated from his earlier one on Waipahu St.). Further in on Pahu St., Darryl Tupinio's grandparents had their family and boarding house for single men working on the plantation. They had a moderately sized pond fed by an artesian well that let them raise taro and gave the kids an opportunity to catch fishes such as the Filipino named *puntat* or Chinese catfish.

Slightly further west of Pahu St. on Farrington Hwy. is the present-day St. Joseph Church (relocated in 1941 from being close-by to Waipahu Elementary School).

The membership of the church increased from 1902 with the influx of Filipino, Portuguese, and Spanish laborers until, in 1936, St. Joseph Church was established as an independent parish. Father Leo Taeyaerts was assigned to the church as its first resident pastor. With help from Hans L'Orange, local contractors, and prominent people in the community, Father Taeyaerts built up the physical plant of the church and rectory. Both buildings were completed in 1941.

In 1946, St. Joseph School was started and the size of St. Joseph Church has continued its growth until today with a mixture of different cultures that today include Filipino, Portuguese, Samoan, Japanese, Tongan, Vietnamese, Chinese, and Hawaiian ethnic groups. The Church serves the Waipahu community well.

Driving west on Farrington Hwy. (from Depot Rd.) the highway takes an uphill climb as it goes over Waikele Stream and the railroad tracks. Through early Waipahu's history, Waikele Stream meandered south from the north [Schofield] plains and then connected with Kapakahi Stream. With every heavy rain, the donburo area (where the Waipahu Cultural Garden Park is today and much of the lower Depot Rd. area) would flood and cause much damage to those living, farming, and doing business in the area.

The old name for Waikele Stream was Poniohua.

Finally in the 1930s, what the old-timers call the Flood Control Project, was begun to divert Waikele Stream to flow directly into Pearl Harbor. The Oahu Sugar Co. (actually, Hans L'Orange) sent engineers at night to survey the area where the stream diversion was needed. This dead-of-night effort was because the stream diversion needed to go through Ewa Plantation's Apokaa lands and the idea was to get the feasibility information without raising the ire of Ewa Plantation. Once

Apokaa Sugar Co., was a wholly owned subsidiary of Ewa Planation. It existed from 1903 to 1936 when it was dissolved to be a part of Ewa Sugar. In 1903 and 1904, its crop size was 610 and 874 tons respectively.

the information was in hand, Waipahu went to the Territorial Government and petitioned the diversion as practical and needed. Dredging was done to divert the Waikele Stream directly towards Pearl Harbor. The dirt that this dredging produced was used as a ramp for Farrington Hwy. to go over Waikele Stream and the railroad tracks paralleling the stream.

The first bridge going over Waikele Stream had a two-lane highway that handled traffic going east and west. Then a second bridge was added that allowed for another two lanes. The highway was now two lanes going east-to-west and two lanes going west-to-east. On the bridge going east-to-west, the end pier bears the name of William A. Patterson (see Chapter 9).

Farrington Hwy. was completed in 1939.

Going further west on Farrington Hwy. is where Waipahu Intermediate School now stands. We earlier described the separation between the high school and the intermediate school but we should mention the football field that the intermediate school retained as Dyson Football Field. It is named after Clarence Dyson as he was a principal of Waipahu High and Intermediate School. Today Dyson Field appears more like a large courtyard next to the Administration Building.

"At the base of the flagpole of Waipahu Intermediate School is a plaque that will be changed to reflect '100 Years of Service' and memorialize veterans (from WWII, the Korean War, Vietnam War, Gulf War, Afghanistan War, etc.), educators, police, and firefighters. This is planned for 2007."
-Cal Kawamoto

Across from Waipahu Intermediate School near the intersection of Farrington Hwy. and Waikele St., the Oahu Sugar Co. had a reservoir that also served as a swimming hole for school kids in the area.

"It was rectangular in shape, about 5000 sq. ft. in area and maybe 8' deep. When the water was drained to irrigate cane fields, we kids used to have a field day collecting all the crayfish in it. The reservoir was just north of the intersection of Waikele St. and Farrington Hwy."
-Darryl Tupinio

The principals of Waipahu Intermediate School are remembered:

Yoshitsugu Yamada   1966-1974
Stanley Seki   1975-1980
Roberta Mayor   1981-1983
Mieko Higuchi   1983-1986
Glenn Tatsuno   1987-1990
Gary Takaki   1990-2000
Edward Oshiro   2001-2002
Randell Dunn   2003-present

Schools in Waipahu:

August Ahrens Elementary
Honowai Elementary
Kaleiopuu Elementary**
Kanoelani Elementary
Lanakila Baptist Schools*
St. Joseph Elementary*
Waikele Elementary**
Waipahu Elementary
Waipahu Intermediate
Waipahu High School

*private
**not in that previous Census Tract area defining Waipahu but these schools are in close proximity to the town proper of Waipahu

References - Chap. 5.

Unpublished manuscript, Kay M. Yamada

Tide and Current, Fishponds of Hawaii, Carol Araki Wyban, University of Hawaii Press, Honolulu, Hawaii, 1992

St. Joseph Church, Waipahu, Celebrates Fifty Years of Service, Lynn Nalani Oamilda, un-dated.

-6- World War II

...we saw the pilots, we waved at the pilots...

"In 1939, my father was called home to Japan because his father was gravely ill and, since he was the oldest son, we sold everything and set sail for Japan. We spent a year there and in 1940, we came home. My grandfather recovered and there was quite a lot of military activity so the Japan family encouraged us to go back to Hawaii. Thankfully, we did as WWII started a year later."

-Jane (Kimura) Arita

Recollections about this period are sketchy but Nina remembers that she was supposed to help with the family laundry.

"My mother told me to help and hang the laundry on the line behind the store. While I was out there, I remember very clearly, Japanese Zeros with the red circle on their wings and bodies, circling the smoke stack of the Oahu Sugar mill."

-Nina Yuriko (Ota) Sylva

This was Dec. 7, 1941, the start of WWII.

"I was 14 years old. We could see the planes. We followed the railroad tracks toward the plantation office on Farrington Hwy. A car tooting its horn came by and the driver told us the ships in the harbor were sinking. We went up by Manager's Row [close by the Oahu Sugar mill and up a hill] and could see the harbor.

I saw dogfights overhead."

-Yasuo Saito

"When the Japanese were firing their guns, I thought I saw almost a stalling of their planes from the recoil of the guns."

-James Serikaku

"We were in the ricefields by our house and we saw the Japanese Zeros circling overhead. My father had just gotten out of bed and was wearing his nightclothes, a simple Japanese kimono.

We kids were with him and waved at the circling planes. They were flying so low we could see the pilots waving back. Maybe it was because my father was in a kimono that they didn't shoot at us. Like, maybe they thought we were Japanese."
-Pete Tagalog

"The grounds of Oahu Sugar were littered with shrapnel."
-Peter L'Orange

"I was eleven years old and at home in the living room with other children sitting on the floor on mats. My Japanese school teacher from the Hongwanji School was coming to teach us about Buddhism and being good and respectful to our parents. I really liked Nakamura *Sensei* [teacher] but somehow that Sunday I didn't want to stay at home for Sunday school class. So I walked to the top of [the hill where we had] our camp of about 8 houses. This was Camp 56 on Kunia Rd. I was outside with Mrs. Diliang Cailing and her young children watching the planes flying overhead going [north] towards Schofield Barracks and Wheeler Field. All of a sudden we were strafed by machine gun fire. Mrs. Cailing, who was carrying her baby on her shoulder screamed that a bullet had just missed her baby's head. We all started to scream and cry and went running into her kitchen. We were all scared and puzzled.

In a few hours, Larry Mirafuentes came home and told us the sad fact that the Japanese had attacked Pearl Harbor and that we were at war.

The planes were flying so low that you could see the pilot's faces. We'll never know if one pilot was only trying to scare us or [if] he was a bad shooter and God spared our lives so we could live this long life and share this experience in 2003."
-Lynn (Serikaku) Tamashiro

"Japanese planes flew low overhead and dropped leaflets. My brother picked one up and since it was blank he just threw it away. We later learned that there was writing on it that could be seen if the paper was dipped in water."
-Ellen (Goya) Miyake

"My father wondered aloud why the people were behaving as they were; without purpose or meaning for the future. As fast as they earned money, they spent it sometimes frivolously because of all of the confusion from the war. After all, a lot of people were Japanese and it was the Japanese [nationals] that were attacking us."

-Nina Yuriko (Ota) Sylva

"As a youngster I remember crawling around under our house on Houghtailing St. and finding lightbulbs painted with a flat black paint. Only the very tip (where one finds the wattage and manufacturer's marks) was left unpainted. This was a circle of about 3/4" in diameter.

I also found replacement automobile headlights similarly painted over leaving a circle of about 1-1/2" diameter open for light to shine through.

In our small front yard, there was a bomb shelter. I never went inside but from the outside you could see that it was built with large timbers (like from railroad ties) and could hold about 6 people. I don't remember a door. The top was covered over with dirt and vines grew all over it.

This would have been well after the war ended that I discovered these things."

-Michael Yamamoto

"I remember that we had to dig and build a bomb shelter in the yard. We had to keep a supply of water and canned goods in case we had to stay in it if we were bombed again. Whenever the sirens went off, we had to go into the shelter. Also we had to observe curfew and be in our homes after 8:00 PM. People on the streets after 8:00 PM were questioned by police or block wardens. There were blackouts every night. No lights could show through the windows after dark. Automobile headlights were painted black with only a blue circle in the center. Civilians could not be on the roads at night except for emergencies."

-Grace (Ota) Takeuchi

"My Dad dug an air raid shelter in the back of our house. We were prepared in case of another air attack.

We were issued funny looking gas masks which we learned to use with efficiency and speed.

We all experienced curfew hours when the lights were turned

off. It was then a complete blackout."

-Anonymous 810

"I was a student at August Ahrens Elementary School and our teacher assigned us the task of making our own gas masks because the real gas masks had not yet been issued at that time. And people were very afraid of a mustard gas attack. We were to take a sanitary napkin and attach a piece of elastic to the two ends so we could secure the pad area as a mask over our nose and mouth. I was so embarassed to carry the "mask" to school that I asked my mother to make me a little bag in which to carry the makeshift mask."

-Anonymous

Sanitary napkins were invented by Kimberly-Clark in 1921. (Someone will inevitably ask about tampons. Tampons were invented in 1937 and with some improvements, came into general use after WWII.)

"We had to practice going into the trenches at school. At home, we sometimes slept under the bed for safety."

-Sumiko (Nakamura) Oshiro

"I had a very large collection of Japanese dolls but with the coming of the war, my parents said I had to destroy all of them."

-Deanne (Nakamoto) Horie

"I remember crawling around under our house and discovering gas masks stored in canvas bags. The masks were of rubber and had round glass openings for the eyes. My parents would get mad when we kids played with the masks. This was about 1947, well after the war."

-Lilly (Takushi) Tokuhara

"I was a student at Waipahu High School and it was where the present-day Waipahu Intermediate School is located. Trenches were dug around the school; I suppose so that defending soldiers could use them for protection. The U.S. Army took over half of the school and had soldiers stationed all over. I felt so sorry for these soldiers. Many were just out of high school and some could not even read or write English! They had been inducted into the Army and came from the eastern part of the continental United States."

-Diana (Hirotsu) Herrst

The trenches around the school were about 6 feet deep and anti-aircraft batteries were around the school grounds.

[Waipahu Intermediate/Waipahu High School is on a slight

knoll or hill overlooking Pearl Harbor and so was a strategic site at that time.]

"My father built a large bomb shelter in our yard. My cousin Ellen's family started to build one and [they] dug up many human bones. This was on the Waipio Peninsula. This led more credence to the fears that the area was haunted!"
-Jeannette (Goya) Johnson

Students from Waipahu High School were enlisted to plant vegetables in the fields of the Oahu Sugar Co. They planted and harvested 10,406,000 pounds of potatoes during the war years.

"We were workers in the offices of Oahu Sugar and were enlisted to do hoe-*hana* [hoe work; essentially weeding with the hoe] in whatever lands that remained for growing sugar cane."
-Helen (Sato) Isono

To preclude air attacks in the future, the mill took on camouflage paints and had batteries of anti-aircraft guns scattered around the fields of Oahu Sugar.

Kipapa Airfield was built and held a large contingent of airplanes and armament. The Oahu Sugar land on the Waipio Peninsula was secured by the US Navy for the war effort. Ford Island had already been secured by the US Navy and in the middle of Pearl Harbor, the island's armaments only brought the reality of war closer to Waipahu.

Close to the mill area, Punahou Schools brought their school and teachers to their students from Waipahu and had their classes in part of the main club house. This main club house is remembered by some as being called the Haole Social Club, built mainly for the supervisors of the Oahu Sugar Co. It had enough floor area for large get-togethers and rooms on the side that served as classrooms during the war years.

"I think that there were two classes; grades 1-5 and grades 6-9 from Punahou. This was because the Army Corps of Engineers took over the main [Punahou] campus in Manoa. The teachers boarded with the nurses at the Plantation Hospital."
-Peter L'Orange

Every attempt was made to secure normalcy for the people of

Kipapa Airfield was on the northern fringes of Oahu Sugar's leased agricultural lands.

Ford Island was originally Moku Umeume [island of the game umeume - an early version of wife swapping]; originally called Marin's Island (1810) for Francisco de Paula Marin, it eventually went into the Seth Porter Ford Trust, then to Seth Porter Ford Jr. in 1885. In 1891, it was sold to the John Ii Estate who then leased some 300+ acres to Oahu Sugar. In 1916, two small parcels were leased from the Ii Estate for gun emplacements by the US Navy. In 1917, the Dept. of the Navy purchased Ford Island from the Ii Estate and Oahu Sugar gave up its lease. In 1919, the Navy built Luke Field on Ford Island.

Waipahu. Teachers were especially mindful for their younger students and from all recorded accounts, there were no incidents of frightful terror that could be attributed to the war.

The Office of Civil Defense, a large volunteer organization of men and women, was formed prior to the start of WWII. District Chairman Hans L'Orange was head of the 280+ member group. This organization had air raid wardens, fire wardens, gas wardens, bomb reconnaissance agents and first aid workers. Still others were responsible for blackout regulations, evacuating civilians, and the immobilizations of enemy sympathizers.

"The Civil Defense had a plan and Oahu Sugar helped to implement the plan. Our home took in families and the young babies. Other places like the gymnasium and emergency shelters took in other families that had older kids. The Plantation Store distributed food and supplies to all homes housing many families."
-Peter L'Orange

Waipahu women volunteered to make bandages under the leadership of Mrs. Hans L'Orange, director of the Red Cross. The women produced 690,000 surgical dressings, 18,531 sewn articles, 724 knitted articles, and in a 3-1/2 month period produced 7,736 penicillin culture pad in jars. Waipahu hospitals were pressed into service for the injured from military duties.

The Waipahu Theater was a common gathering place for servicemen needing a diversion.

The Oahu Volunteers group was organized in the early days of WWII. Two regiments were formed and in Waipahu, a full battalion was formed. There were approximately 320+ volunteers. They served without pay and were trained by regular army officers and non-commissioned officers. They were trained with rifles, went on maneuvers, and guarding of installations. These volunteers were to be used if the enemy landed on beaches and infiltrated into the cane fields. They never saw actual combat but their existence allowed the army to send additional regular troops to forward areas.

The 442nd Regimental Combat Team was the most decorated army unit in WWII.

Waipahu had approximately 600 men that volunteered for the army when WWII started. Many of these were a part of the 442nd Regimental Combat Team.

"Due to various circumstances, I realized that the Japanese

were second-class citizens. They were employed only in low-paying positions. Because of this prevailing attitude towards the Japanese people, I felt that by joining the military, present and future generations could be elevated to first class citizens and not be mistreated. I volunteered and was inducted into the army on March 23, 1943.

We eventually ended up at Camp Shelby, Mississippi, where the 442nd Regimental Combat Team was formed."
-Mitsuo Oshiro

"I was working for the Oahu Sugar Co. as a field irrigation supervisor. I was drafted into the Army and Oahu Sugar said that my position was critical so they could get me a deferment. I felt that this country was very nice to me and so elected to not accept the deferment and so served in the Army from March, 1941, until December, 1945."
-Yuzuru Morita

WWII ended in Europe on May 7, 1945, and in Japan on August 14, 1945.

Older Japanese were sent to internment camps. In many cases, only the men went to camps and the wives and families were left at home.

"My father was interned at a camp in Santa Fe, New Mexico."
-Tajiro Uranaka

Others were interned in camps at Sand Island (in Honolulu) and still others, in a camp in Honouliuli (near Ewa).

"People made *senninbari* [belt of 1000 knots] to send to their loved ones in the war. These waist belts were of white muslin and people would be asked to 'put a stitch in' with red embroidry thread. One loop through the belt and a knot to secure the thread would be all that would be asked by those getting belts for loved ones. These belts were supposed to give good luck to the wearers so they wouldn't be injured or killed during the war."
-Bernice (Tamura) Hamai

"My dad was originally supposed to go to Brazil. He and some others jumped ship in Honolulu and he was therefore an illegal immigrant. He looked up a 'Suzuki' who vouched for him and he therefore began to work at Oahu Sugar. (For years I used to wonder why people would call my dad 'Suzuki'!) When WWII came, the manager (Hans L'Orange) and Cranky Watanabe

111

vouched for him. So my dad could stay in Hawaii and didn't have to go back to Japan or even to internment or re-location camps. Right away after the war, he became an American citizen!"

-Kenichi Watanabe

The Waipahu War effort gave $19,010.92 to the Red Cross. War Bond sales yielded $1,828,025.00 additionally.

Waipahu Filipinos gave $10,154.39 as relief funds for the war being fought in the Philippines.

"My friends and I had just gone to an early YBA [Young Buddhist Association] meeting in Honolulu and were returning to Waipahu by bus. We were near the entrance to Pearl Harbor and we could see the black smoke from the attack. I think it was about 8 AM. When we got back to Waipahu, we learned that my grandfather had sustained a shrapnel wound in his thigh and was in the hospital."

- Diana (Hirotsu) Herrst

"It was a Sunday but I was in my office above the Kawano Store in Waipahu and the Japanese Zeros were strafing the area. I moved from one spot and heard a whizzing sound and turned around to see a bullet hole in the floor where I had just been standing. Downstairs, another bullet went through the center of a mattress in the Kawano Store!"

- Stanley Yanase, D.D.S.

Shigemi Arakawa remembers the times they went through during the war years.

"Our family were retail merchants and WWII meant severe rationing (5 gallons of gasoline per month) among other things. Punahou School was the designated site for gasoline rationing coupons and we had to drive in to Honolulu to get the coupons. The people of Honolulu were not able to get pork as one commodity. So we would load up pork from Waipahu, drive into Honolulu and trade pork for gasoline coupons and what ever else our community back in Waipahu needed."

- Shigemi Arakawa

"We would sometimes have to buy goods at full retail in Honolulu and return to Waipahu to resell the goods at a small mark-

up; but everyone got what they needed."
- Goro Arakawa

We started this book originally as a story about Tatsuichi Ota and the town in which he lived. As we did research, we discovered that the story about Waipahu and its people is a richer story and worthy of recording. For this next chapter, we present the story of Tatsuichi Ota and what is remembered about him in Waipahu.

The reader can make a detour and skip this following chapter on the Ota family and just continue on with the story about Waipahu. At the very least, the Ota family story might be like one story of many in the history of Waipahu.

References - Chapter 6.

Waipahu at War, R. H. Lodge, division overseer, Oahu Sugar Co., Honolulu, Hawaii, un-dated.

Geology of the State of Hawaii, Harold T. Stearns, Pacific Books, publishers, Palo Alto, California, 2nd ed., 1985.

Oahu's Hidden History, William Dorrance, Mutual Publishing Co., Honolulu, Hawaii, 1998.

World Almanac Book of Inventions, Valerie-Anne Giscard d'Estaing, World Almanac Publications, New York, New York, 1985.

-7- Tatsuichi Ota

...one of many immigrants...

Fig. 7-1. A ceramic tile in the Pahu St. residence of Tatsuichi Ota.

The characters read, from top to bottom,

**O
TA
TATSU
ICHI**

As we noted in the preface, our story originally centered around Tatsuichi Ota. When researching material, we changed direction such that the focus of the book became a story about Waipahu. So now we take a brief excursion and tell the story about Tatsuichi Ota.

Japan

The history of the Ota family can be traced in recorded history to as far back as the Meiji Restoration (1868-1912) in Japan. The oligarchs who ruled the country saw that the preceding Tokugawa rule had failed Japan. With the ascension of the new Emperor Meiji, these oligarchs saw an opportunity to create a new and possibly better future for Japan. They elevated Emperor Meiji to near god-like status and set about to restructure Japan. In education, finances, business, communication, and transportation, reform was carried out in the name of Emperor Meiji. Samurai warriors were done away with and became business-class members of their communities. In some cases, the samurai had no income and resorted to selling their samurai name and status as a means of having money. In the case of the Ota samurai, their problem was compounded by the fact that they had no male heirs to carry on their family name of Ota.

The Nakaya family, merchants in Hiroshima, decided that they wanted a name change and the stature of a brave samurai class. Akizo Nakaya bought into the name of samurai Ota and the family Ota that was to become Tatsuichi and Kaoru Ota in Hawaii was started. (The remaining Nakayas became Nakamoto.) The first Ota in this part of our history was Sawazo Ota.

Sawazo Ota produced first son Minesaburo Ota who married first daughter Tsune Hashioka of Masajiro Hashioka.

Minesaburo and Tsune Ota produced first son Tatsuichi. The fourth son, Kaoru, is also of interest.

At age 15, Tatsuichi Ota was a school teacher in the Oko District (pier area) of Hiroshima, Japan. At age 21, he sailed on the

S.S. China (China Maru) from the port of Yokohama, Japan, on Oct. 30, 1901 and arrived in Honolulu on Nov. 9, 1901. By this time, Tatsuichi had learned the English alphabet.

The ship's manifest shows that Tatsuichi was a farmer. This listing differs from another version as a reason for his coming to Hawaii.

At a time when most Japanese were coming to Hawaii to work on the sugar plantations, Tatsuichi Ota came to Hawaii because he had been offered a position as bookkeeper of Shimamoto Store in Waipahu. He went on to be the manager of the store and eventually bought the store in 1903 and changed the name to the T. Ota Store.

Kaoru Ota, Tatsuichi's younger brother, told Nina Yuriko (Ota) Sylva, at Tatsuichi's funeral, that Tatsuichi had come to Hawaii to earn money to send home to Japan. Their family had a large debt and Tatsuichi was to earn monies to send back to Japan thereby helping his family. Whether the large debt was a result of buying into the Ota Samurai name or just a result of the then poor Japanese economy, is not known.

But upon seeing Waipahu, Tatsuichi decided that Hawaii was where he wanted to settle and start his own family. This decision caused him to look towards being a landowner in Hawaii.

[Much of the previous section has been reconstructed from conversations with Grace (Ota) Takeuchi, Irene (Ota) Yamamoto, Nina (Ota) Sylva, and from the family tree obtained by Randy Sylva through the City of Hiroshima, Japan.]

(Other Japanese immigrants had come to Hawaii to work on sugar plantations and thereby earn large sums of money. With this money they planned to return home and possibly acquire land in Japan. Still others came to Hawaii, learned of possibly even greater earnings on the continental United States, and moved on to the West Coast.)

Early Hawaii and Tatsuichi Ota
Yasu Yamada arrived in 1909 aboard the Chiyo Maru and married Tatsuichi Ota in an arranged marriage (*omiai*) on July 15, 1909. A photo of Yasu Yamada as she appeared at that time is shown in Fig. 7-2. This photo is one of many appearing on identical postcards found among papers of Tatsuichi Ota giving

Fig. 7-2. Yasu Ota from one of many postcards found in the Pahu St. residence of Tatsuichi Ota.

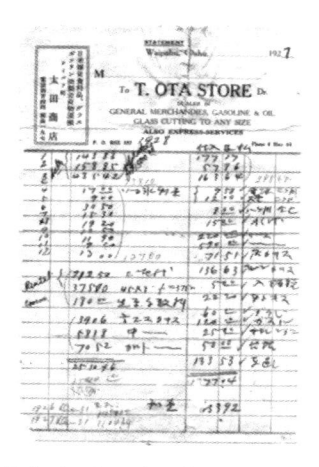

Fig. 7-3. An invoice from the T. Ota Store.

Fig. 7-4. The T. Ota Store, ca. 1903.

credence to the term "picture postcard bride." The Tatsuichi Otas resided in back of the store. (A copy of an invoice from that store is shown in Fig. 7-3.) The site of the store is where the present Saiki Motors is on Waipahu St. Waipahu St. was called (Main) Government Rd. at the time that Tatsuichi Ota managed the store.

Tatsuichi and Yasu Ota had children Irene Ayako, Aileen Shizuko, Nina Yuriko, and Tatsuo while living at this store/house.

Aileen Shizuko never did like her given English name and later came to use Sadie as her English name.

Nina Yuriko remembers that the family as a whole always had dinner together. Laughter at the dinner table was encouraged. There was to be no talk of money nor was criticism of anyone to take place at this time as well. Bragging was also discouraged.

"My father used to scold us when we came home and related to him about how this person or that had done something naughty or bad.'You have enough good things to keep in your head! You should not concern yourself with things like this!'

About 1920, my mother went back to Japan with Shizuko [Sadie] because my mother was asthmatic and my father thought the change in climate might help her regain her health."
  -Nina Yuriko (Ota) Sylva

"In 1925, I lived in a downstairs room with the Ota family. While my family lived only a few doors away, my family was large and so I went to stay with another family, the Tatsuichi Ota family. I remember having one room across a hallway from other rooms that held the Ota family children.
  -Buster Takayesu

Tatsuichi Ota felt he had familial obligations and while not planning to return to Japan, he did want to help the rest of his family still in Japan. He saved about $8,000 and sent it back to Japan.

The first world war, WWI, did not seem to impact Tatsuichi Ota in Waipahu, Hawaii.

About 1928, Tatsuichi sold his store to Buster Takayesu's father, Giyei, for about $1,500. With this money Tatsuichi began buying land in what is now known as Ota Camp. These were rice paddies at that time and probably appealed to Tatsuichi Ota as the going price at that time is estimated to have been about $0.02 per square foot.

Fig. 7-5. Waipahu ca. 1920. Looking south from the Oahu Sugar mill site. Note the rice fields. The top horizon area eventually became Ota camp. (Note the Bank of Hawaii building in the lower left of the photo.) Photo courtesy of Georgine (Takayesu) Morita.

"About 1938, my father went back to Japan with the intent of staying about six months to study more calligraphy."
                                    -Nina Yuriko (Ota) Sylva

He had taken to calligraphy as a cultural and art form, and as a hobby. In Hawaii, he was considered by some as quite adept in his writing of Japanese characters; he was even given an award (Fig. 7-6). The *sumi* [black ink] used in the calligraphy comes from rubbing a black ink stone in a well with water (Fig. 7-9). The writing is done on rice paper. All works of significance are signed with the *han* (Fig. 7-9a) in a manner similar to how modern day rubber stamps are used. Brushes (Fig. 7-7) are used for writing.

Fig. 7-6. T. Ota with award from the Japanese Calligraphy Educational Association, denoting his title of Master. Presented Mar. 31, 1973. (Note medal described in a later paragraph.)

For those interested, Japanese characters are read from the top down, in columns. Then from the rightmost column to the top of the next column to the left.

Therefore, the single horizontal stroke, upper right, in Fig. 7-8 is the number 1. Then the next column to be read is the column to its left starting at the top with three horizontal strokes, being the number 3.

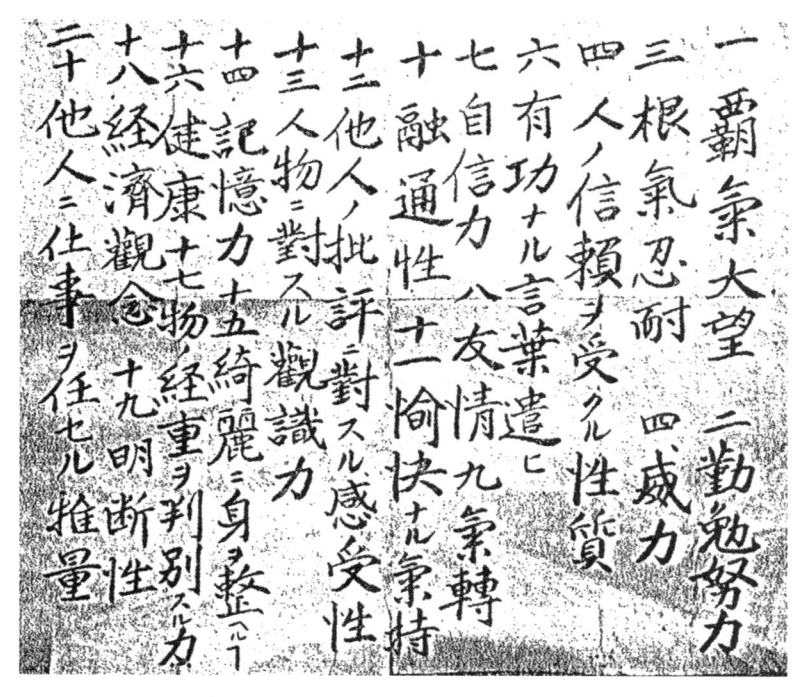

Fig. 7-8. Philosophy of how to live one's life.

From right to left these are translated by our Albuquerque translator, Grace (Tanaka) Santistevan. Brackets [ ] indicate additions for clarification.

1) Be ambitious with great hope
2) Be diligent and make [great] effort
3) Perseverance and patience
   [Persevere and be patient]
4) Power and authority
5) Character to be trusted
   [Be of good character to be trusted]
6) Effective speech
   [Have good use of words]
7) [Have] Self confidence
8) Friendship
9) [Be of] quick wit
10) Accommodate
11) [Have a] Delightful attitude
12) Acceptance of others' criticism
13) Observation and Evaluation of others
14) Memorization ability
15) [Be of] Neat appearance
16) [Be of good] Health
17) Power of sorting priority
18) [Have] Knowledge of economic[s]
19) [Be of] Fair judgment
20) Have the ability to choose to whom responsibility should be delegated

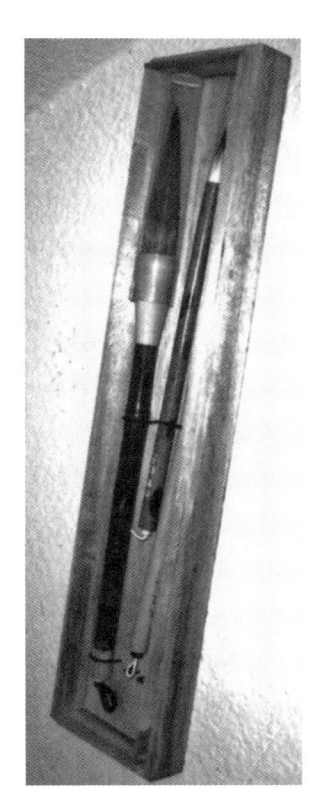

Fig. 7-7. Brushes for calligraphy.

Fig. 7-9. (L) Hand-carved wooden box with sumi stone.
Fig. 7-9a. (R) Han of Tatsuichi Ota.

The *han* or seal (carved out of wood) of Tatsuichi Ota is shown. One han presents a positive image when inked and pressed onto the paper; the other han presents a negative image. The ink was in a small container as a red-orange oily paste; wet when it was applied to the han and drying once transferred to the paper. The original inks that Tatsuichi used are still in containers and in a wet form today some 75 years later.

Kaoru Ota
Kaoru Ota, 18 years younger than Tatsuichi, arrived in 1914 at age 16, and stayed with Tatsuichi and Yasu Ota.

"Kaoru's and Tatsuichi's father had remarried and Kaoru did not like his new mother. He wrote to Tatsuichi and Tatsuichi told him to come to Hawaii."
-Grace (Ota) Takeuchi

Kaoru stayed in the back of the upper part of the store and the Tatsuichi Otas stayed in the downstairs of the store. This lower level of the wooden structure was built on the slope down and away from (Main) Government Rd. Outside the lower level of the house was the yard and a clothesline for the family laundry.

One of the tasks that Tatsuichi assigned his brother was the gathering of *warayose* [stalks leftover from harvested rice] for sale to other animal owners. Kaoru had a difficult time with the horse that pulled the hauling wagon and complained to his older brother about having to deal with the animal.

Tatsuichi decided to purchase a truck and thereby replace the troublesome horse. But first he instructed his brother to study automobiles: how they ran, how they were to be maintained, and how to repair them if they broke down. Only after he was convinced that Kaoru had mastered the automobile, did they go to Castner Garage in Wahiawa and purchase a truck.

In May of 1924, he purchased a Ford truck from Castner Garage in Wahiawa for about $711. In July of that year, he bought another Ford truck, this time smaller than the first, as the receipts he kept show that he paid about $470.

It is interesting to note that family and friends considered Kaoru a better driver than his older brother Tatsuichi ... even in later years.

The Kaoru Ota Family
Kaoru Ota, for some reason, was visiting at the newly built Japanese Hospital (this later became Kuakini Hospital and then the present-day Kuakini Medical Center). His wife-to-be, Shizuyo Furukawa, was born in Hiroshima, Japan, but had received training as a nurse in Tokyo. She had just come to Honolulu to work at the Japanese Hospital. She and Kaoru both happened to be in an elevator when it got stuck between floors. Their meeting eventually led to marriage on Feb. 13, 1926, and the family of Kaoru Ota was started.

> -Nina Yuriko (Ota) Sylva as related to her by Irene (Ota) Yamamoto and also related to Michael Yamamoto by Grace (Ota) Takeuchi

Older brother Tatsuichi hosted their wedding reception in Waipahu and Kaoru Ota and his wife Shizuyo stayed with the Tatsuichi Ota family on the upper level of the store for about a year. Daughter Lillian was born while they were living in Waipahu. They later moved to the Palama area of Honolulu and stayed in a two-story structure close to where the present-day Tamashiro Market is now located at the intersection of King and Palama Sts. Kaoru started running the Liquid Sunshine Soda Shop there and later moved it to the corner of Austin Lane and King St., diagonally across from the Palama Fire Station on King St.

Fig. 7-10. Liquid Sunshine Soda Shop.

By this time Kaoru had the rest of their family: George, Eleanor, Grace, Betty, Dorothy, and Franklin. Kaoru was raising his family in a rental unit across the Palama Fire Station and the opportunity to purchase the property came up. Kaoru approached Tatsuichi to partner with him in buying the property but Tatsuichi felt that a partnership within a family was not a good idea and suggested that Kaoru look elsewhere and make an investment by himself.

The Kaoru Otas and Tatsuichi's children

"While Kaoru and his family were staying on King St., Tatsuichi sent his oldest daughter, Irene, to stay with the Kaoru Otas. She was being sent to McKinley High School and travel from Waipahu was very tiring for her. Staying with the Kaoru Otas saved her a lot of travel time but she was lonely so Tatsuichi sent daughter Shizuko to keep Irene company.

This circumstance is how Shizuko went to Royal School and eventually graduated from McKinley High School in 1933. Older sister Irene graduated from McKinley High School in 1929.

Third daughter and child, Nina Yuriko, resided in Waipahu. Her early schooling started at August Ahrens Elementary School. While there, she was selected to be part of the English Standard

Charles Ishikawa shares a limerick in Japanese:

Soda-ya no,
Soda-san ga,
Soda nonde, shinda soda,
Soda, soda,*
Sonna hanashi-ga,
Atta soda.**

In English, the meaning appears to be:

The soda-man of the soda company
Died after drinking some soda.
Oh yes, oh yes
There was such a story going
  around.

*Note the clever use of "soda, soda" in the Japanese version as being English for the actual drink. and in the English version, "soda, soda" becomes translated instead to "Oh yes, oh yes."
**And again

Grace Santistevan, our translator in Albuquerque, New Mexico, gives us her interpretation:

Of the soda shop
Mr. Soda (as the subject)
Drank some soda
I heard (he) died
Oh yeah yeah (or) Yes, I can recall (or)
Yes, I've heard a story like that existed,
I think (or) that's what I heard.

Tatsuichi Ota's own records shows registration of a Packard truck to the Liquid Sunshine Soda Shop at least for the year of 1926.

(The Sunrise Soda Co. is not the same concern. This company was also located in the Palama area and at about the same time.)

School program and skipped the 3rd grade. She remembers paying for this dearly as she had a lot of catching up on math as a result!

After August Ahrens and Waipahu Elementary Schools, she got picked up by a neighbor (Mr. Takeshita) each morning where the present-day Farrington Hwy. and Depot Rd. meet, to go to Central Intermediate School. She then graduated in 1939 from Farrington High School.

Son Tatsuo went to Waipahu Elementary School and later commuted to Iolani School with neighbor James Yonge.

"Tatsuo and I stayed with Uncle Kaoru after one Japanese Summer School (month of August) to help with labeling of soda bottles. When Tatsuo wanted to go home that summer, Uncle Kaoru told Tatsuichi that Tatsuo was only eating and not helping so he can go home. That's when my father took us home and never sent us to help my uncle again."

-Nina Yuriko (Ota) Sylva

WWII
"We were going to Grandma's [Yasu Ota] to make pancakes for her. She liked my pancakes and as a Sunday treat, we were going from Kalihi to Waipahu. We got as far as the intersection of Kalihi Stream and Dillingham Blvd., when the local police stopped us and told us to go back: 'This is the real thing: we are being attacked.'"

-Irene (Ota) and Jack Yamamoto as related to Michael Yamamoto in later years

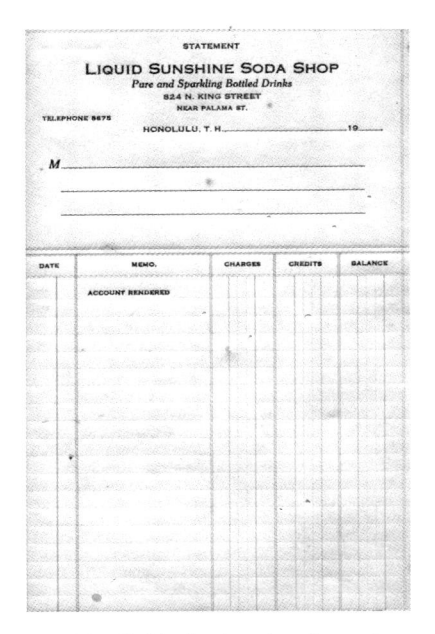

Fig. 7-11. An invoice from the Liquid Sunshine Soda Shop.

"During those war years, younger brother Kaoru Ota was living in Honolulu and as a result of being close to urban Honolulu, learned that Tatsuichi was being 'watched' and suspected of being a sympathizer to Japan. Kaoru urged Tatsuichi to purchase Liberty Bonds as a show of support to the United States. Tatsuichi had no reason not to do this and amassed quite a few of these bonds. And this was at a time when a person could not keep more than $200 in cash.

By the time that the FBI came to interview then alien Tatsuichi Ota, he was able to show them the bonds. They asked if he was going back to Japan and when he replied that he wasn't going

back, the next question was 'Can you prove that?' He then went to his bedroom, came out with a stack of bonds and declared, 'You think I buy this if I planning to go back Japan?' He and our whole family were never sent to an internment camp as a result of this confrontation."
-Irene (Ota) Yamamoto as
related to Michael Yamamoto

"There were about twelve interviews similar to this during the course of the war."
-Nina Yuriko (Ota) Sylva

In Feb., 1943, Tatsuichi had to fill out a Personal History Declaration form. This was apparently the way the U.S. Government kept track of Japanese aliens. Aside from the listings of family members and addresses, past travel declarations, and the like, Tatsuichi gave his age as 63 and being 5 ft. 4 inches tall and weighing 130 lbs.

"I remember your grandfather well. He used to wear khaki overalls and walked straight upright."
-Masuye Akiyama

"These were *apronpansu* (apron pants); we know them today as overalls."
-Alaric Sokugawa

Tatsuo Ota, the only son of Tatsuichi, had graduated from Iolani School and he enlisted in the 442nd Regimental Combat Team. He was wounded during the war and had taken his discharge from the Army in San Francisco. He wanted to use his GI Bill to go to school on the mainland. He wrote home that the monies were not quickly forthcoming and that his plans were at a standstill. Yuriko dutifully sent her brother all of his pay that he had designated sent to her and so he was able to go to school.

"A year later Tatsuo returned to Waipahu where my father [Tatsuichi Ota] asked Tatsuo how he was able to go to school.

Tatsuo told Oto-san [father] that the Army pay that 'Y' (Yuriko) had been saving made it possible as she sent it all to him when he was discharged. I remember a stern look from Oto-san almost admonishing me for seemingly delaying his seeing Tatsuo back from the war."
-Nina Yuriko (Ota) Sylva

Tatsuo eventually went back to Iowa State University and graduated with a Bachelor's Degree in Commerce.

Kaoru Ota and WWII
"Shortly after WWII started, Kaoru was called in by the Federal Government for interrogation about his loyalty to Japan because he had made a few trips as a group tour leader before the war. His family was very worried because if he were interned, there would be no bread-winner. However, being the friendly person that he was, he sought the help of a friend, U.S. Army Chaplain Major Young, who vouched for him and maintained that Kaoru was not a spy. With six children who were born in the U.S. to raise, his allegiance was no longer to Japan. Kaoru had bought property in Honolulu and did not intend to go back to Japan to live. After an overnight stay at the Detention Center he was released and never called in for any more questioning."
-Grace (Ota) Takeuchi

Postwar Years
By 1945, Tatsuichi Ota had leased land holdings on the east side of Depot Rd. between (Main) Government Rd. (now Waipahu St.) and Farrington Hwy. The approximate location of this land began a few structures down from Waipahu St. (The Bank of Hawaii was the first structure at the corner of Waipahu St. and Depot Rd. See Chap. 3).

The Ota property extended down a slight slope towards Farrington Hwy. to about where Hikimoe St. is today. The land was originally leased from Oahu Sugar by another person. When that man went back to Japan, Tatsuichi bought the lease from the man and began dealing with Oahu Sugar directly thus becoming a landlord in that area.

"I remember your grandfather well as he used to come by and collect the rent from my parents."
-Anonymous 810

"Tatsuichi Ota was an unpretentious man. There were no airs about him and his daily outer wear consisted of a plain shirt and khaki overalls with *geta* [wooden slippers or clogs] footwear.

He loved his Hayden mangos and I remember one time we caught up to him walking down Depot Rd. with a mango in one hand, peeling the skin off with the other ... dripping mango

juice all over his overalls."
-Michael Yamamoto

"Oh, yes. He loved his Hayden mango. So much that he didn't want to give me any ... and I was his next door neighbor! His tree would drop fruit into my yard and I wanted to pick it up. But no, he said I had to give those to him."
-Mac Flores

A favorite place that Tatsuichi would meet friends at was the taxi stand on Waipahu St. near the Kawano Store. This was the site of *shogi*, *hanafuda*, and *go* games.

Shogi - Japanese board game with tiles and strategies like chess.

Go - Japanese board game with black and white stones and strategies of surround and capture.

Hanafuda - Japanese flower card game with strategy of match-and-combine to collect points.

"I can still remember your grandfather sitting there playing shogi or go ... the total concentration on his face!"
-Lilly (Takushi) Tokuhara

"I used to see him there quite a lot and even if I didn't see money change hands, I think there was a lot of gambling going on."
-Mac Flores

"Your grandfather enjoyed shogi. Our neighbor, Wakamatsu Matsuo, always had men over to play shogi. They sat on the porch and played all day during the weekends!"
-Bernice (Tamura) Hamai

Tatsuichi and Kaoru maintained their ties to Japan. As a commemoration to the two Otas, Grace relates:

"When I visited Oko Town in Hiroshima, Japan, my cousin Toshihiko Nakamoto (a connection to the early beginnings of the Nakaya family becoming Ota and Nakamoto), who lives there, took my husband George and me to a small Shrine there.

It was built on a mountainside with a long stairway of concrete and stone. There were two stone lanterns about 7 or 8 feet tall, flanking the entrance to the Shrine at the top of the stairway. The engravinging on the back indicated that this pair was donated by Kaoru Ota. There was another pair below donated by Tatsuichi Ota.

I was impressed that they remembered their "roots" and left a legacy in their hometown.

Fig. 7-12. Lanterns at Shrine in Oko, Hiroshima, Japan. The woman in the picture is Grace (Ota) Takeuchi, daughter of Kaoru Ota.

I believe the commemorative gesture was also because they both were awarded the medal: 5th Order of Merit with the Order of the Sacred Treasure from the Emperor of Japan and awarded in Honolulu by the Consul General of Japan at the Japanese Consulate."
-Grace (Ota) Takeuchi

Ota camp
Ota camp today is roughly bounded by Kapakahi Stream, Farrington Hwy. and Pahu St. Originally, Tatsuichi had owned about 32 acres extending towards West Loch of Pearl Harbor but through various sales, it was reduced to the present day 16 acres.

At one time, Ota camp was known as the site of infamous cock fights. Some people would not know where Ota camp was located but almost everyone would instantly remember its location if asked, "Do you know where they always hold the cock fights?"

Tatsuichi never had anything to do with the cock fights; those running the fights just naturally gravitated to the open area in Ota camp and held the cock fights there ... until police shut down the operation in the late 1970s.

In 1962, Oliver Kinney acquired a lease to several properties owned by Tatsuichi Ota. Kinney sold and assigned the "Master Lease" a few years later to Amity Waipahu, Inc. After Amity Waipahu announced plans to develop an apartment complex, it evicted many Ota camp residents in early 1972. The evicted families were relocated to an area west of their original homes. Wanting to retain their connection to their former tightly knit community, the residents formed the Ota Camp *Makibaka* Association and sometimes call themselves 'Ota camp,' leading to confusion among some non-residents.

'Makibaka' in the Tagalog language of the Philippines means 'struggle.' Pete Tagalog founded the association 'to fight for our rights.'

Some recollections about Tatsuichi Ota

"Lots of times your grandfather (Tatsuichi) would ask me to help him carry some wood he had found back to his place [Pahu St.] so he could use it to heat up his *furo* [bath] water."
                    -Pete Tagalog

"Your grandfather was a frugal man. There were times that he would be carrying a piece of wood with nails in it ... he said to take home so he could use the wood for his furo water and the nails to re-use."
                    -Anonymous 810

"In the early 1960s, when the building at the corner of Hikimoe St. and Depot Rd. was being built, your grandfather would come by and ask the construction people if he could have their scrap wood for use in his furo."
                    -Dale Claggett

"Your grandfather was not beyond asking for free help. One day my father came home and said that he had been helping Ota-san. My mother asked him what help he was giving Ota-san. My father replied that it was something to do with repairing a gas line. My father got a scolding from my mother: 'You could have been hurt!' And, 'Did he pay you?' With a negative reply, my father really got a scolding from my mother."
                    -Lincoln Uyeno

Jack Ujimori was enlisted by the State's Hawaii Housing Authority to develop the new homes for the evicted residents on City-owned land. Misunderstandings, demonstrations, turmoil, lawsuits, and counter-lawsuits would be an encapsulated description of what ensued over the 30-year period of struggle.

In 2001, the original 31 evicted families became owners of their properties. In this twist of irony, property ownership is something that might not have happened had they not been evicted from their original Ota camp homes.

Lincoln and his family were not living in Ota Camp. They lived close-by in homes owned by the Oahu Railway & Land Co. Lincoln's dad was part of what people referred to as "the railroad gang" as these people were employed by OR & L to maintain the railroad tracks in the Waipahu area.

Later years of Kaoru Ota

"In 1949, Kaoru bought a beautiful old colonial-style home on a one-acre parcel on the slopes of Punchbowl. By that time, he had learned how to borrow money by taking out a mortgage. He

knew that paying his bills on time gave him good credit with the banks. He got to know the bank managers because of his business and he maintained good relationships with them."
-Grace (Ota) Takeuchi

Kaoru Ota was active in community service. Representing the Japanese community in Hawaii, he traveled extensively. He helped to found the United Japanese Society and became its president on May 20, 1962. He was also president of Kaiulani Elementary School PTA (Kaiulani Elementary School was almost across King St. from where they lived) and when Grace (Ota) Takeuchi was a student there and they had the Sunshine Soda Shop. He was also president of Hawaii Kiin, a club that promoted the Japanese board game of Go. Other notable community contributions: President of the Honolulu Japanese Chamber of Commerce, Oko Jin Kai, Hiroshima Ken Jin Kai., and the Hawaii Calligraphy Association.

"Through association with friends in Japan, Kaoru was asked to be the Hawaii liaison of Japan Air Lines (JAL) in 1952. He located office space in the Dillingham Transportation Building on Bishop Street for JAL. Offices of PanAm, United, and Philippine Air Lines were also located there at the time. He advised the JAL Managers who were assigned to Hawaii about protocol in Hawaii and the Hawaiian way of doing things. In appreciation for the cooperation, he was given lifetime first-class flying privileges with JAL. He and Shizuyo were invited on the inaugural flight from New York to London as well as the inaugural flight from Tokyo to Australia. They were privileged to make many trips by JAL to their homeland in their lifetimes."
-Grace (Ota) Takeuchi

On July 14, 1968, he was awarded one of the most important and highest honor a citizen of Japan could receive: 5th Order of Merit with the Order of the Sacred Treasure. This award was bestowed on those making special contributions to their adopted country and who succeeded in improving relations between Japan and the United States.

At this time, he was one of seven receiving this honor. Six Islanders received this award in 1966 and only a few others before then.

Statehood
Tatsuichi Ota became a naturalized citizen on August 18, 1955.

He was very proud of the fact that he took the examination in English and passed with a grade of A-. He registered to vote on June 27, 1956, and first voted in that year.

In 1959, Hawaii became a state. Tatsuichi's house on Pahu St. in Waipahu, had numerous mementos of the achievement of Hawaii's people in obtaining Statehood. Newspaper clippings, some program material of the celebration at Iolani Palace, and collections of commemorative stamps and postcards tell of his pride in being a part of the State of Hawaii and the United States.

1966-1990

"Michael Yamamoto was getting a haircut at a barbershop in the Ala Moana Shopping Center. He overheard a conversation between two men of how one of them tried to repay Tatsuichi Ota back-rent due from either the Depression years or during WWII. Tatsuichi refused to accept the money because, 'Those were hard times for all of us. And therefore it was not necessary to repay the money.'

The man owing the money was obviously taken aback and thankful to Tatsuichi for the kindness shown."

> -Karen Yamamoto as retold to Michael Yamamoto. (He had long forgotten the conversation.)

More recollections

Tatsuichi drove an automobile till very late in life. His family was concerned that he was a hazard on the road but was reluctant and unable to tell him that he should stop driving so he would not cause serious accidents. Fortunately, the insurance company's agent came to their rescue. The agent told Tatsuichi that due to age, they would no longer be able to insure him. "Yosh!" [okay] was Tatsuichi's response and he stopped driving much to the relief of his family!

"When I was a grade-schooler, I would go and stay with Grandpa and Grandma on weekends. The main house in those days was raised up on stilts so that the floor level was about five feet above the ground. There was a separate wooden building about 35' long by about 15' wide about 15' away from the main house on the ground level. This housed the kitchen on one end, a *furoba* [bath house] next to that, and the furo fire-making/water heating section. The actual water heating "fireplace" was stoked from the outside of the building and the heat warmed the bath water inside the furo box of water inside the bath house. To take a bath, the daily routine would be to heat the water by making a large fire in the outside fireplace, go into the bath house, scoop out enough of the now very hot water into a large tub and mix in enough cold water to make the water temperature tolerable. Using this water, one could soap himself down as well as rinse off with clean, warm water.

One "firing" a day of the fireplace produced enough hot water for the entire family.

The kitchen had a true "icebox." Somehow, ice was always inside the top of the chest-like box. (Where the ice was obtained was never explained to me.) This box served as their refrigerator. It seemed to have been made of hardwood and was about 24" wide and 24" deep and about 48" high and had glass paneled doors on the front.

One "job" that I had for breakfast was to scrape very blackened toast and butter it. The toaster at that time had almost no control for dark or light...all toast came out very dark!

[I must have either liked the job or dis-liked it! I still remember the toast-scraping to this day!]

Eventually, the bath-house/kitchen was torn down and a kitchen added to the rear of the main house. And change to even this arrangement came when that kitchen was torn down and the house was moved. A picture of the house is shown in Fig. 7-16. Now the house faced Pahu St. and a small kitchen and bath room were added to the rear. A portion of the yard had the vegetable garden, a few macadamia nut trees and a clothesline.

Across this Pahu St. house, Tatsuichi raised a limited number of turkeys, geese, and chickens. Eggs and meats were sufficient for the family. I can still remember a large truck without a cab or bed on the roadside, rusted into uselessness but with a wooden steering wheel, pedals and a bench-like seat that allowed for my imagination to stray. Also close-by was a garage-like shed that had a well about 8' in diameter with a wooden protective wall around it. The water was so dirty brown, I can't imagine how it could have been used for anything but watering plants. The well is no longer there and I imagine it was filled in long

Was this the old truck the Otas bought to displace the horse or was this the truck registered to the Liquid Sunshine Soda Shop from 1926?

133

ago for safety concerns. I don't think it was an artesian well.

The railroad tracks ran about 100 yards away. Nina would take me to the tracks and teach me to listen for yet unseen oncoming trains. She told me to hold my ear to the tracks so I could hear the trains coming even before seeing them.

I later discovered that the trains coming by would slow down enough that I could wave to a railroad worker sitting on an open-top car full of pineapples ... and sometimes the worker responded by heaving a pineapple to me!"
                                    - Michael Yamamoto

While not living in Ota Camp but instead being in Camp 56 off Kunia Rd., life was not much different when recalling furo baths and railroad cars with pineapples.

"When we took our baths, the water was heated by oil burners and piped into the bathhouse. The hot water was mixed with cold water and piped into the furo, a box about eight feet by ten feet and maybe three feet deep. We would soap outside the furo and then rinse off and dive into the furo and make like we were swimming. This would be from about 1944 to 1947.

I remember that the train tracks ran almost just outside our house. When we got the train worker to heave pineapples to us, we somehow always missed catching them and they splattered on the road. We just carefully washed off the dirt and ate them right there. They were good!"
                                    -Chris Gibo

Nishi Health System. Kaoru Ota had expressed an interest in the Nishi Health System.

"In Kaoru Ota's younger days, he wasn't very healthy. He suffered from sinus problems and allergies. He was always looking for ways to improve his health. He read a book called *Nishi System of Health Engineering* by Dr. Katsuzo Nishi of Tokyo based on a new theory of blood circulation and began the regimen of health advocated in the book. By exercise and diet, Kaoru's health really improved ... his sinus cleared and allergies disappeared. He wanted to help others and founded the Nishi Kai of Hawaii. He invited Dr. Nishi to come to Hawaii and speak to the Japanese community about his theory. Kaoru founded chapters in Honolulu, Hilo, Kailua, Wahiawa,

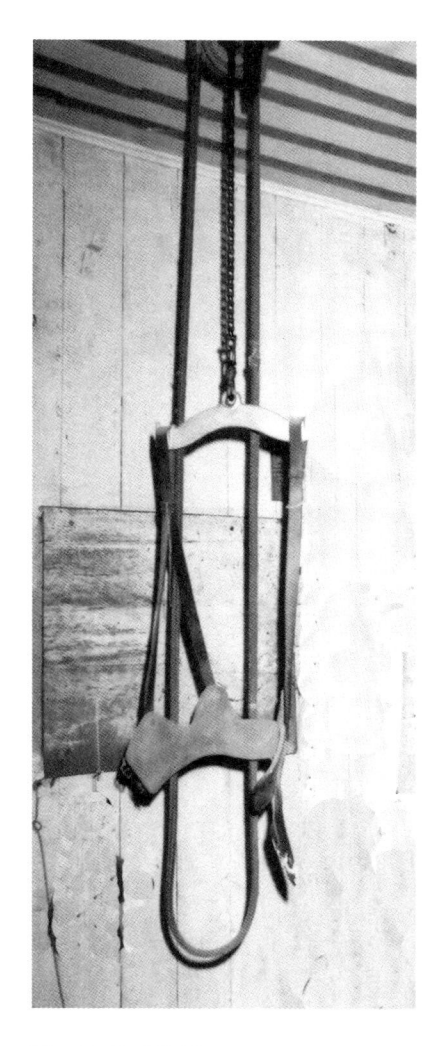

Waialua, and Ewa where he would go there monthly and teach others what he knew about Nishi-shiki. There are many people in Hawaii still living by Dr. Nishi's System of Health. All their lives Kaoru and Shizuyo practiced the teachings of Nishi-shiki. Shizuyo lived till age 82 and Kaoru lived till age 85."

-Grace (Ota) Takeuchi

With Kaoru's urgings, Tatsuichi also took up the Nishi system and invested in a spine stretching device and what can only be described as an upside-down bicycle. Fig. 7-13 shows the devices as Tatsuichi had them installed in his Pahu St. residence. The system advocated alternating hot and cold showers to invigorate the circulatory system, eating 5 different vegetables at least three times a week, and living a simple if somewhat frugal life. Tatsuichi often told of how he lived on $2 a day. Shigemi Arakawa remembers that Tatsuichi would buy cases of cup-o-noodles [like freeze-dried noodles] from their store.

"He would always tell me that this was a part of his Nishi-shiki eating program."

-Shigemi Arakawa

"I remember visiting him in the late 1960s and aside from general pleasantries, he talked about Richard Nixon and how the President was doing this or that and what he should be doing instead. The Nishi System of Health was also a favorite topic of his and the conversation bordered on a lecture about life."

-Michael Yamamoto

Fig. 7-13. Nishi system apparatus. Top - spine stretching device; Bottom - upside-down bicycle.

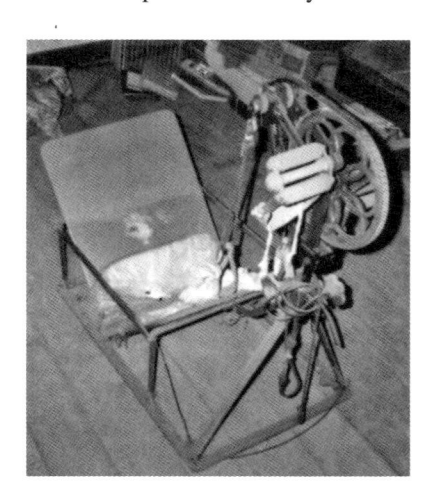

Fig, 7-14. Tatsuichi and Yasu Ota.

In 1970, wife Yasu Ota passed away. Until this time Tatsuichi

135

had maintained that he would live to age 100. But once his wife died, he no longer mentioned this goal.

His family was concerned that he was living alone but he refused to go and live with any of them. The family decided that if this is how he wanted to live, they should allow him to do so. The one concession they asked of him was that he would call one of them (it was generally Shizuko) at 6:30 AM everyday to tell them he was okay. Having "reported in," the conversation would end and both parties went on with their day.

As time went on, Tatsuichi maintained a healthy demeanor. He was not hard-of-hearing, his lungs, heart, and other internal organs were good and his mind was sharp. He did wear glasses, however, but these were primarily for reading.

"He walked with short staccato steps and usually wore a vest over his shirt. His hair was very short and his skin was well tanned."

-Dorothy (Ota) Nakamura

Tatsuichi's Order of Merit
In 1974, Tatsuichi was awarded the 5th Order of Merit with the Order of the Sacred Treasure (Fig. 7-15). This was the same honor bestowed on his brother Kaoru, in 1968.

In the late 1970s, the Ota family held a Father's Day get-together at a restaurant at the Hawaiian Village Hotel in Waikiki. Tatsuichi insisted that he did not want to be picked up in Waipahu. He said he would catch the bus to Waimalu where the Sylvas [Stan and Nina (Ota)] were living. From there he went to the restaurant with them.

Fig. 7-15. Medal— 5th Order of Merit with the Order of the Sacred Treasure.

When he arrived at the restaurant, he told of waiting at the bus stop on Farrington Hwy. in Waipahu. Because he was dressed as perhaps a very poor person might be dressed, others waiting at the bus stop felt sorry for him and gave him their pocket change. At the luncheon table he proudly held out a handful of change! This when he was already a landowner with sizable holdings in Waipahu!

"My last memory of Uncle [Tatsuichi] Ota was at a Hiroshima Ken Jin Kai picnic at Ala Moana Park during the summer in the late 1970s. He came by bus from Waipahu because he wasn't allowed to drive by then. He was a frugal and health-conscious man so for lunch he brought a sliced papaya and a couple of boiled eggs."

-Dorothy (Ota) Nakamura

"A memory I have of Tatsuichi Ota's independence and stubbornness happened when my brother Frank[lin] got married to Gayle in 1974. My father said that Uncle Tatsuichi was coming to the wedding. I asked who was bringing Uncle, and my father said Uncle was planning to come on the bus to the Sheraton Waikiki Hotel from Waipahu. He was 94 years old so I was afraid he would get lost. I phoned him to tell him that we would pick him up. He said, 'If you come, I'm not going!' So I relented and waited on pins and needles for his arrival. After everyone arrived and the dinner service started, he still had not arrived. I went out of the banquet hall to look for him, and as I was going down the escalator, there he was coming up on the other escalator. He was only 30 minutes late. I was amazed that he was able to find his way. After the party, he insisted that he was going home on the bus but I told him that the Waipahu bus was not running at that late hour, so he reluctantly let us drive him home."

-Grace (Ota) Takeuchi

"He often sat just inside his front gate on an aluminum beach chair that perhaps someone had discarded. He would doze and enjoy the fresh air, chatting with people as they came by. They would therefore all know he was well."

-Pete Tagalog

Fig. 7-16. Pahu St. residence of Tatsuichi Ota.

Until one day, a neighbor of Tatsuichi saw him on the ground at the base of the front steps to his Pahu St. house. They called an ambulance and Tatsuichi refused to go to the hospital. Initially, he seemed to be all right but he later died that day of heart failure. He was 98 years old.

Fig. 7-17. Possibly the last scroll Tatsuichi produced. He died at age 98.

The scroll reads "Fortunate to be able to reach my 98th birthday in good health; with all four limbs and five senses intact; to be living in Paradise (Hawaii), the world's finest place where all races live harmoniously and safely."

References - Chapter 7.

Numerous newsletters of Hawaii's Plantation Village.

Ota camp, Gordon Y.K. Pang, Honolulu Star-Bulletin, April 15, 2001.

-8- Life in Waipahu

. . . life in this little town . . .

Our treasured source at Hawaii's Plantation Village tells us about the gummy fluid.

"The sticky bean plant is Klu (*Acacia farnesiana*). The Hawaiian name is Kolu. Kolu in Hawaiian means glue. The bean pod is the part that has the really sticky sap.

Klu was introduced to Hawaii with the hopes of establishing a perfume industry. The plant is a shrub and has very fragrant, ball-shaped, yellow flowers. Klu grew abundantly in Waipahu due to a high germination rate and agreeable climate. The perfume industry never became successful."
-Yoshiko (Tamashiro) Yamauchi

Remembrances

Activities during non-school hours were varied. From walking on crushed cans with sticky tree sap stuck across the arches of feet, to going to various culture classes, kids were kids.

"We liked uncrushed Carnations ® cream cans for walking. These didn't have high edge-seams and so wouldn't hurt when you stood on one end where sticky tree sap was used. Sometimes we punched holes and passed string through the sides of the cans. The string would be looped up to our hands and would help to keep the cans stuck to our feet as we clopped along."
-Georgine (Takayesu) Morita

The sticky tree sap is remembered to be the gummy fluid that could be squeezed from the green pod of a plant and the clip-clopping was thought to imitate walking on getas.

"One activity I can remember was crabbing. We would first go to Pang Kui Market on Waipahu St. to get meat. Then we would go down Depot Rd. to its very end where it met Pearl Harbor. Off a rickety pier, we would tie the meat to a nail and with a string, let the bait sink into the water. As the string got taut, this would signal us that crabs were pulling on the meat and we pulled the string up quickly! We caught white crab and blue crab; the backs were as much as three inches across! The area was called sho-buro."
-Anonymous 810

"You had to be quick with a scoop net [wire hooped net with a short wooden handle] under the crab being hoisted up so it wouldn't let go of the meat and drop back into the water!"
-Ron Ichiyama

"Clamming around the Waipio Peninsula was always fun! We waded into the waters of Pearl Harbor and used an empty upside-down gallon can to sit on in the knee-deep water. The clams were so plentiful, you could just feel around and get a lot in a short time. Then you would take them home and let them blow out the dirt and sand by letting them sit in a pot or large can filled with sea water. A day or so later, you could boil them and have sand-free clams to eat!

Samoan crabs were plentiful too. You could take a scoop net and chase them along the bottom to net them.

As time went by, the waters were polluted enough that you couldn't see the bottom. Clamming had to be by shovel to scoop a bunch of bottom mud. The whole lot would be poured into a bottom-screened box floating on the water. Then, like gold panning, you had to shake the whole box and let the dirt wash away to leave only the clams. Crabbing, likewise, had to be done by crab nets with bait sitting on the bottom to lure the crabs."
-Richard Hirata

"The clams were about the size of silver dollars and Samoan crabs were about 8" to 10" across the back!"
-Edith (Correa) Valdriz

"My parents had the Beta Shoe Store in the Aloha Shopping Center. The shoes would come in large boxes and we would take these in the back of the store and pretend that they were ships or boats or whatever, sometimes rocking back and forth in them as we played.

When I was born, my parents didn't have a name picked out for me in advance so they looked at the various models of shoes and the names on the shoe boxes. They picked my name from one shoe box label."
-Myrna (Manuel) Tsinnajinnie

"The cherry Cokes® at Hanaoka Fountain were superb."
-Bernice (Tamura) Hamai

"The sundaes were terrific too! There was something about how Mr. Hanaoka made his crushed pineapple for the sundaes that made them extra *ono* [tasty]!"
-Robert Anuba

"Hanaoka's ice cream was my favorite. Ice cream was five cents. Ice cream soda was 10 cents ... that was one of my favorite treats."
-Yasuo Saito

Some other things that kids entertained themselves with are remembered. These are almost at no cost to the kids ... money was scarce and there was no TV!

maman-goto (play house)
five hole marbles/agates (remember the kini and the bambucha?)
milk covers (now called pogs)
flattened soda cap buzz saws on a string
kite flying
swimming in Waikele Stream
picking guavas, purple plums
wooden tops where the original tip was replaced with an extra-long sharpened nail
steal eggs (a kid time game)
alabia
Saturday Bookmobile at L'Orange Park
Texaco Metropolitan Opera radio broadcasts
catch grass-hoppers to take to school
trap bees in hibiscus blossoms
lids from canned goods bent over and used as makeshift knives
playground swing and see-saw at L'Orange Park

Hawaii's Plantation Village has an excellent display of mid-wife implements and a description of the services of mid-wives. These are based on donations from Mrs. Misao Tanji.

"In the late 1920s, even a penny found on the roadside was valuable. The penny could get you a small bag of crackseed!"
-Lillian (Oshiro) Oshiro

"While there were hospitals, our entire family of ten kids were each delivered by a midwife."
-Diana (Hirotsu) Herrst

"Our family of many kids were all delivered by a midwife. I think that her name was Ishikawa. I remember that my parents told me how the placenta from a birth was saved in a tea can and buried beneath our house almost as a ritual of birth. When the umbilical cord of a child fell off, it was labeled as being from each specific child's birth, dried, and saved in a *tansu* [chest]. Later, if that child got sick, the specific umbilical cord was taken out and a tea brewed from it so the child could drink it and recover from the ailment."
-Anonymous

"The Plantation Hospital was across the Plantation Store on Waipahu St. It had about four wards with eight beds per room and four private rooms. Hospitals were only for the really sick people."
-Elsie (Fernandez) Moniz

"I used to take my kids and some of their friends to the area where Waikele Stream met Pearl Harbor. This was in the late 1950s and early 1960s. They could go swimming because the water was so clean. Tilapia were also plentiful and opai was so easy to catch with a scoop net. We would take the opai home and salt and fry them.

My daughter used to get a $2 fishing license from Buster's place [Waipahu Bicycle & Sporting Goods], and very patiently fish in the area. I used to see oysters about 6" long dangling from the mangrove roots ... not today! Too polluted."
-Mildred (Tsutsumi) Makii

"In the late 1930s, the area had a fishing village with about 15 or 16 families. Fish were plentiful and the waters [of Pearl Harbor] were clear and clean."
-Henry Morisada

"I can't recall the exact annual celebration but there was always a greased pig contest. A pig was greased up and released. Who-

143

ever caught the pig got to keep it. The same man would win every year! His chest was so hairy, the greased pig never had a chance!"
                              -Marlene (Okada) Hirata

Are these events related?

"I had a pig that was like a dog. He followed me everywhere. He was a true pet. I remember the community was having a party and the next day I noticed that my pig was no longer around! I think I know where it went!"
                              -Ron Ichiyama

Talking about pigs, many remembered about *buta kau-kau*. Here is an example of Japanese, Hawaiian and Pidgin:

> buta, Japanese for pig;
> kau-kau, Hawaiian for food;
> food for pigs, Pidgin

"I think almost every household put out their *buta kau-kau* [aka slop] cans. These were for the piggery people so their pigs would have food. And we went as far as sorting out the slop so there wouldn't be any cans or paper products ... the pigs ate almost everything else.

There weren't any disposals. And this was from the 1940s to the early 1950s."
                              -Mel Bello

"I remember that I had the chore of doing the family laundry. This was by hand on a wooden washboard. In the 1940s, we had a washing machine. I also remember that in the 1930s, ironing was done with a burning charcoal-filled iron and the stove was kerosene fired. The icebox was a box-like cabinet with ice inside that was covered with burlap bag material."
                              -Helen (Sato) Isono

"My grandparents lived in Higashi camp (1920s-1930s) and they had a lot chickens and a vegetable garden. Food was never a problem for them and I, coming to visit from Honolulu, would always be amazed at the number of eggs that my grandmother would fry up for us. I can still remember the smell of frying eggs on their kerosene stove to this day. And chicken *hekka* [chicken pieces stir-fried with various vegetables] was a com-

---

Tofu is soybean curd.

For the curious, tofu is made from soybeans, peeled from their pods, boiled and crushed. The beans are put into a cloth strainer, crushed, and squeezed to release all the juices. The juices are combined with Magnesium Chloride and allowed to harden to become the tofu blocks we know. What remains in the cloth strainer is called okara; eaten plain or with julienned vegetables such carrots and burdock root, it is a delicacy itself.

mon part of main meals."
-Rachel (Hiramoto) Fukuda

"We used to buy bread for a nickel. A peddler came to sell fish and bread. The *tofu* man (Watanabe) came with his cans of tofu. He carried the tofu cubes in water in large cans on both ends of a thick pole across his shoulders. Mr. Watanabe lived on Depot Rd. and his kids were nicknamed #1 tofu, big tofu, and small tofu."
-Yasuo Saito

Manju and anpan are Japanese pastry delicacies with a filling of sweet red beans.

"The manju-ya had kids nick-named 'manju' and 'anpan'."
-Thayer Nakamoto

"People used to catch *dojo* from fresh water streams and rice paddies and put them in a pot with a block of tofu. To escape the heat, the dojo would burrow into the block. Eventually the whole block with the dojo would be boiled and when the block was pulled out and sliced, you would have tofu with pieces of imbedded dojo. With rice and *shoyu* (soy sauce), you would have a scrumptious meal! [With a high protein content.]"
-Anonymous

"Dojo (weather loach, oriental weatherfish), *Misgumus anguillicaudatus*, family *Cobitididae*, was introduced to Hawaii from Asia (most likely China or Japan) in the late 1800's. They grow up to 9 inches long but most are 4 inches long and about 3/8-inch in diameter. They have an elongated, eel-like body and 3 pairs of barbels on the snout.

The Chinese catfish (*Calarias fuscus*) doesn't get as large as the channel catfish (*Ictalurus punctatus*)"
-George Arita

"The Filipinos would clean the dojo and gut it. Then it would be cooked in a vinegar broth with sweet chilies, onion, and tomatoes. Sometimes we would pan-fry the dojo."
-Espy Garcia

"Dojo is also good bait for papio (crevally, jack, or pompano)."
-John Tasato

The weather loach's swim bladder sensed changes in weather and the dojo would swim erratically to the surface of the water and back down again when low barometric pressure associated with a storm system moved in to an area.

In Japan, the dish of dojo in tofu is called dojo-nabe (dojo pot) and is a delicacy.

If you talk about fish, *puntat* invariably comes up. This is the Filipino name for the Chinese catfish! If you want to see one, go to Hawaii's Plantation Village at the Waipahu Cultural Garden Park. Yoshiko Yamauchi pointed out the black, 10-incher that she placed in their aquarium when it was about 2" long over 12 years ago! It has survived for these many years on a diet of fish food and insects fed to it by the staff.

"We lived in Ota camp a few hundred yards in from Farrington Hwy. There was an artesian spring that fed a pond about 12' in diameter in our backyard. We had taro growing there and the water ran off into Kapakahi Stream.

By taking a net with small eyes strung out between two hand-held bamboo poles, we could thrash the brush around the streams and get the puntat up to where we could scoop them up. These were about 5" or 6" long and we would sell them for pocket change or candy money.

My grandmother would buy larger ones and cook them up for family dinners. Grandma cleaned and gutted the catfish and flavored it with salt, pepper, and garlic before frying. Sometimes, *shoyu* [soy sauce] would be added at the table."
                                          -Darryl Tupinio

"My mother would gut the cafish, scrape off the slimy skin, put salty black soy bean paste (*dau see*), garlic (grated or chunks), and green onion. The head was the best part. If the catfish was about 12" long, you could cut it up into about four chunks and steam it for about 1/2 hour.

We had 11 kids in the family so if you came late to dinner, you didn't eat!"
                                          -Mildred (Seu) Kam

"During the war, sometimes things would be hard to get. Many of us added food to the family meals by fishing. Where Waikele Stream meets Pearl Harbor, fish, crab, and oysters were plentiful.

I didn't know how to make a fish [throw] net but a friend taught me the procedure and knots and so I made a giant 30' diameter throw net! My friends all laughed at me because it was so large and hard to handle.

It came in handy when, one day, a 4' barracuda swam up Waikele stream to where the dirty water met the clearer ocean water. I threw the net, got the barracuda and had to jump in after the fish to wrestle it to shore. My friends all thought I was crazy!

One time, I found a place where the oysters were *this* big. [He gestures and I confirm that the oysters were 10" to 12" in length! - Mike Yamamoto]

The biggest Samoan crab I got in that area was about 24" across the back. I wish I had a picture. An older guy had to help me land the crab and told me that since he had helped me, he got the crab and I got the giant pincer. The pincer I got was

Harold T. Stearns writes in *Geology of the State of Hawaii*, that fossil remains on the Waipio Peninsula confirms the sizes of these huge oysters (12" in the longest dimension) as far back as 39,000 years ago.

In the 1930s, tiny pearls were found in some pearl (*pipi*) oysters in Pearl Harbor. The lochs of Pearl Harbor also were home to a speckled clam that had perfectly spherical, white pearls.

Pearl Harbor, as a Naval Base, was started by the U.S. Navy in 1909.

Pearl Harbor was known to the Hawaiians as Puuloa.

The Anuhulu River in Haleiwa has a narrow two-lane road with a double arch bridge across it. Crabbing from the bridge, even today, yields very large Samoan crabs!

'this long.' [Again, I confirm size; the main part of the pincer was about 12" long according to Albert. - Mike Yamamoto]"
                                        -Albert Empron

"I've seen oysters shucked from their shell that were about 6" long so I think the shell that they came from could very well have been about 12". I've also seen Samoan crabs that were 12 inches across the back and when their legs were spread out, it was about 30 inches."
                                        -Steven Bello

And while not in Pearl Harbor and perhaps a decade later in time, we were able to closely substantiate Albert's story.

"I believe the size of that Samoan crab! In the 1950s we went crabbing off the narrow bridge in Haleiwa. We caught a Samoan crab that was 14" across the back! I know it was 14" because it was so large, we measured the shell when we got it home!"
                                        -Moana Espinda

"In the 1960s, I happened to visit a friend in the Honouliuli area. On the wall of his house there was the shell of a Samoan crab that must have been at least 16" across the back!
I never imagined that they grew that large!."
                                        -Paul Suyama

"Macadamia nut trees were abundant in and around Waipahu. Grandpa Tatsuichi's yard on Pahu St. had several and it was a challenge to try to crack the nuts for the meat within the very hard, very round, very crack-resisting protection. I always wondered how rats (or mice) were able to gnaw their way thru the hard outer shell to get to the nut meat before I did. The intact nuts that I found on the ground, I attacked with a hammer and many hammer blows only caused the entire nut to fly off into space rather than get cracked!"
                                        -Michael Yamamoto

Macadamia nuts were introduced in Hawaii from Australia in 1892.

Kid times are always remembered especially when the after-school hours are concerned.

"We used to find a way to get into the Plantation Store after hours and get at the pickled green olives! We would open jars, take out and eat what we wanted, replace the lids, and sneak out again."
                                        -Anonymous #3

"There were times that we used to go to the swimming hole that we had created by damming up Waikele Stream. It was during my first grade year and while we were swimming in the early morning hours, we would hear the Waipahu Elementary School bugle telling us that school was starting. It was usually too late to change and make it to classes so we just ignored school for that day.

At the end of the year, I wasn't passed to go to the 2nd grade and my mother went down to the school to ask why I was being flunked. They showed her my attendance record with all the missed days!"

-Norman Kurata

Norman had the nickname *waru-bozu*.

In Japanese, *waru* - from *warui* or naughty; and *bozu* - slang for boy

"Kids would get at the Coke® chest-like machines. These were the ones that held the bottles upright. The bottles had to be slid to the end where the paying mechanism would allow release of a bottle. Instead, kids would figure out a way to un-cap the upright bottles and stick straws in to drink the contents of the bottles! I guess this was a drawback of that type of bottle dispenser so it was discontinued eventually.

We used to go into Arakawas with old, ragged rubber slippers. Of course, the whole idea was to go in with old slippers and go out with new replacements without getting caught!"

-Anonymous #3

"In the plantation camps, there were trees with purple plums. They were really sour but if you put enough salt on them, you could eat them! And the streams had *opu* and the reservoirs had tilapia. Lake Wilson [near Wahiawa] even had snails that we could catch."

-Edith (Correa) Valdriz

Opu is properly spelled Oopu and is a goby; of which there were as many as five species in fresh water streams in Hawaii.

Most students might have continued their education from the elementary school grades to completion at Waipahu High School.

Concurrent education might be Japanese language school after regular school hours, or dressmaking school, floral arrangement classes, or tea ceremony classes.

A community as small as Waipahu produced many sports figures of national and international recognition. Baseball, track, volleyball, boxing, bicycling; these were but a few sports in which Waipahu produced notable athletes. (See also the listing at the end of Chap. 9)

"There was the 120-lb. limit barefoot football league; no age limit, just 120-lb. weight limit. There were about 4 or 5 teams:

Associates	— from Higashi camp
[Brownies]	— from Higashi camp
Danes	— from Nishi camp
Trojans	— from Spanish, Filipino, and the "leased" camps
[Townies]	— from Machi

I cannot remember who the sponsors were but each kid had a helmet, shoulder pads, and hip pads. I think this was in the late 1940s."

-Mel Bello

What started in the 1930s and 1940s as a city-wide league led Waipahu to form the Jack Rabbits team(s). WWII intervened and in the mid-1940s, Rusty Hamada and Sparky Okamura re-organized the Waipahu league. Initially, shoulder pad and helmets were the only "uniforms" and the players often used their own shirts and pants to play in.

In 1948-49, the barefoot football league came to an end. But the Waipahu Jack Rabbit Athletic Association continued with youth football, basketball and baseball.

"Takemi and Kazuo Arakawa were both Junior Olympic Champions in different events. Walter Gouveia was a one-man volleyball team who challenged a whole team of players on the West Coast in Los Angeles.

Hans L'Orange, former manager of Oahu Sugar was the patron saint of all sports in Waipahu for 30 years. The athletic field [on Waipahu St.] is named after him."

-Dr. Stanley Yanase, D.D.S.

Goro Arakawa recalls that brother Shigemi was obsessed with marbles. So much so that their father told Goro to take all of Shigemi's marbles and dump them into Kapakahi Stream. This is in the donburo area behind present-day Saiki Motors. Shigemi quietly smiles as Goro relates the story.

"We lived in Ota Camp and our back yard was right up to Kapakahi Stream. We had a vegetable garden that had a lot of Jikima. Our front yard had the Marungay (horseradish) tree."
                                            -Myrna (Manuel) Tsinnajinnie

"My grandmother had a farm fronting Pearl Harbor and on the west side of Kapakahi Stream. As a grade-schooler, I remember taking the train from Honolulu and getting off at the Waipahu Depot [Train Station]. From there, I would walk across the railroad bridge [still there today in 2005] to my grandmother's farm. There were fish ponds, rice paddies, pigs, chickens and other fowl. I remember that we used to catch the black crab *alamihi* and toss them to the pigs for them to eat. Of course the crabs were still alive and very fast and would clamp on to the pigs' snouts and the pigs would be in a fit to get the crabs off! So we fed the crabs to the pigs one at a time. Eventually, each crab was flung off and eaten by the pigs.

The fish pond gates were opened at low tide and when they filled with the high tide, the gates were closed. You had to get up at all hours to keep the ponds filled. The fish pond was interconnected with the rice paddies and the duck ponds. Gates controlled water draining from the ride paddies and the duck ponds to keep the salt water from going into the rice fields.

During the day, the ducks would swim into the salty fish pond and get thirsty and would race back to their duck pond to get a drink of fresh water.

The area is no longer there and mangrove thickets cover the entire area and Kapakahi Stream is all polluted."
                                            -Ed Yamada

"I remember one occasion when I was looking out over the [donburo] farm area when my grandfather was met by local police. I was afraid that he had done something wrong as they talked for quite a while. I was too far away to hear what the conversation was about. After a few minutes, my grandfather went into the banana patch area and returned with two bottles which he gave to the policemen. I think I saw money changing hands.

I never asked about the encounter but I think that the police were buying *okolehao* [moonshine]. And I never did ask grandpa more about that kind of thing or where he had his still!

I was a grade-schooler at that time."
                              -Diana (Hirotsu) Herrst

"My father, who worked very hard in the cane fields all day, enjoyed having *sake* [rice wine] or whiskey with his evening meals. I think it helped him to relax.

During the prohibition days, when these relaxants were unavailable to him, he decided to produce some home-brewed beer. My job was to assist him by washing out bottles and capping them once they were filled by my father. As a reward, he'd give me the leftovers.

I used to set up a bar on our front porch by enclosing a portion of it with straw mats (goza) and serve [the leftover brew] to my siblings. Did we get giddy and happy!

Some families made sake, but my father used to say that it was too smelly during the fermentation process. We heard about raids, so I was happy that my father stuck to beer."
                              -Anonymous

"There was the Machi Club that was started up by Shigemi Arakawa. There were sports activities with about four groups challenging each other; and sort of a 'good citizen' organization where the kids were not to smoke or throw rubbish around the streets. The kids would police themselves and they even had a court system with penalties for infractions. The kids would police themselves."
                              -Masuye Akiyama

"In the late 1940s and early 1950s, there was swing music by the *Orchettes* at the Ewa gymnasium. There were some Waipahu boys in the orchestra. Waipahu never had a basketball gym so we used to go to Ewa gym for dancing on Saturday nights.

Even people from Honolulu used to come for the music and dancing.

During the summer months, there were Bon Dances (usually weekends at either Ewa or Waianae). After the dances, we used to go body surfing. This was at Kahe Point or Ewa Beach. Kahe point is next to Waipahu Beach, the beach that Oahu Sugar owned.

I still have scars from body-surfing into shore from 50 or 100 yards out!"

-Mel Bello

Students seeking higher education sometimes had unexpected experiences filled with new adventure and eventually culminating in a productive, lifelong career. The following story is somewhat typical of students from Hawaii going off to colleges in the continental U.S. That is, a college education was generally four years away at school with hardly any opportunity to go home for summers or holidays. (In contrast, today's students have ample opportunity to go home for various holidays and breaks during their college education.)

"I was a student at Waipahu High School and was going to go to the University of Hawaii; hopefully, on an athletic scholarship.

A book salesman, Lyle Ashcroft, from the D.C. Heath Co. was calling on Waipahu High School trying to sell books. He was also scouting for the Southern Oregon College of Education, his alma mater. He made an offer to me of a scholarship from there. I went there from 1950 - 1954.

While there, I found out that Kenny's Steakhouse in Ashland, Oregon, was paying the $40/quarter scholarship and $20 out-of-state fee for me to attend the school! It was a small school; maybe 500 total enrollment with about 250 each males and females. Meals were 50¢ or so for lunches and dinners.

You can imagine a young kid like me going by myself from Hawaii to San Francisco to Medford, Oregon, and then finally to Ashland!

I came home only one time a year. One summer I was able to get a job at a Brookings Lumber Yard. That's how I made my 'go home for summer' money!

I was amazed that one day, recently, I was at a home-improvement store and I saw a stack of plywood with 'Brookings' stenciled on the side! Hey, that's where I worked when I went

to school!"
                    -Ken Kimura

Ken eventually became a teacher at Waipahu Elementary School and then a Vice Principal at Waipahu Intermediate School.

"Our parents had language difficulties. They taught by their actions and the way that they lived. They believed in honesty, hard work, kindness, compassion, living and working together, humbleness, respecting your parents, elders, teachers, and minister. If you strongly believe in things, if principles are important, endure and persevere till the end. My parents use to say '*ishi ni kajitte mo.*'

'Even if you have to scratch or eat stone,' do not give up. I don't know if the saying came from Japan.

Our Royal Hawaiian Band members, when old Hawaii was overthrown, protested and refused to perform. Their saying was 'even if we have to eat stone, we will not perform in the band.' "
                    -Zen Abe

"We didn't have much in terms of material things but we sure had quality of life - so much fun and happiness."
                    -Arlene (Kobashigawa)
                         Kuniyoshi

"I know that my parents always told me: '1) do your best, 2) be good to people, 3) be helpful, and 4) keep on learning. Whatever good that you do will come back to you.' I think all families, not only Japanese, say that when they're trying to bring up their kids."
                    -Yuzuru Morita

"We had nine kids in our family. My father worked in the cane fields all his life and my mother ran our store. She took in laundry as well and my Dad even had a pig farm for a while.

She used to always tell us, 'education main thing in life.' I think you could say that my mother was the driving force in putting the family through school."
                    -Steven Bello

"I know that my parents made tremendous sacrifices so that I could go to school. They even came up to South Bend, Indiana, for my graduation. I can still remember her glowing face at the graduation."
-Mel Bello

"My mother always told us 'to succeed in the world, you have to be educated.'"
-Laura (Shigeura) Harimoto

Table 8-1 - Nicknames in Waipahu

In every community, nicknames are more colorful than given legal names. John Tasato shared an original list collected by Hiro Ito. Adding to the list were Helen Isono, Grace and Ken Kimura, Marge Kodama, Ted Okada, Lillian Okada, Calvin Ebisuya, Sumiko Oshiro, and others. Can you give the owner of these nicknames their legal names? And add more nicknames?

A brando	Chicken	Fly	Ma ka pe	Pum pe	Tojam
Abura	Chico		Makuji	Pun jab	Tomahawk
Among	Chief	General	Makule	Puntat	Toronko
Amonk	Chocolate	Ghandi	Manju	Put (Poot)	To-to
Andong	Cho lon	Gigantic	Manoa		Trigger
Anpan	Choriso	Glon Glon	Man tok	Q	
Ap-pe	Clark	Greenie	Mariano		U ma ku
	Clumsy		Matug	Rat	
Baba	Copper	Hene	Me da ka	Red	V
Balloon	Cranky	Herman	Me ga ne	Ree sa	
Banana	Cupie	Hinkle	Mi lu ku	Rock	Walan
Ba-yan		Horse	Moge	Rocky	Wa pa
Bento	Dan go		Mo lok	Romeo	Wa shi
Big Head	Den ga	Ish ka	Monkey	Rubber	Winsela
Big John	Depo	Junko	Mo yan		White man
Big Shot	Dinky		Munchy	Savage	Whitey
Biggie	Diver	Ka-don	Musubi	Scratchy	Wimpy
Bi-lik	Doc	Kakio	Mutt	Sen-cho	Windy
Blackie	Do-don	Ka ne	Negi	Shaggy	Wiper
Blondie	Dollar	Kan ko		Sha ke	
Bolo	Donkey	Ka-nute	Oomp	Shorty	X
Bones	Dumbo	Kayo		Skit	
Bon ko	Duffer	Killa	Pajo	Slim	Yankee
Boto	Dynamite	Killer-la	Pake	Sloppy	Yat
Boyan		Kilroy	Pakko	Sparky	
Bozu	Ebo	Knuckles	Pak-sung	Specs	Zik
Brown	Embo (or	Kope	Pa le a	Spike	
Buffalo	Enbo)	Krong	Panko	Spud	5¢
Bull	Et te	Kukai	Pa sha do	Squanto	99
Bull Dog	E bi	Ku ri ka	Pepe	Sun Down	
Bumpy			Pi no-tch		
Butch	Farina	Lefty	Pio	Tarzan	
	Fat	Long leg	Pogo	Tatan	
Caesar	Five Times		Pogot	Tengara	
Caramen	Freckles	Mabo	Poi tat	Thunder	
Casey	Frenchy	Magoo	Poka	Tiger	
Chabo	Froggie	Ma-gua	Professor	Tiny	
Chick	Fudge	Major	Pu loot	Tofu	

155

References - Chapter 8.

Hawaii's Native & Exotic Freshwater Animals, Mike N. Yamamoto and Annette W. Tagawa, Mutual Publishing, Honolulu, Hawaii, 2000.

Numerous newsletters of Hawaii's Plantation Village.

Many articles, *Waipahu 75th Diamond Jubilee Edition*, Sunday Star-Bulleting & Advertiser, Honolulu, Hawaii, Nov. 5, 1972.

Geology of the State of Hawaii, Harold T. Stearns, Pacific Books, publishers, Palo Alto, California, 2nd ed., 1985.

-9- Notes on the history of Waipahu

... more about people, places, and events in Waipahu ...

Waipahu has had many people that significantly contributed to its growth. People are behind movements, social events, and political directions shaping towns like Waipahu. In the shaping process, people themselves grow ... and some returned to their roots in Waipahu, others moved forward in other communities. While writing this book, we encountered many people willing to come forward to contribute stories, anecdotes, and photos and to allow us to record what they remembered of their town of Waipahu. Here we present even the smallest and sometimes almost forgotten memory that tells a story. The overall attitudes of helping others, being generous with time, and sharing have never left the people and town of Waipahu.

Names of people, events, and descriptions of events that people felt contributed to the growth of Waipahu are given. These are not listed in any particular order but they are all significant in the history of Waipahu.

Hans L'Orange, worked for Oahu Sugar from 1912 to 1957. He came from Norway and was an ice-skater in his home country but his father wanted a seafarer's life like his own for the 20 year-old son. So the younger L'Orange came to Hawaii with the hope of eventually being nominated by Prince Kuhio to the U.S. Naval Academy. He settled in Waipahu and first worked as a field hand tending to mules for the Oahu Sugar Co. He is said to have remarked that "the people of Waipahu are the nicest in all the world," thus starting a union that would benefit thousands in the history of Waipahu. He became Oahu Sugar's manager in 1937 and retired in 1957. During his tenure as manager, he treated the people of Oahu Sugar and Waipahu fairly and they reciprocated. Aside from managing a sugar giant, he was a considerate and kind community leader. He is said to have never fired anyone; choosing instead to let natural attrition keep his staff balanced. He encouraged participation in community sports uniting the people of Waipahu as one and frequently led community jaunts and challenges in sporting events to other towns. That he loved Waipahu and Waipahu loved him is evidenced in part by the fact that the Oahu Sugar's Waipahu Field was named the Hans L'Orange Park in 1924. In 1969 the park was officially turned over to the City & County of Honolulu. In 1972, it was officially dedicated as Hans L'Orange Park and further still, in 1983, the city installed a plaque calling it the Hans L'Orange Park.

Those who personally knew him still speak only kindly of and with much adoration and love for Hans L'Orange.

"Dad loved the people he worked with and for. He was a caring person but a tough man. He was not an 'easy guy'; he lived by 'Army rules' saying 'that's how it's supposed to be' for many things."
-Peter L'Orange

"I think Hans L'Orange was fired by AMFAC 2 or 3 times because he gave so much back to the community [of Waipahu] and yet Oahu Sugar was the most profitable [sugar operation] in Hawaii. He helped private companies within Waipahu and Waipahu schools with their athletic facilities. Sometimes the workers from Oahu Sugar beat the schools by building the facilities before [the school] had even applied for the permits to build the facility! He used to say 'happy sugar workers produce sweet sugar.' He let us cultivate vegetables on land above the mill for our soup kitchen and families during the 1946 strike!

The welfare of workers, families and the entire community of Waipahu was his concern.

In the 1930s, he had about 6 or 7 acres set aside for vegetable gardening in the area that is now close to the Mililani Graveyard. We, as 3rd and 4th graders, had to work one day a week tending to the garden and the vegetable stand. We were trucked to the site. As I look back on the time, it was a vocational experience for all of us. We learned about gardening, learned math (making change with vegetable sales), learned how to be counter clerks, all while producing vegetables for the plantation community at a low cost.

What a guy! So caring and forward-thinking!"
-Zen Abe

Hans L'Orange was instrumental in forming the Waipahu Juvenile Patrol in 1948. With WWII, many parents had been pressed into service for the war effort and many of their kids remained at home with little or no adult supervision after school hours. To curb juvenile delinquency, pairs of adults from all walks of life were organized to regularly patrol Waipahu in the evening hours after 8PM. In cooperation with the Honolulu Police Department and with their full blessing, the patrol counseled and observed youths. Then Chief of Police Dan Liu said that the Waipahu Juvenile Patrol reduced incidents of juvenile delinquency to almost nothing in Waipahu.

Masao "Cranky" Watanabe got his nickname at age 14, when he was being cheated at cards by older boys. Not allowing this, he put up such a fuss that the older boys started calling him "Cranky." At age 16, he started work at Oahu Sugar and spent some 50-plus years working there. Interspersed with work were many years spent improving himself by going to night school and eventually the University of Hawaii. Years of community service and his knack of dealing with people was evident when he was pressed into service during WWII as Hans L'Orange's representative in Civil Defense and later, at the end of the war, in retrieving equipment loaned by Oahu Sugar to the military. Cranky's most recent service years were as Director of Industrial Relations at Oahu Sugar.

When interviewed by Lani (Ishikawa) Nedbalek in 1984, Cranky reflected that work at Oahu Sugar was a way of life when he started but now plantation work is just a job.

A Honolulu native, Clarissa Haili, later Clara Inter, got her entertainment name, "Hilo Hattie," from performing a hula to Don McDiarmid's 1932 song *When Hilo Hattie Does the Hilo Hop* and some other comic hula songs; this after leaving the education field. She was popular in San Francisco, Los Angeles, and Hawaii. She was also featured in several films.

A local garment manufacturer later purchased the Hilo Hattie name and became Hilo Hattie, the company.

Clara Inter was a teacher at Waipahu Elementary School teaching (1923-1940) all grades 1 through 8 except the second grade. From all accounts, she was a good teacher and well-liked by students and peers. She later went into the entertainment industry and many today only know of her as Hilo Hattie. Hilo Hattie, the company, is today a tourist industry giant dealing primarily in Hawaiian wear.

"In the early 1940s, I got very sick and had to stay at home. Clara Inter was a teacher who went from school-to-school and she would come to give me lessons. She was such a nice and vibrant teacher."
            -Jane (Kimura) Arita

At the other end of Waipahu St. was August Ahrens Elementary School and its principal, Lulu Corbly.

"Lulu Corbly was a strict disciplinarian. She had a piece of rubber hose on the wall above her desk and you kinda knew that she would not be afraid to use it if you weren't doing the right things.
-Anonymous 810

"I spent summers going to her house and getting extra education sessions."
-Bernice (Tamura) Hamai

[While Bernice offers no explanation for the extra summer sessions, it appears that she was part of a select group of students showing exceptional promise and therefore had the benefit of Lulu Corbly's extra attention. We would like to think that even at this early time in Hawaii's educational development, teachers felt that going beyond formal hours in classrooms was a good and professional thing to do.]

Shigeru Serikaku came to Hawaii in 1906 at age 16. Earlier, in 1903, the Wright brothers had made their famous flight and Serikaku had learned of this and was so intrigued that he began studying everything he could about flight. With help from friends and donations from a fan club that started up, he eventually built his flying machine and flew it ... firsts in Hawaii. The year was 1913. With the approach of WWI, plans for further flights were denied by the authorities nor was the first flight recorded in formal documents.

"Mr. Serikaku was a quiet, unassuming man. If I may use the term, a 'very Christian man.' He never announced or advertised his Christian beliefs and he didn't preach Christianity."
-Elsie (Jinbo) Suyenaga

"I admire the man. You could say that Mr. Serikaku was a true mechanic."
-Al Watanabe

"I was a youngster living closeby to Mr. Serikaku. He was a very nice man. One day, he invited me to have a sort of breakfast with him. He gave me toast with mayonnaise on it. I really liked it!"
-Ron Ichiyama

Pat Patterson was a youngster growing up in Waipahu near Shigeru Serikaku.

Emiko (Kadohiro) Serikaku, daughter-in-law, and Ellen (Serikaku) Ujimori, daughter, of Shigeru Serikaku, kindly shared this information as compiled by Thomas Taro Higa.

Serikaku's airplane had:

French-built aircraft 4-cylinder, air-cooled engine weighing about 85 lbs generating 35-HP

Aircraft itself:
wingspan - 28 feet
fuselage - 25 feet
height - 6'8"
propeller - 5' 10"

The first flight was about 40 feet long at the Moanalua Park/Gardens with Shigeru Serikaku as pilot and was witnessed by 20 regular supporters of his endeavor.

The location of the remains of this first airplane built and flown in Hawaii is not known.

William M. Patterson's name was originally Paterson but when August Ahrens presented him with a watch, it was engraved as Patterson with the extra t so from then on, the elder Patterson used that as his family name.

William A. "Pat" Patterson was born in 1898 and the son of the first head *luna* (overseer) William M. Patterson of the Oahu Sugar Co. When Pat Patterson was 13, he was sent to the Honolulu Military Academy by his mother, Mary (Castro) Patterson. He ran away from the school and joined his mother in California going by way of ship. He found work at the Wells Fargo Bank in San Francisco. Originally an office boy, he quickly became an executive in the department dealing with aviation companies.

At a time when aviation companies where forming and merging at an alarming rate, United Airlines was formed as a result of acquisition and mergers of National Air Transport, Pacific Air Transport, Boeing Airplane-Transport and Varney Airlines. As a result of his being closely associated to these aviation companies, Pat Patterson was recognized as valuable to the newly formed United Airlines. In 1934, Pat Patterson became the President of United Airlines.

In 1950, United Airlines introduced a fleet of Boeing Stratocruisers to start regular service to Hawaii. The first was named *Waipahu* and christened with a scoop of sugar showered over its nose by Mrs. Hans L'Orange on Jan. 14, 1950, at the Honolulu International Airport.

Pat Patterson acknowledged his roots in Waipahu ... a very warm gesture of Aloha by any measure. The people of Waipahu acknowledged Pat Patterson's part in the history of Waipahu by having the bridge on Farrington Hwy. over Waikele Stream named as the William A. Patterson Bridge.

The bridge goes over Waikele Stream going west on an up-sloping Farrington Hwy.

"On one of his visits to Hawaii, he was brought to Waipahu to view the bridge bearing his name. A ceremony was held and he was moved to tears by the honor.

The bridge name appears on the westernmost end-pier of the bridge on the right of auto traffic lanes. **Do not stop in the area.**

From the bridge, you can see the area beyond Waipahu Cultural Garden Park and up on the plateau that is the mill site, is the place where his home was located when he lived as a youngster in Waipahu."

-Al Watanabe and Eddie Uemori

Robert Castro tells us that he would like to think that young Pat Patterson was somewhat influenced to go in the direction of flight as a lifelong endeavor because he lived closeby to

Serikaku. But then, Robert tells us, the very rough sailing that Patterson made when he ran away to the mainland could also have influenced him as Patterson is said to have told friends that "I will never again ride on a ship!" [Perhaps not a seagoing sailing ship!]

Roy Tokujo grew up in Camp 46, Koalipea (aka koro pea), of the Oahu Sugar Co. He was one of four recipients of a scholarship sponsored by Pat Patterson of United Airlines. Roy, an honor student at Waipahu High School, wanted to be a nuclear physicist and elected to go to Cal-Berkeley. His advisor was Edward Teller. Roy became homesick and consulted with his advisor only to be told that there was no future for a nuclear physicist in Hawaii; the jobs were in Alamogordo or White Sands both in New Mexico, leaving Roy with a future even farther away from Hawaii. He went to Chicago, home of United Airlines and consulted with Pat Patterson. Patterson told him that the future as he saw it, was tourism for Hawaii. So Roy went to the Michigan State University, one of two schools at the time with a program in tourism (the other, Cornell, was farther east). In completing his studies in tourism, he organized a *luau* for 10,000 people in Michigan! Food and entertainment, the likes of which will probably never be equaled again on the mainland, told Roy that really, his future was with tourism. On return to Hawaii, he followed the direction of tourism and eventually became the head of Paradise Cove Entertainment. Roy Tokujo now produces the *Ulalena* show on Maui, and is active in many other business and community endeavors.

luau - party with much Hawaiian food, entertainment, and dance.

Most recently, Roy Tokujo is involved in the makeover of the Royal Hawaiian Shopping Center in Waikiki. His part is a Waikiki-themed show equalling or exceeding the presentations at Paradise Cove and on Maui.

Hideo "Major" Okada worked for the Oahu Sugar Co. for 41 years; in later years as a lead man in its processing department. The sidebar lists some of his many, many involvements in the community of Waipahu and Hawaii.

His daughter, Marlene (Okada) Hirata, a dynamic personality in her own right, shares some memories of her dad.

"Major" Okada was a pretty good baseball player in his youth. His friends thought that he was good enough to play in the major league, hence the nickname that stayed with him for the

Major Okada:
Leader in creating Waipahu Cultural Garden Park; active in Waipahu Community Assoc.; active in the Democratic Party of Hawaii; active at a very high level of ability and integrity in the labor movement in Hawaii; active in sports activities in Waipahu; recognized in national books for his prodigious contibutions to his community.

"Major Okada and my Dad were good friends. Even when Major was active in labor, and therefore 'on the other side', they respected each other with mutual trust, admiration and understanding."
    Peter L'Orange

rest of his life.

Marlene and her two brothers always looked forward to times when his work schedule at Oahu Sugar would allow the family to go to "Waipahu Beach" (across from Hawaiian Electric's Kahe Power Plant), or clamming at Hoaeae, or picking seaweed at Ewa Beach.

Major helped everyone seeking his help. Middle-of-the-night beckonings at his house from Filipino workers needing help to community efforts whether they were dealing with labor unions, fundraising for athletic programs, assisting in educational programs, or for any other endeavor in Hawaii calling on Major, he was always there.

He did well to instill in his children how important it was to help others and the community. Witness daughter Marlene (Okada) Hirata's boundless and tireless energy in helping individuals and community organizations.

Even with his full schedule in life, he was able to create the start of Hawaii's Plantation Village in Waipahu. The Educational Center there is named in his honor.

"Any project or program that had his support took on a special kind of legitimacy. Major always came through and never misled people. If he gave you his word on anything, he delivered. He had a vast network of people whose lives he touched."
-Docent Manual, Hawaii's
Plantation Village,
Nov. 2003.

Hawaii's Plantation Village (HPV) was conceived by Major Okada as a means to preserve the heritage of plantation life in Waipahu and Hawaii. With Goro Arakawa, who envisioned the museum aspect of the facility, and many others in the Waipahu community, HPV became a reality in 1992.

Goro Arakawa and his siblings received their education through the 12th grade in Hawaii. However, Goro went to NYU for his college education. While on the East Coast, he was able to visit many museums and this caused him to wonder why there were no museums in his hometown that preserved Hawaii's plantation life.

To get to the Waipahu Cultural Garden Park where Hawaii's Plantation Village (HPV) is located, find the intersection where Depot Rd. begins on Waipahu St. (there are several directions from which you can find your way here).

Go west on Waipahu St., past Saiki Motors, and past another curve. The entrance to the park will be on your left.

On his return to Waipahu, and while still helping in the family business, Arakawas of Waipahu, he was able to interest others in the community in the idea of a museum on plantation life. This effort, eventually melded with the idea of a model plantation camp to become Hawaii's Plantation Village which is part of the Waipahu Cultural Garden Park.

Waipahu Cultural Garden Park has 45 acres that were originally a flood plain. With the Flood Control Project of 1939, the area became more usable. In the late 1960s, plans were started for a botanical garden on the site. By 1970, plans were expanded to include a historic plantation village to be enjoyed by all of Hawaii.

"Early in the planning stages, we enlisted the aid of George Fan, an architect, and Spencer Leineweber, a preservationist-architect. These two helped to bring the initial concept into fruition with the plans for various houses and buildings. (Spencer Leineweber was recognized nationally as a preservationist-architect and so the association of her name to the park gave a lot of credibility to the project.)

Then, as we began to solicit funds for (at the time) mainly the Waipahu Cultural Garden Park, an executive committee formed for fund-raising realized that we needed a broader base from which to solicit funds. So Hawaii's Plantation Village (HPV) became a part of the Park. This covered all of Hawaii's Plantaion past . . . not only from the Waipahu area but from all over Hawaii."
                                        -Cal Kawamoto

"We did 'legwork' type of research. The HSPA library, the Hamilton Library at the University of Hawaii, and of course, the many plantations all over Hawaii to see typical construction of structures.

It was an intellectual exercise in research because we first had to find the old structures. Some had been moved from their original locations and put to another use by the time we were viewing them. Then we had to find and use old documents to recreate their original design so we could have drawings for Waipahu's Village to use.

When it finally came together in the early 1990s, HPV won the first award in Hawaii from the AIA (American Instute of Archi-

tects) in Washington, D.C."
                                                -Spencer Leineweber

A museum of old-time artifacts from the era of sugar plantations is in the main building, the Okada Educational Center. The village is comprised of buildings that tell a story of the era thus helping to preserve the heritage of plantation life in Hawaii.

With much fund-raising, planning, and dedicated efforts from many individuals, the Waipahu Cultural Garden Park became reality in 1992.

"I remember that the Big-Way Supermarket owners were especially strong supporters of HPV. When we were in dire financial need, they could be counted on for an 'on-the-spot' check. This is not to say that there weren't others that helped us immensely as well."
                                                -"Andy" Anderson

"HPV maintains a small bookstore and gift shop. Their cookbooks are not only about cooking but they include little tidbits about the various ethnic groups and their cultures."
    -Cal Kawamoto

Fig. 9-1. The Okada Educational Center Building. This has the Administrative Offices, a Museum in the Goro Arakawa Exhibit Rooms, archives, and the Gentry Auditorium, for Hawaii's Plantation Village.

Typical buildings in Hawaii's Plantation Village and the year represented:

Chinese cookhouse (1909)
Chinese Society Building (1909)
Portuguese house (1918)
Puerto Rican house (1900)
Japanese duplex (1910)

Japanese house (1930)
  related: Tofuya
        Wakamiya Inari
          Shrine
         Community furo
         Barber shop
         Sumo ring
         Garage
Filipino dormitory (1919)
Filipino house (1935)
Okinawan house (1919)
Korean house (1919)
Hawaiian hale (1850)
Plantation store (1900)
Infirmary (1915)
Camp office (1930)
Social/Union hall (1920)

"When the Puerto Rican house was being built, there was an elderly woman who came by to watch the progress. When the building was finally finished and we were putting furniture into the house, she came by and reached into her pocket. She pulled out a Crucifix, donating it to HPV saying, 'Now mama can finally come home.'

This moved me to tears."
                     -Spencer Leineweber

Of special note on the grounds of HPV, is a memorial stone (Fig. 9-2) originally erected in 1930 at one of the Oahu Sugar Co. cemeteries (on Waikele St. south of the St. Joseph cemetery) as a tribute to Japanese countrymen who came to Hawaii.

Many of these died penniless and away from their families. Master stone carver Zenichi Karioka inscripted "Fellow countrymen who have gone before us, this tower is erected for you." The words were chosen by Keiho Soga and calligraphy was by Toraichi Okita.

The Memorial Stone was to go from its original location in the Oahu Sugar Cemetery in Waipahu to the new cemetery in Mililani.

The stone fell or was dropped from the delivering truck and lay

Fig. 9-2. Memorial Stone.

Zenichi Karioka was in the Garage department of Oahu Sugar. These men made the tools for other shops as well as kept the field equipment maintained.

"Mr. Karioka was also a master stone carver. There were many times when others could not break rocks, Mr. Karioka would do it without much talk; I think he knew how to read the 'grain' of the rocks"
                     -Zen Abe

Keiho Soga was the pen name of Yasutaro Soga of the Nippu Jiji Newspaper.

face down by a roadside for almost 30 years. It was discovered by a road crew in 1988 and appropriately placed permanently at HPV. It serves as an entryway sentinel to a time tunnel that leads to the old plantation structures.

The Wakamiya Inari Shrine at HPV was built in 1914 in the Kakaako area of Honolulu by the Rev. Yoshio Akizaki. In 1919 it was moved to the Moiliili part of Honolulu. When Ben Takayesu (Buster Takayesu's son) bought the land, he arranged to have the shrine moved to the HPV. The shrine shows the religious side of plantation workers and is named after the Japanese God Inari, the god of good rice crops.

The leading founders of the Waipahu Cultural Garden Park are recognized as

Goro Arakawa
Hideo "Major" Okada
Jack Lindsey
Mitsuo Shito
Charles Nishioka

Charley Nishioka, still as humble and gracious as he was when Raymond Sokugawa approached him to run the Aloha Service Station in the Aloha Shopping Center, recalls when he was a farmer in Ewa. Charley had just delivered a load of cabbage in Honolulu and Raymond Sokugawa found him and explained that he wanted Charley to run his service station. Noting that the advertised asking price for the service station was $10,000 and that he only had a few hundred dollars in his pocket from the cabbage delivery, he told Sokugawa that the money in his pocket was all that he had. Sokugawa accepted and Charley began a career that started on December 24, 1951, as the owner-operator of an auto and repair service station that grew to include an auto parts store, tire sales store, and a 1-hour photo service store.

Charley gives much credit for his success to his immediate family: wife Elsie (deceased), son Saxon, and daughter Elaine. He also always mentions the strong support of his loyal employees. Charley retired in 1989. But before then he was chosen as the 1986 Small Businessman of the Year for the State of Hawaii.

With this selection, he became Hawaii's nominee for the Small Business Association National Small Business Person of the

Year for 1986.

Elaine helps to recount her father's trip to Washington, D.C., where all the nominees from all the states were interviewed by the selection committee.

"They were all interviewed and then they retired to their hotel rooms. The next morning they were assembled together for the announcement of who was going to be the SBA's National Person of the Year.

They annouced that my dad was that person ... and I wasn't there!"
-Elaine (Nishioka) Yoshioka

Charley was congratulated by then President Ronald Reagan and a photo as a memento of that occasion hangs in his home.

Charley is a firm believer in giving service ... when he ran his service station; giving back to his community ...when he served on numerous boards and organizations and donated much time, effort and money to: the Boy Scouts, the University of Hawaii, the Rotarians, City of Honolulu government, the American Cancer Society, Waipahu community organizations, Waipahu educational institutions, Chambers of Commerce, Better Business Bureau, . . . the list is endless.

Thank you, Charley!

He always insisted that his employees understand and practice the philosophy: "The customer deserves to get the very best service possible in exchange for the business that he brings us."

And his dedication to helping others came back recently.

At Commencement exercises on May 14, 2004, the Leeward Community College, a division of the University of Hawaii, bestowed on Charles K. Nishioka, the degree of Honorary Doctor of Humane Letters!

"Charley has passed on to his son, Saxon, the philosophy of helping others. He helps Waipahu High School with their business education program and Waipahu's community programs."
-Lillian (Kitamura) Yonamine

Arakawas of Waipahu ... in the last century, Arakawas was *the* department store in Waipahu. With advertising slogans such as "the big store in the little lane" to radio programs with a crowing rooster as part of a message, almost all of Hawaii came to be aware of the store that was Waipahu's claim to fame in the retail world. Goro Arakawa recounts that his mother told him that their very first store was where a concrete pad now sits on the left side of a sloping roadway on the left side of Saiki Motors on Waipahu St. From there, the retail effort moved to another location on Waipahu St. and then to Depot Rd. where, on the first floor, they had their start of selling dry goods and the second floor above that were hotel rooms. Still on Depot Rd., they moved across the street to a location they maintained until they closed their doors in 1995.

This location is remembered as "the old Magoon theater" that at one time also had been home to a roller skating rink. Today the old Arakawas store is home to a religious organization.

Zempan Arakawa came from Okinawa in 1904 and began working in the fields of Oahu Sugar as a water boy. He was a diminutive young man that struggled with the task of taking water to field hands. He was resourceful enough to recognize the need for various articles of clothing for the field workers.

What began as a one-man, after-hours tailoring effort eventually led to his hiring some plantation women to sew for him as demand grew for his shirts, pants, food bags, and other articles. In 1907 he sent for Uto from his native Okinawa and she came to Hawaii to be his wife. She bore him two children, Okiyo and Shigeo. Shortly thereafter, Uto passed away.

Tsuru Tamanaha, from the same village in Okinawa as Zempan and Uto, befell similar circumstances. That is, through various hardships, she lost her husband and had a daughter Shizuko to support.

Zempan helped them with credit and places to stay. Tsuru's daughter, Shizuko, was the same age as Zempan's Shigeo and so Tsuru helped to take care of him.

Eventually Tsuru and Zempan married and had six more children: Leatrice, twins Kazuo and Takemi, Shigemi, Joan, and Goro.

Zempan was an entrepreneur venturing into farming (pineapples), running a taxi and hotel as well as the drygoods store. His

---

When Arakawas business peaked after WWII, their offerings included:

Hardware and gardening items, toys, foodstuffs, jewelry, appliances, athletic equipment, drygoods, and clothing. One of their advertising slogans said it best:

If you don't know what you want, you'll find it at Arakawas.

The crowing rooster, Palaka yardage and clothing, and snappy one-liner advertising are all remembrances of the store that did so much for Waipahu.

Palaka is a cotton material having a plaid design; durable; easy to care for; comfortable to wear; originally thought to have been brought over in the mid 1800s by whalers.

An innovative and needed item was the *kappa*, a raincoat that Arakawas produced. A family effort, the raincoats were made of muslin and treated first with persimmon tannin (*kaki-shibu*) then with boiled linseed oil and turpentine. They bought the raw materials from the Theo. H. Davies Co., made the raincoats, and resold them back to The Theo. H. Davies Co. for distribution throughout Hawaii.

children all worked for the family business and he raised them all stressing the virtues of treating people well and fairly and treating oneself such that mental and physical good health was a part of their everyday lives; all of this while expanding the range of products the store offered for sale.

Oftentimes, Takemi could be seen out side the store greeting customers with a warm and sincere welcome.

With the newer outlet type malls and shopping centers, Araka-was decided to close in 1995 ... coincidentally the same year that the Oahu Sugar Co. closed down their operations.

Sports activities always brought the town of Waipahu together. Hans L'Orange did much while manager of Oahu Sugar but there were others that should also be remembered. See the listing at the end of this chapter.

Another interview that Lani (Ishikawa) Nedbalek conducted, this one in 1985, was with Walter Gouveia.

Walter Gouveia, started at age 14 or 15 in the Oahu Sugar Co. sponsored 4th of July race from Waipahu to Pearl City. Winning that race, he was encouraged by Hans L'Orange to enter the city-sponsored Kapiolani Park-Diamond Head race. This led him to enter the Olympic trials race in Los Angeles. He placed in that race and that led him to the New York trials and ran with the likes of the great Jesse Owens but didn't place and therefore was not able to go to the 1936 Olympics in Berlin.

On the way back to Hawaii, he entered the Boston Marathon and finished 10th ... most noted in all these races was the fact that he ran bare-footed!

Walter fondly remembered that there were many photographers around taking his picture. But mostly, the pictures were of his feet!

He later took up one-man volleyball. Just before WWII, the USO asked him to play one-man volleyball games as morale boosters and entertainment for troops. He took on teams with 6 players ... and quite often won!

"Danny Barcelona's parents worked for the Oahu Sugar Co. and I think the family lived in Camp 9. He was a '47 or '48

grad of Waipahu High School. He eventually became the lead drummer for the Louis Armstrong Band. I think he is now retired and living in southern California."
-Mel Bello

Our interview with Mac Flores was laced with stories of the times when he lived in Ota camp, worked at various occupations, the war years, and his interest in sports in Waipahu. Distilling all of this, the display at HPV probably best summarizes Mac Flores' character and beliefs for youth sports:

"Dedicated, undaunted, enthused, and energized, it's a fanatical belief in the need to:
   1) contribute in a meaningful way to the betterment of the community;
   2) provide fun, affordable, and confidence-building experiences for our kids;
   3) ensure maximum development of our youth

For him, 'Nothing's impossible if it's for the kids!' "

Lincoln Uyeno, an 'ace' pitcher in his youth, nominates Mitsuo Fujishige as a notable in the history of Waipahu and gives us the following and sidebar information on Mits Fujishige.

Mitsuo Fujishige was at Waipahu High School from 1946 to 1953 as Athletic Director and Coach. By doing a masterful job in Waipahu High School's athletic program, he united the town of Waipahu rallying them around the student athletes.

He also coached the track and swimming teams, the Waipahu AJA team in 1949, and in the Hawaii Baseball League, the Asahis from 1957 thru 1961.

"Fugay [an affectionate nickname for Mits Fujishige] used to tell us 'what you touch, you can catch.' "
-Tsune Watanabe

Before Mits retired, he encouraged Masa Yonamine to move to Waipahu High School to pass down the sports programs that Mits had started. Masa inherited Mits' fervor and skill that continued Waipahu's athletic supremacy reign for many more years.

Masa Yonamine stepped down from coaching in 1970 but con-

Championship years of Waipahu High School during Mitsuo Fujishige's tenure are noted:

Football 1947-49-50-51
Basketball 1948-49-50-51-52
Baseball 1948-49-50-51-52-53

Masa Yonamine's contributions to Waipahu High School championships are:

Football 1957, 1958, and 1960 (tie) in the Rural Oahu Interscholastic Assoc. (ROIA)
Baseball 1954 - 1957, 1959, 1964, 1966, 1968 (ROIA)

tinued to serve as the schools's attheletic director until retiring in 1986. During his years at Waipahu High School, he helped many of his players obtain athletic scholarships so they could continue their higher education. Many of these became successful and respected businessmen and leaders in the community.

For 32 years of outstanding service towards developing the athletic program at Waipahu High School, the school's athletic complex was dedicated in his honor.

Masa's wife, Lillian, was a counselor at Waipahu High School for many years. She speaks fondly of the students she saw pass thru the halls of Waipahu High School.

"They were ALL good, industrious kids. There was no talking-back. They were honest, down-to-earth kids who respected their peers, family, and school personnel. I even saw some kids, when they had nothing else to do, sit down and read the dictionary! So wonderful!"
-Lillian (Kitamura) Yonamine

We are very fortunate that Lani (Ishikawa) Nedbalek interviewed many people in Waipahu a long time ago and allowed us to use her works for our book today. Among the people Lani interviewed was Dallas C. McLaren, the first principal of Waipahu High School when it was Waipahu High and Intermediate School in 1938.

From teaching in Illinois, to teaching in Hilo, Hawaii, to becoming a principal at Waimea, Kauai, Dallas McLaren was tapped to be the principal of the new Waipahu High and Intermediate School. There was no physical plant and students were shuttling between Waipahu Elementary School, the Waipahu Continuation School and the Hongwanji Japanese School near the mill site. McLaren eventually got the school operating. Being the first high school in Leeward Oahu, the student body consisted of students who had been going to high schools at McKinley, Mid-Pacific (Mills School), Farrington, and Leilehua. These students came from anywhere between Aiea to Ewa to Waianae.

WWII interupted the growing process of the school and the school coped with military activities in and around the school. Eventually, the school graduated its first class in 1941. From the very beginning, Dallas C. McLaren laid the foundation for the school as memorialized in the bronze plaque at the dedication of Waipahu High School in 1939:

To the growth of sound minds and sound bodies,
To character building, sportsmanship, and fair play,
To industry and the will to succeed,
To friendliness - the spirit of aloha,
To thoughtful concern for the common good,
To loyalty and the love of country,
To the boys and girls of today,
To the men and the women of tomorrow.
                               -Dallas C. McLaren

Lani Nedbalek has doggedly tracked the whereabouts of the plaque and its last known location was "at the current Waipahu High School." But it cannot be found at this writing.

Notable at Waipahu High School in the early 1950s, was Janet B. Faye, English teacher and advisor to the College Club. She touched many by encouraging students to seek higher education and not only at the University of Hawaii, the most common choice of island students. Money was always a problem for a college education but Mrs. Faye had her students writing away applying for scholarships, taking exams, and applying for admission to many schools in the continental U.S.

"Out of our class of 300+ students, we had students accepted at Columbia, MIT, Notre Dame, Princeton, Washington State, Colorado State ... all mostly with scholarships! Graduates became college professors, veterinarians, and aerospace engineers to name a few. All this because of the prodding and encouragement of Mrs. Faye."
                               -Edwin Kato

As a side note, Barbara related that she learned how to use a computer at age 68! This to write her papers and her book. She recalls how she would get chided by her kids: "Mom, we told you how to do that yesterday!"

Barbara (Oyama) Kawakami really began her career as a young girl interested in dolls and doll clothing; a young girl fascinated with watching her mother mending the family's clothing. This interest in fabric and like things eventually parlayed into a life work and she is today considered an authority on plantation clothing. Her book *Japanese Immigrant Clothing in Hawaii, 1885-1941*, is a winner of two awards and a must-read.

Barbara Kawakami is one of nine children. She is the only one born in Japan but later returned to Hawaii with her family to grow up in the Oahu Sugar Co. camp community in Waipahu. Her formal education ended at the 8th grade but later in life she began pursuing upper level education. First the GED (General Equivalency Diploma) and then at age 53 (!) she started at the Leeward Community College. Eventually she attended the

University of Hawaii where she graduated with a Bachelor of Science Degree in Fashion Design and Merchandising (now Textiles and Clothing). Her daughter and two sons have been an important link in encouraging Barbara's pursuit of higher education. Barbara relates that her husband displayed little encouragement when she was pursuing her later education and even as she progressed through college. She eventually earned a Masters of Arts Degree in Asian Studies in 1983.

In 1979, while at the University of Hawaii, she began research on Japanese immigrant clothing. The lack of available information at that time led her on a quest for information that culminated in her book. After the book came out, Barbara's husband showed how proud he was of his wife's accomplishment ... even she was surprised with the joy and pride he displayed! On the day that she graciously gave us time for an interview, she told us about the clothing hanging in her living room. People from the Smithsonian Institution in Washington, D.C., had heard about her and were coming in a few days to interview her and possibly invite her to put some of her collection into the national museum!

She has since donated over 20 authentic clothing items (such as kimonos) to the Smithsonian and over 120 to the Japanese American National Museum in Los Angeles, California. The latter is planning a world-wide tour of her work at this writing.

In 1972, Waipahu celebrated its 75th or Diamond Jubilee at the Waipahu Cultural Garden Park. *Kaulana O Waipahu*, Song of Waipahu, was composed especially for this occasion by Ivy Kalani Hanakahi Woo. The Hawaiian and English words to the song are given below.

1. Kaulana o Waipahu
   Napua aloha aina
   No ka hale wili ko
   Eo
   Kaleo aloha o Waipahu

2. He wahine no Kahuku la

   Kaa puni no oia la
   Loaa nei ika pono

   Eo

1. Famous is Waipahu
   Their love for the land
   With its grinding sugar mill
   Answering - With a voice
   of love o Waipahu

2. There was a lady from
     Kahuku
   Who traveled afar
   Found her lost anvil
     (tapa beater)
   Answering - Walking

Keone kuilima laula o Ewa	hand in hand throughout the breadth of Ewa
3. Mai Kaala kamakani huihui Ke kahawai o Kaahupahau Ika wai aniani Eo Kapuna wai o Waipahu	3. Oh, the coolness of Kaala To the stream of the Shark Goddess Kaahupahau Answering - To the beauty of the swirling pools of Waipahu
4. Haina mai ka puana Kaulana o Waipahu Ika lehulehu hookipa Eo Kaleo aloha o Waipahu	4. Haina ends the song Famous is Waipahu Generations of blossoms to keep Answering - With the voice of love, oh Waipahu

In 1997, Waipahu celebrated its 100th Anniversary. Tri-Chairs Mervyn Ah Tou, Edward Uemori, and Michael Isobe guided the community through the many events.

The theme of the celebration, *Waipahu's Centennial Celebration — It's People and Heritage*, was conceived by Sharon Quidilla. At the time, she was a Junior at Waipahu High School. From a press release about the Centennial Celebration:

Sharon's father was a 17-year employee of the Oahu Sugar Co. and they resided in Ota camp. Sharon was active in a variety of community activities. She was a member of the Senior Class Council, a secretary for the Leo Club and tri-chair of project graduation for her class of 1988 at Waipahu High School. She was the school's first Student Athletic Trainer, completing 274 hours of First Aid and CPR training to be able to administer aid to athletes on the field and during rehabilitation. At the time of the Centennial, Sharon was studying telecommunications and was hoping to enter the nursing program at the University of Hawaii.

Fig. 9-3. Logo and Theme of Waipahu Centennial Celebration.

The Waipahu Centennial logo was created by Harold Balatbat, a Senior at Waipahu High School. Harold came with his family from the Philippines in 1990. He was an honor student (3.8 grade point) and a member of the National Honor Society at Waipahu High School. He attributed his drawing talents to his grandfather, uncle and auntie. After graduation, Harold was hoping to go to either Seattle University or the University of

Hawaii to study architectural engineering.

The Centennial Celebration was centered around Hans L'Orange Park, the Waipahu District Park, and Hawaii's Plantation Village. The events began on June 21, 1997, and ran through November of that year. Included was a well-planned series of events that included: the honoring of old-timers, veterans and sports figures in Waipahu's history, and cultural and educational displays recalling the ethnic and cultural heritage of Waipahu. Food, music, and crafts were interspersed in the giant celebation. Many, many community members took lead roles in putting the celebration together and these were able to involve the City, State and military components of the community in the half-year long event.

"You gotta know the past, where you came from, to know where you're going."
                                        -Hideo "Major" Okada

The stories that we have presented are but a small part of the history of Waipahu. So now, people of Waipahu, you know some of the history of where you came from and you can have direction in where you may go.

We wish you well on what could be *your* incredible journey!

Table 9-1 - People of note in Waipahu's Athletic History

The following is a list of people we found in the rich athletic history of Waipahu. We have probably not listed all, missed many, not intentionally but by chance, and suggest that you add to the list to make it more complete and include the sport(s) in which these people participated. And what about nicknames?

A
Zenichi Abe
Goro Arakawa
Kazuo Arakawa
Takemi Arakawa
Kelly & Colin Auerbach
Joe Awa

B
Barcelona Brothers
Barcenilla Brothers

C

D
Fred Daguman

E

F
Gilbert Fernandez
Mousey Ferreira
Doug & George "Dumbo" Fujishige
Mitsuo Fujishige
Itsuto & Koso Furukawa

G
Walter Gouveia

H
Nanao "Rusty" Hamada
Tato Harada
Fred Hashimoto
Stan Hashimoto
Shigeo "Mariano" Higa
Risa Higa
Warren Higa

I
George "Chicken" Ikenaga
Inoshita Brothers
Clarence Ishii & Dad Ishii
Tora Ishikawa
Mike Isobe

J

K
Ken Kimura
Yoko "Froggie" Kiyabu
Charlie Kobayashi
Katsuji "Kats" Kojima
Ichiro Konno

L

M
Crispin "Chris" Mancao
Jack Masuda
Mike Miike
Jack Mitsumoto
James Moniz
James Mundon
Jimmy Mundon

N
Haru Nakamura

O
Rick "Cadon" Oamilda
Henry "Nutsky" Oana
Hideo "Major" Okada
Masa Okada
Joe Olivares
"Amonk" Oshiro
Shigeo "Shaggy" Oshiro

P
Phil Paculba

Q

R
George Richardson

S
Sei Saiki
"Chief" Saito
Razo Saito
Don Sakai
"Gute" Santiago
"Honny" Sato
Masa Sato
"Sencho" Sato

179

Toki Sato
Larry Shigeyasu
"Miruku" Shimizu
Sadao Shinno
Albert Silva

T

U
Eddie Uemori
"Toronko" Umeno
Lincoln Uyeno

V

W
Mitsuru "Brown" Watabu
Tsune & Riki Watanabe

X

Y
Ryoto and Chester Yasui
Yasui Brothers (Johnny, Tommy, Fred, Eddie)
Shinsuke "Shin" Yogi
Masa Yonamine

Z

References - Chap. 9.

Many articles, *Waipahu 75th Diamond Jubilee Edition,* Sunday Star-Bulleting & Advertiser, Honolulu, Hawaii, Nov. 5, 1972.

Hans L'Orange Field, Common Ground, Uncommon Glory 1924-1999, Hans L'Orange Baseball Park Council, Waipahu, Hawaii, 1999.

Website of United Airlines, Inc.

Selected papers from the family of Shigeru Serikaku.

Selected papers from Lani Nedbalek.

Selected papers from the family of Charles Nishioka.

Selected papers from the Arakawa family.

Docent Manual, Hawaii's Plantation Village.

Japanese Immigrant Clothing in Hawaii, 1885-1941, Barbara O. Kawakami, University of Hawaii Press, Honolulu, Hawaii, 1993.

Program notes of the 75th or Diamond Jubilee of Waipahu, 1972.

Notes from the 1997 or Centennial Celebration of Waipahu, 1997.

History Makers of Hawaii, A. Grove Day, Mutual Publishing Co., Honolulu, Hawaii, 1984.

Epilogue
At the end of our story . . . *along the way* . . .

As we conducted interviews, we were asked some of the following questions by many people. Here are some of the more frequently asked questions and our responses.

Why the chapter divisions and how did we select what was included in each chapter? When we began the interviewing/fact gathering process, the interviewee's responses naturally seemed to create the chapters and chapter headings. While each interview covered many topics, there came a point in time when, for example, we thought that "this" belonged grouped together with another's "that" and soon we had many "this's" and "thats" when taken together, formed the basis of a chapter. Consider Chapter 6–World War II. While many people could remember many things about life in Waipahu, WWII memories always seemed to come up and so all the memories about WWII from many people eventually became Chapter 6. And so it went.

It seemed logical to define Waipahu and locate it for the benefit of readers who might not know about the town or its location. So Chapter 1–Locating and defining Waipahu ("water bursting forth from the ground") began our story. If it were not for Oahu Sugar, Waipahu as a thriving community might not have come to be . . . hence, Chapter 2–Oahu Sugar ("a horse ride and a broken leg") followed and included life on the sugar plantation. Life in the surrounding community was covered as Chapter 3–Along Waipahu St. and down Depot Rd. ("the road curved this way and then that way").

Then, if people's lives were important, and these were all immigrants, their contirbutions from their home country was interesting. This is Chapter 4–Some culture we retain to this day ("we brought this and we brought that") that really could be another book in itself.

Chapter 5–Along Farrington Highway ("a connector highway, a by-pass highway") was covered separately even if, later in time, it was still an important part of Waipahu. It seemed like a natural and geographical way to continue to describe the town.

Chapter 6–World War II ("we saw the pilots, we waved at the pilots") had made such an impression on many people, that we decided to treat it as a separate chapter.

Tatsuichi Ota and the story of his family really started this book but as we mentioned in the Preface, the more interesting story is about the town of Waipahu. We still included T. Ota as he was a part of the Waipahu immigrant community. This is Chapter 7–Tatsuichi Ota ("Ota, one of many immigrants").

There were so many little tidbits of information and anecdotes that could have been presented and duplicated in several chapters but instead we collected and included these only once in this Chapter 8–Life in Waipahu ("life in this little town").

Finally, Chapter 9– Notes on the history of Waipahu ("more about people, places, and events in

Waipahu") in the history of Waipahu. In brief one-paragraph stories, we recorded *some* of these and their impact on Waipahu.

Some background stories on interviews.

A) One of the first interviews we conducted was with Hideo Ishihara. We had called him from Albuquerque to ask if he could share some memories of old Waipahu as we had heard that he was an 'old-timer.' In a very nice way he said that he didn't think that he had any memories and so could not help us. On the next visit to Hawaii, we visited his Ishihara Senbei-Ya to pick up some senbei (they are very good) and while there, we told his daughter-in-law Michelle, to please thank Mr. Ishihara for the time he had spent with me on the phone. I was going to leave that evening and so wanted the senbei to take home and also to leave my 'thanks, anyway.' I left my business card and left for my friend's place in Pearl City.

Minutes after arriving at my friend's place, I got a call from my wife, at home in Albuquerque, saying that Mr. Ishihara's daughter-in-law had spoken to Mr. Ishihara, called my wife, and the conversation went on that Mr. Ishihara said that if I had taken the time to go to his shop, get senbei, and thank him, maybe he could at least give me a few minutes of his time. Would I go back to his shop to talk with him?

I rushed back to Waipahu and sat with Mr. Ishihara for nearly *two* hours as he gave me, *from memory*, the location of stores along Waipahu St. and Depot Rd. in the 1920s! I wrote furiously and made sketches. This began our wonderful interview process.

I stopped at Mr. Ishihara's place again on our next trip and he took me over to see Goro and Shigemi Arakawa. We spent another few hours taking in Goro's, Shigemi's and Hideo's memories.

This led to the next meeting when I saw Goro; he asked if I knew Mac Flores. When I replied in the negative, Goro told me "You should, he was your grandfather's neighbor." With that he gave me a piece of paper with Mac Flores' name and current phone number!

We interviewed people on the phone, in their homes, in a quiet corner of a local restaurant, and in Torrance, California!

B) What started as the passing of my grandfather Tatsuichi Ota's only son, Tatsuo, led to the family having the Bank of Hawaii (BoH) handle the estate of Tatsuo Ota. The BoH representative, Sharlyn Miyahara, told us about the group of Waipahu people living in Torrance, California, and surrounding areas. Sharlyn contacted her aunt in Torrance and we found out the exact date the group would meet. We made a trip there to coincide with the monthly luncheon "meeting" at their local Marukai store. It is a gathering of people; what binds them together is the fact that they all went to Waipahu High School.

The meeting was (and probably still is) a loose gathering of people eating plate lunches gathered around many tables. Each table having their own topic of conversation: the most recent Vegas trip, the most recent golf game, the next formal dinner gathering, etc. They have a roster of names and phone numbers but there seems to be no president, manager, or group leader.

While there, we passed out bags of senbei and that seemed to open the door a bit for our book project but each table invariably returned to their topic of the day. We were able to get a few interviews and the roster allowed us to later conduct some phone interviews.

C) In the fact gathering process and in trying to describe the town of Waipahu in its early days, it occurred to me that something should be mentioned about the water system. So I called the Board of Water Supply in Honolulu. What follows is the conversation as best as I can remember.

MTY: Hi, I'm writing a book about Waipahu and I'm trying to find out about the water system there.
Phone receptionist: Let me put you through to the department that might be able to help you.
Department: Hello, [cough] [cough] [cough]. Click!

On re-dial.

MTY: Hi, I think we got cut off, can you put me through to that department you connected me to a minute ago?
Department: Hello, can I help you?
MTY: Hi! Were you the fellow I was just talking with? Are you over your coughing spell?
Department: No, that was another person. Can I help you?
MTY: Yes, I'm writing a book about the town of Waipahu and need some help. In particular, about the water system there wa-a-a-y back when.
Department: What kinds of things did you want to know? I can't tell you a lot of things because of 9-1-1. What is this for again?
MTY: Well, this book I'm writing is about the history of Waipahu. And I thought that the reader might want to know about water, electricity, sewers, etc. and so I'm contacting the Board of Water Supply to fill in that part of the information that I need. I'm also interviewing people that lived in Waipahu for their memories.
Department: Would you be interested in interviewing my aunt?
MTY: Sure. Who is she?
Department (by now we have his name: Glenn Oyama): My aunt is Barbara Kawakami.
MTY: Didn't she write a book?
GLENN: Yes.

I'm searching my bookcase as I talk to Glenn.

MTY: It was a book on plantation clothing. I have it here. I would love to interview her.
GLENN: OK, I'll call her and explain that you would like to interview her. Now, on your next trip here, I'll have information gathered about water and Waipahu.

This led to Barbara (Oyama) Kawakami and her book, *Japanese Immigrant Clothing in Hawaii, 1885-1941*.

Glenn later took us to the site of the Spring Waipahu (aka Pump 8), and a trip through rugged terrain to see other pump sites. He also shared much information about *water* on Oahu that we did not use in this book. We are so much more educated on the topic of water as a result of the knowledge he shared.

D) We used a modified form of the technique of triangulation to validate information given by an interviewee. That is, when we felt that the information given might not be correct, we tried to validate it from another source, i.e., another person or in previously recorded documents. After many interviews, we began to be able to judge or have a "hunch" about the accuracy of the information we were receiving from the many people. But recall that the book is about "Recollections," and so we trust that what we have recorded is accurate to the degree that was best recalled by the many people we interviewed!

We found that giving ample response time or wait-time to our questions led us in many directions. For example, if a person was telling us about "after school" times, if we didn't try to hasten a response, he might also stray into "having ice cream after school." Letting a person stray a bit gave us another direction (and topic) to pursue. Controlling the amount of wait-time was important but allowing enough wait-time gave us some interesting topics during each interview.

During many interviews, we led the interviewee by suggesting "tell us about after school" or "can you remember about the war?" or "what kinds of food did you have at home?" to jump-start the conversation. We tried to avoid descriptive adjectives such as good, bad, wonderful, happy, or sad, to lead the interviewee towards a prejudged response.

E) We had VERY few people tell us that they did not want to be interviewed. Our records show that we contacted about 200 people and interviewed some more than once. Only three declined to be interviewed or felt that they would not be able to share any memories. We have no record of anyone missing an interview appointment; a postponement, only one.

F) As an interviewee, you may be wondering why we used and credited the *other* person's story when your story was the same or at least very similar. The reason is that we used the first story that came our way and we did not want to be prejudicial about *who* gave us the story.

G) We had a very interesting interview with Mel Bello that culminated with a question: "If there was anything you would like to see for Waipahu and its future, what would that be?"

Mel's answer: "You know, I left Waipahu when I was 17 years-old but when people ask me where I'm from, I always tell them that I'm from Hawaii and the town of Waipahu in Hawaii. I still have a lot of Aloha for that fine town!

I think that the best thing that could happen for the town to continue to grow, is for parents and retirees to have a mentoring program for all students at all levels of education. And this is not only in formal school subjects, but in spiritual, emotional, religious, psychological, etc., areas."

More end-notes.
This book was printed and bound by McNaughton & Gunn, of Saline, MI. The book is printed on white, 60# Offset 444 PPI paper and the cover stock is 10 Pt. C1S with gloss lay-flat film lamination. The color of the cover is a light blue designated in graphics and media as Pantone 297C. The binding is called Perfect Binding in the trade.

Typefaces are *Times Roman* for the text; *Helvetica* and *Brush Script* are also used; *Shelley Allegro Script* is used for the title. Font sizes are varied as are *bold* or *italic* character style selection. *InDesign* and *Photoshop Elements* software put it all together on an Apple iMac G5 computer; an Epson 2480 scanner and a Xerox Phaser 8400 Printer were our image processors.

The format of three vertical columns per page seemed appealing to the eye. Using the two outermost columns of each page for the major material makes for easy reading as text close to the center (spine of the book) does not force the reader to "flatten" the book to read it. The inner third column was useful for "tidbit" information related to the main text.

We learned a lot from the whole interview process. Some simple examples: Nishi and Higashi are not names of famous people. **Nishi** means **west** and **Higashi** means **east**! So much for our knowledge of Japanese! And **donburo** is **down below** and **shoburo** is **shore below**. (See Chapter 1 for more about donburo and shoburo.)

And, of course, we learned a lot of the history of Waipahu. There is so much more that can be told but we felt that we had to present what we had before too much time elapsed. We also learned a lot about people . . . most people are genuinely warm, sharing, caring, generous, and honest. And every person has a story that could fill a book by that one person.

And finally, we want to emphasize that our intent from the very beginning was to only record a part of history. We did not want to make judgements of people or criticize them. We only wanted to evoke memories of long ago for the enjoyment of all.

On our last interview trip, Eddie Uemori asked "Are we having fun?" to which I responded, "Everyday! It's been a heck of a journey . . . so-o-o-o **very** satisfying and enjoyable!"

About the Authors

Michael T. Yamamoto, principal author, is the grandson of Tatsuichi Ota (Chapter 7). A native of Honolulu, he grew up in the Kalihi area and graduated from Farrington High School. Mike attended the University of Hawaii, first majoring in Electrical Engineering, then worked with the U.S. Weather Bureau on Wake Island for a year, and returned to the University of Hawaii to graduate with a Bachelors Degree in Science Education. He taught chemistry, physics, and mathematics for one year at James Campbell High School in Ewa Beach. He later returned to the University of Hawaii as a research assistant and technician in the Department of Physics and Astronomy.

While working at the university, Mike's interest in mechanical things became a hobby. He was later able to combine this hobby with being a salesman of machine tools and eventually opened his own machine tool distribution company. He has contributed several magazine articles to the *Home Shop Machinist* and is the author of *Repair of Mechanical Dial Indicators and Calipers*.

Nina Yuriko (Ota) Sylva is the third daughter of Tatsuichi Ota. Her major contibution to this work is her excellent memory and recall of events dating back to her early childhood. Nina attended elementary school in Waipahu and graduated from Farrington High School. She also attended the Galusha School of Business in Honolulu.

Nina was employed by the Army Corps of Engineers, the Pearl Harbor Naval Shipyard, and retired from the Navy Finance Office. She lives in Aiea and is an active participant in the Hauoli Kupaa Senior Club. Nina is widowed and has two sons and two grandchildren.

Karen N. (Kina) Yamamoto, Ph.D., is the wife of Michael T. Yamamoto. She researched most of the materials for this book at the University of Hawaii Hamilton Library's Hawaii-Pacific Collection, State of Hawaii Archives, and Hawaii's Plantation Village. Karen grew up in the Kalihi area of Honolulu and graduated from Farrington High School. She attended the University of Hawaii where she earned a Bachelors and a Masters Degree in Education. She taught physics, chemistry, and general science at McKinley High School and at the University Laboratory School.

As an Education Associate at the University of Hawaii College of Education/Curriculum Research and Development Group (UH/CRDG), Karen was one of the principal authors of the first editions of *Foundational Approaches in Science Teaching (FAST 1 & 2 Student Book and Teacher's Guide)* and *Developmental Approaches in Science and Health (DASH K-2 Teacher's Guides)*. She was also an Education Consultant to and an Education & Consumer Affairs Analyst at the Hawaiian Electric Co., writing energy and environmental education resource materials. Karen then attended Stanford University where she received a doctorate in Science Education in 1996. She later joined the American Indian Science & Engineering Society (AISES) in Boulder, Colorado, and relocated with the non-profit organization to Albuquerque, New Mexico.

Both Karen and Mike are retired and living in Albuquerque, New Mexico. They have one son and one daughter.

Index

Contributors are listed by the name that they are best known. Selected topics of interest are listed in **bold print**.

A
Abe, Charmille iv
Abe, Zen 35, 64, 69, 73, 153, 160, 168
Ah Tou, Mervyn 177
Akiyama, Masuye vii, 6, 68, 126, 151
Anuba, Robert 142
Anderson, Andy 167
Arakawa, Goro 6, 64, 68, 113, 149, 165, 169, 184
Arakawa, Shigemi 6, 8, 37, 59, 62, 112, 135, 149, 151, 184
Arita, George 39, 64, 145
Arita, Jane 56, 105, 161
Artesian springs/wells 192
Athletes -
  List of 179
  Others 172
Author Profiles 189

B
Baist, Margo 58
Balfour, William Jr. v, 42
Behasa, Pete 72, 87
Bello, Mel 22, 37, 51, 144, 149, 152, 154, 173, 186
Bello, Steven 147, 153
Bunda, Darrlyn 63, 65

C
Camps -
  Map of 24
Castro, Robert iv, 25, 27, 29, 39, 163, 192
Celebrations - see Chap. 4
  Waipahu 176-177
Chong, Douglas 10
Chronology of events 77-79
Claggett, Dale 130

D
Dela Cuadra, Sandra iv

E
Ebisuya, Calvin 155
Empron, Albert 147
Espinda, Moana 147

Ethnic groups - see
  Camps
  Immigrant Groups

F
Flores, Mac 128, 173, 184
Fujioka, Harold iv
Fujioka, Sharon iv
Fukuda, Rachel 23, 35, 41, 145

G
Garcia, Espy 145
Gibo, Chris 134
Goya, Takemi iv

H
Hamai, Bernice iv, 38, 40-41, 52, 55, 62, 67-68, 111, 128, 142, 162
Hamai, Jay 27
Harada, Rachael 61
Harimoto, Herbert 26
Harimoto, Laura 154
Hawaii's Plantation Village (HPV) iii, 5, 23, 84, 165-169
Hayashida, Judy 20, 54, 56
Herrst, Diana iv, 51, 64, 66, 72, 108, 112, 143, 151
Higa, Roy 98
Hirata, Marlene v, 40-41, 51, 54, 144, 164
Hirata, Richard v, 142
Hirotsu, Harry iv
Holokahi, Carole iv
Honke, Karen 35
Horie, Barney iv
Horie, Deanne iv, 108

I
Ichiyama, Ron 64, 68, 73, 84, 141, 144, 162
Ifuku, Gail 7
Immigrant groups -
  Arrival dates 11
  Culture see Chap. 4
  Chinese
  Japanese
  Korean

Portuguese
Puerto Rican
Ishibashi, Anita 40
Ishihara, Hideo iv, 62, 67, 184
Ishikawa, Charles xvi, 72, 124
Isobe, Masa 62
Isobe, Mike 27, 62, 177
Isono, Helen 13, 109, 144, 155
Ito, Hiro 155

J
Johnson, Jeannette iv, 53-54, 63, 109

K
Kagemoto, Ray iv
Kam, Mildred 85, 146
Kanechika, Harue 33, 84
Kaneshiro, Liz iv
Kato, Edwin 175
Kawakami, Barbara 10, 175-176, 185
Kawamoto, Cal 101, 166-167
Kawamoto, Carrie iv
Kawano, Irwin iv
Kessner, Ali iv
Kimura, Grace 155
Kimura, Ken 65, 153, 155
Kimura, Mildred iv
Kodama, Marge 155
Kokubun, Francis 53
Kuniyoshi, Arlene 66, 153
Kurata, Norman 148

L
LaPierre, Paul iv
Leineweber, Spencer 166-168
Leonard, Sue iv
L'Orange, Peter 34, 106, 109-110, 160, 164
Los Banos, Domingo 91

M
Makii, Mildred 143
Maps -
  Census Tract 3
  Locating Waipahu 2

New Pathway for Waipahu St. 49
Oahu Sugar Fields and Camps 24
Points of Interest, 1930 9
Sewerage System 28
Town - Significant Locations 70
Marsteller, Ann iv
Matsuda, Charlotte iv
Matsunaga, Jane 38, 57
Matsuo, Shiro 66, 88
Mauricio, Mike iii, 1, 5, 14, 83
Mayeda, Christine iv
Miyahara, Dennis xv
Miyahara, Sharlyn xi, xv, 184
Miyake, Ellen iv, 106
Miyasaki, Lorna iv
Miyashiro, Debra 7
Moniz, Elsie 12, 26, 29, 34, 39, 143
Morisada, Henry 11, 55, 61, 143
Morita, Georgine iv, 120, 141
Morita, Hugh iv, 23, 25
Morita, Yuzuru iv, 111, 153
Murata, Wally 14

N
Nabarrete, Cornelio 26, 53, 57, 59, 63
Nakamoto, Thayer 56, 99, 145
Nakamoto, Tyler 99
Nakamura, Dorothy 124, 136-137
Nakamura, Grace iv
Nedbalek, Lani iii, 5, 49, 161, 172, 174-175
Nicknames, list of 155
Niino, Evelyn iv
Nishioka, Charley iv, 169-170
Nishioka, Saxon iv, 169

O
Oahu Sugar Co. -
  Labor and Strikes see Chap. 2
  Lands & Camp Locations 24
  Personalities, various 159, 161
  Production Tidbits 43
Okada, Lillian 155
Okada, Ted 155
Oshiro, Lillian iv, 37, 40, 55, 143
Oshiro, Dr. Milton iv
Oshiro, Mitsuo 25, 40, 111
Oshiro, Sumiko 57, 108, 155

Oyama, Glenn 185, 186, 192, Back Cover

P
Pang, Glenn iv
Pearl Harbor 4, see also Chap. 6
Pedersen, Patricia iv, 97

R
Rulers of Hawaii - list of 79-80

S
Saito, Mary Ann 52, 84
Saito, Yasuo 105, 142, 145
Sakuma, Amy 20, 55
Santistevan, Grace iii, 121, 124
Schools -
  August Ahrens 50
  Waipahu Elementary 69
  Waipahu High 97
  Waipahu Intermediate 101
  Others 101
Serikaku, Emiko 162
Serikaku, James iv, 20, 73, 75, 105
Sewerage system 28
Sienkiewicz, Keith iv
Sokugawa, Alaric 98, 126
Songs - Words to
  Alma Maters 69, 97
  Hole Hole Bushi 32
  May Day 72
  75th Anniversary 176
Sports Figures -
  see **Athletes**
Sugar -
  Facts 45
  Production Tidbits 43
Sumile, Hazel 54
Suyama, Paul 147
Suyenaga, Elsie 162
Suzuki, Brian iii
Sylva, Nina iv, xv, 105, 107, 118-120, 123-126

T
Tagalog, Pete 106, 130, 137
Takayesu, Buster iv, 61, 119
Takeuchi, Grace 107, 118, 122-124, 127, 129, 131, 135, 137
Tamashiro, June 20, 38, 57, 69
Tamashiro, Lynn 106
Tanji, Tom iv
Tasaka, Jack iii

Tasato, John iii, 29, 66, 145, 155
Togo, Dennis 90
Tokujo, Roy 31, 164
Tokuhara, Lilly 14, 20, 42, 53, 56, 66, 108, 128
Tsinnajinnie, Myrna 12, 38, 52, 88, 142, 150
Tupinio, Darryl 69, 73, 100-101, 146

U
Uchigaki, Harriet iv
Uemori, Edward 22, 37, 163, 177, 187
Ujimori, Ellen 162
Uranaka, Tajiro 111
Uyeno, Lincoln 130, 173

V
Valdriz, Edith 87, 142, 148
Voorhees, Tiffany iv

W
Waipahu -
  Cultural Garden Park see
    Hawaii's Plantation Village
  Naming 13
  Spring 68, Back Cover
Watanabe, Al 53, 162-163
Watanabe, Kenichi 73, 112
Watanabe, Tsuneo 173
Whalen, Stephanie iv
World War II (WWII) see Chap. 6

Y
Yamada, Ed 64, 150
Yamada, Kay iii, xiv, 31
Yanase, Dr. Stanley 55, 112, 149
Yamaoka, Iris 7, 29
Yamauchi, Yoshiko 13, 141
Yasui, Tommy iv
Yonamine, Lillian 170, 174
Yonamine, Masa 173-174
Yoshioka, Elaine 169-170
Yoshitake, Shige iv, v, 6, 7, 40-41

Back cover notes.
Right column photo credits, top to bottom:

Honolulu Star-Bulletin & Advertiser, Waipahu 75th Diamond Jubilee Edition, Nov. 5, 1972.

Anonymous contributor.

Robert Castro.

Photo of Glenn Oyama (Board of Water Supply, City & County of Honolulu) by the author.

Basic map insert from Phears Mapbooks, Honolulu, Hawaii, 2004. (The heaviest line running roughly top to bottom [11 o'clock to 5 o'clock] is Waikele Stream.)

Water information.
42.5 cubic feet per second is about 27.5 million gallons per day. A fire hydrant's flow, with its top structure sheared off, can be about 1,000 gallons per minute = 60,000 gallon per hour = 1,440,000 gallons per day = 1.44 million gallons per day. The Spring Waipahu was ejecting about 19 times this amount in its early history!

An *artesian well* is the result of boring into the earth, reaching water that is under presure, and allowing the water to fountain upward. A *spring* would fountain water up through a natural opening in the earth. The source of the water would be an aquifer beneath the earth or floating above salt water; the cross-section of such an aquifer would resemble a lens, often referred to as a Ghyben-Herzberg lens.